Bob Kiener

MUSTANG DESIGNER

MUSTANG DESIGNER

Edgar Schmued and the Development of the P-51

Ray Wagner

Orion Books ■ New York

Published by Orion Books, a division of Crown Publishers, Inc., 201 East 50th Street,
New York, New York 10022. Member of the Crown Publishing Group.

ORION and colophon are trademarks of Crown Publishers, Inc.

Manufactured in the United States of America

Library of Congress Cataloging-in-Publication Data

Wagner, Ray.
      Mustang designer Edgar Schmued and the development of the P-51/
   by Ray Wagner.
         p.   cm.
      1. Schmued, Edgar.   2. Aeronautical engineers—United States—
   Biography.   3. Military engineers—United States—Biography.
   4. Mustang (Fighter planes) I. Title.
   UG626.2.S355W34   1990
   629.13′0092′273—dc20   89-36701
                                                                        CIP

ISBN 0-517-56793-8

10 9 8 7 6 5 4 3 2 1

First Edition

Book design by Deborah Kerner

To Edgar Schmued

───────────────

and the men who made the
fighters that protected freedom

.

Contents

Acknowledgments

In preparing this book I have been helped by many people, and I have tried to include their names here. Special thanks are due to Mrs. Christel Schmued for suggesting this book and making her husband's papers available, to the San Diego Aerospace Museum for use of its extensive research files, to the Air Force Historical Research Center for its research grant and resources, and to Ed Schmued's coworkers, who provided much helpful information.

Christel Schmued not only was the first to suggest this book, but also obtained much information by her determination to track down each lead and win the cooperation of those who could help. Her insight, faith, and encouragement made the work an enjoyable task.

Many of Ed's coworkers provided interviews, letters, pictures, and documents, beginning with a meeting chaired by Bill Wheeler at the SDAM, April 27, 1986. They are listed below, with specific citations in footnotes at the end of each chapter. Exact quotations have been used wherever possible to tell the participants' story. Sole responsibility for the text and other assessments belongs to the author. Special thanks for their patient help go to Mary Wagner and to my associates at the San Diego Aerospace Museum.

Major General John R. Alison (USAF, retired)

Norman Avery

Bill R. Barker

Colonel William F. "Bill" Barnes (USAF, retired)

Charles Barr

General Mark E. Bradley (USAF, retired)

Ronald Bulinski

Dustin W. Carter

Dr. Ira Chart

Robert Chilton

George W. Cully

George Gehrkens

Carl J. Hansen

Alice Hofferber

Edward J. Horkey

Richard Hulse

F. J. "Buddy" Joffrion

Alfred F. Kustra

Jerry Landry

Sam Logan

Marc W. Malsby

Dr. Raymond S. Ross

C. F. Ruckdaschel

Richard L. Schleicher

William A. Schmitz

Dr. Richard K. Smith

Vernon A. Tauscher

Liesel Thaiss

Gordon Throne

Margaret Villepique Tyson

John W. Underwood

Deke Warner

Herbert K. Weiss

William "Bill" Wheeler

John W. Young

PHOTO CREDITS

The pictures in this book are held by the San Diego Aerospace Museum *(SDAM)* or were provided by the author and by admirers of Mr. Schmued. Wherever possible, they are credited to the organization or individual with whom the image originated. If the originator is not known, they are cited as *SDAM*, the present location of these prints. The major sources are:

NAA: North American Aviation, now Rockwell International. Many of these were obtained via C. F. Ruckdaschel, who spent many hours searching company files.

Smithsonian: used by permission of the Smithsonian Institution; usually manufacturer's photos.

USAF: United States Air Force

IWM: Imperial War Museum

Individual contributors include Norman Avery, Peter Bowers, Ron Bulinski, Dusty Carter, Jerry Kishpaugh (via Dick Morley), Michael O'Leary, and most of all, Christel Schmued *(CS)*.

Introduction

Many stories about the design of the P-51 Mustang have been told, most of them out-and-out fabrications, or not really reflecting the actual history. This has prompted me to tell the real story as it happened, and here it is.

With these words, the late Edgar Schmued began what was intended to be his own account of how the P-51 Mustang, the most successful fighter of World War II, was designed and developed. Unfortunately, his death in 1985 prevented the fighter designer from completing a book for publication. But the importance of the Mustang makes its design of prime concern to those interested in aviation history.

The names of World War II's most famous American fighter planes, such as the Lightning, Warhawk, Thunderbolt, or the best of all, the Mustang, are well known, but those of their designers have not been heard by the general public. Only years after the war did Kelly Johnson receive book-length attention, and then it was more for the postwar successes of "Skunk Works," his experimental shop at Lockheed, than for his wartime P-38. Don Berlin and Robert Woods, as well as Edgar Schmued, were names best known to their fellow workers rather than to the public.

It isn't surprising, after all, that it was the fighter pilots and their generals who were at the center of the wartime stage. Yet neither the courage and skill of the pilots nor the strategies of their leaders could win, unless the engineers were able to plan weapons equal to their missions and industry was able to build the huge number of planes necessary for victory.

This is a design biography, different from other fighter books in that the story is told from the designer's point of view. It uses original documentation to give a more accurate and complete account and shows the personal qualities of those who produced the airplanes. I have tried to tell here the story of American wartime fighter development, including engines and armaments, as part of a nationwide program of aircraft builders and fliers, reminding the reader of men like Don Berlin, Kelly Johnson, Alexander Kartveli, and Robert Woods, as well as the work of our central figure, Edgar Schmued.

It is important not to think of an aircraft design in isolation but in the context of its history. At the beginning of the war, American fighter squadrons had to use aircraft inferior to the Spitfires and Messerschmitts that would fight the Battle of Britain. When design of the P-51 was begun, the Army Air Corps already had ordered four promising fighter types into production and didn't seem to need others. To understand the Mustang's success, we must know about its predecessors and their designers and see how wartime needs dictated the path of American efforts.

The fighters designed before the war were planned as defensive weapons, to protect friendly troops, cities, and resources from enemy air attack. Such missions required only enough fuel for flights of two hours or less. Long-range air-offensive operations were left to the bombers.

To defeat Germany from the air, United States Army Air Force leaders planned to have hundreds of bombers penetrate Germany in mass formation, protected by their own gunners. When the Luftwaffe fighter force proved too strong for unescorted bombers, the Allied bombing offensive could not continue without suffering unacceptable losses.

The Mustang entered the war at a critical moment. For the first time, the Allies had a long-range fighter that could go all the way to Berlin with the bombers, flying more than seven hours on a mission. The P-51 Mustang became the decisive weapon in the air war, defeating the enemy fighters deep within their own territory. Many factors were involved in winning the war against the Axis in Europe, but few were as important as the North American P-51 fighter.

Another reason for the Mustang's popularity is that it looks like a fighter should: it is sleek and businesslike. The fiftieth anniversary of its first flight is here, but air shows still find the P-51 to be a surefire crowd pleaser.

The war was won in the air by an extraordinary combination of American and British technology focused on the creative design of an immigrant from Germany. How this happened will be described in the detail necessary to understand the development process. Along the way, we will correct some of the errors that have become embedded in more traditional accounts.

No one man designs a fighter. Within each aircraft company, an engineering team is at work, pressing fighter performance upward. While it is convenient to refer to the team leader's name as each type's designer, the fighter should always be understood as a group product. Ed Schmued himself always insisted that design was a team effort, and in that spirit, his coworkers at North American have contributed their memories of the projects and of the man himself, who is remembered with respect and affection. Using the designer's own words wherever possible, I've shown how the P-51 team drew on the best ideas available to produce the most successful fighter, bar none, of the war, and how the P-82 Twin Mustang was begun.

A warplane can be no better than its power plant and its armament. This book describes the way engines determined fighter performance and how the P-51 itself owed its success to the Rolls-Royce engine, while the P-82 suffered from an inadequate power plant. The increase in firepower for Air Force fighters is also explained.

Each engineering team works within a corporate environment, and its military products must be sold to a military hierarchy whose outlook is shaped by its nation's economic conditions and wartime experience. Both the corporations and military procurement must be described if the design and use of a combat plane is to be understood.

Since the operational history of American fighters has been detailed in other books, I have limited this history to the overall wartime picture of the Mustang's air battles. This text concentrates on the creation of these aircraft, leaving stories of the day-to-day flying to the men best qualified to tell them: the combat pilots themselves. Both the factual record in this book and the words of these pilots will testify to the claim that the P-51 was the most successful fighter of World War II.

But the Mustang story did not end with that war, for the Korean War added another chapter, and civilian pilots began setting new records and winning air races with their private Mustangs. Forty years after the last P-51 came out of the factory, a Mustang still held the world's record for the fastest piston-engine aircraft.

Jet propulsion added new dimensions and complications to fighter design, and Edgar Schmued led design teams that began a new generation of fighters. The most im-

portant of these were the North American F-86 and the Northrop F-5, and the story of their development will show how much the industry changed in the decade following 1945.

To maintain the focus on Air Force single-seaters, the development of both carrier-based Navy fighters and of heavy night fighters has been excluded from this study, for they represent very special design problems. I invite the reader to learn the story of this era of combat aircraft design in America, and of Edgar Schmued, one of the men who made successful fighters possible.

MUSTANG DESIGNER

CHAPTER ONE

Choosing Fighter Designs, 1935–1939:
From P-30 to P-50

The first Air Corps fighter of modern pattern in squadron service, the Consolidated P-30, was an all-metal low-wing monoplane with retractable wheels and an in-line, liquid-cooled, supercharged engine. *SDAM*

**W**hat does a fighter plane do? At first the answer seems obvious, but consider the specifics. Will it only fight enemies in the air or will it fight those on the ground, too? Where will it fight: in what climate, near to the ground or far above it, and near, or far from its base? And when, in the day or night?

What will it cost, how many can be made, and when will they be ready? Who will fly them, a few very experienced professionals like the famed German *experten,* or thousands of hastily trained ex-civilians? Who will be able to design such aircraft, and how will the best designs be chosen? Some of these questions were asked in 1935 when our story begins, but some were not asked early enough, or often enough.

Choosing the best designs for the Army Air Corps, as it was called then, meant the open bidding by competing aircraft companies required by a law intended to foster free enterprise and avoid possible political influence. According to the Air Corps Act of 1926, aircraft should be chosen by circulating requests for bids among private manufacturing companies, by comparing their proposals, and then purchasing the best offer. The task of selecting the best design was up to the Air Corps' Materiel Division, whose technical executive was Major Oliver P. Echols at Wright Field near Dayton, Ohio.

Edgar Schmued. *CS*

Unlike today's agencies, this was not an especially large bureaucracy and had many other tasks. Coordination of engineering and procurement was the task of project offices. The Air Corps Pursuit Project Branch itself consisted of one first lieutenant, one civilian engineer, and a secretary. Benjamin S. Kelsey, an MIT graduate, became chief of this office in 1934 and held that post for nine years. He personally examined, and usually flew, each prototype offered.

The actual selections, however, were made by a Board of Officers set up for each competition to evaluate these proposals by awarding points for a "Figure of Merit." The project officer acted as the board's recorder and could talk directly to company officials about their proposals. Company officials were not allowed meetings with board members themselves.[1]

In 1935, the different boards set up to choose new bomber and pursuit types met in critical times. Many of the warplanes that became famous in World War II made their first appearance that year, including the Boeing B-17, Hawker Hurricane, Messerschmitt 109, and the Consolidated PBY flying boat. While other famous warplanes, like the North American P-51 of 1940, came later, their design shapes usually followed the general patterns established in 1935.

That was also the year that Hitler publicly ended the Versailles Treaty's limits on German rearmament and announced the new German air force, the Luftwaffe. The arms race preparing for World War II had begun, even before Mussolini began his invasion of Ethiopia. All around the world, airplane designers bent over their drawing boards to plan new air weapons.

At the beginning of 1935, U.S. Army fighter squadrons still used planes whose open cockpits and exposed landing gear showed their descent from the Spads and Fokkers of World War I. Most of these fighters were Curtiss P-6 and Boeing P-12 biplanes with fabric-covered wings, while the Boeing P-26 was a metal-covered, wire-braced monoplane. Biplanes also equipped all the Royal Air Force squadrons, and even the fighters then rolling out of German factories for the new Luftwaffe were biplanes.

A new generation of fast bombers, begun by the Martin B-10 monoplanes, was faster than the Army biplanes in service. Since these bombers could attack their targets before being intercepted by enemy defenders, it seemed that the bomber would always get through. Bomber proponents felt that pursuit aviation had lost importance and that bombers alone were the decisive air weapon.

The argument about the power of bombers had important implications. Only air bombardment could affect the course of the war by attacking strategic targets. If bombers were not fast or well enough armed to penetrate enemy territory deeply, then airplanes could be used only for the close support of ground troops. From this dispute emerged the political issue most on aviation minds since the days of airpower advocate Billy Mitchell: should air power remain a part of the Army or be organized as a third service, equal to the Army and Navy? The perception of bomber effectiveness often determined official attitudes toward that question.

While wartime publicity had made fighter aces like Richthofen and Rickenbacker famous, it could be argued that their

Fokkers and Spads had not changed even one day's course of World War I. But Claire Chennault, then an instructor at the Air Corps Tactical School at Maxwell Field, argued that pursuits (as fighters were called then) could defeat bombers, given enough warning by ground spotters. Defenders of the pursuits realized that speed, rather than maneuverability, had become the main criterion for acceptance.

Among some 368 fighters the Army had when 1935 began, only the Consolidated P-30 displayed what would become the classic lines of a World War II fighter: an all-metal low-wing monoplane with retractable wheels, enclosed cockpits, and cantilever (without external bracing) wings. Powered by a supercharged 675-hp Curtiss liquid-cooled in-line engine, this two-seater had been designed by Robert Woods. Four P-30s had been delivered for service tests in 1934, and 50 more had been ordered for delivery in 1936 as PB-2As (PB = Pursuit Biplace). Of all Army fighters, only the P-30's top speed of 256 mph was fast enough to catch the Martin bombers.

It was now evident that a new generation of monoplane fighters was necessary. Looking forward to the funding for fiscal 1936 (the budget year from July 1, 1935, to June 30, 1936), the Army Air Corps planned to buy new fighter types. On January 15, 1935, the Air Corps announced a design competition for pursuit planes. An all-metal monocoque fuselage and cantilever monoplane wings were desired. Bids were to be opened May 6 on proposals to fit two specifications: X-602 for pursuit, two-place, and X-603 for pursuit, one-place.

In a design competition, the Air Corps invited private companies to offer prelimi-nary drawings of proposed aircraft to fulfill an Army specification. The winning designs would be given an Army designation and a contract for engineering data, an experimental prototype, or perhaps even a service test contract for 3 to 15 planes.

At the same time, the Army needed to buy about 80 pursuits in fiscal 1936 to replace aircraft in service, so bids were also requested for two-place and one-place pursuits, to be opened May 27 and August 9, 1935, respectively. To enter a production contract competition, private builders had to submit a sample aircraft, built at their own expense, for testing at Wright Field. As it turned out, the result of this complicated procedure, required by the law intended to encourage competition among private enterprises, was that not a single aircraft was purchased during 1935.

The winner of the design competition for two-seaters had been designated XP-33 and was essentially the Consolidated P-30 with a new air-cooled, Pratt & Whitney Twin Wasp R-1830-1 twin-row radial. For the production contract, a colorful Russian immigrant, Alexander de Seversky, offered the only sample plane, but it was damaged on the way to Wright Field and didn't arrive in time.

Meanwhile, service tests were convincing the Army that two-seaters were too lacking in maneuverability to be good fighters and that the single .30-caliber hand-operated gun in the rear cockpit was unlikely to be of much help in a battle. No more two-seater fighter production contracts were to be made, and the Consolidated XP-33 was canceled while still in the blueprint stage.

The single-seat fighter competitions were much more active, and the patterns of

World War II fighters were firmly established. No less than 16 bids were opened in the May design competition. After five months of evaluation, an unexpected choice was made. The fastest American plane then was the Wedell-Williams racer, built in a Louisiana hangar, without blueprints, by a pair of brothers who were amateur engineers. Although they had no real factory, the little company was awarded a development contract for an XP-34 design based on their racers.

No XP-34 ever appeared, due to the death of the Wedell brothers and their backer Williams in flying accidents and the inability of their survivors to complete the contract requirements. The lesson learned was that a company with mass-production capacity was needed.[2] Fortunately, the next production contract competition produced prototypes whose performance exceeded the unfulfilled XP-34's promise.

The most successful pursuit effort of 1935 was the Curtiss design, by Donovan R. Berlin, that became the P-36. Berlin had been hired away from Northrop as chief engineer by the Buffalo, New York, firm because of his experience with all-metal construction. Born in Romona, Indiana, on June 13, 1898, he was a mechanical engineering graduate of Purdue University.[3] His P-36 would be the first American fighter to down German planes, the first to pass the 1,000-plane production total, and was developed into the P-40, the principal U.S. production fighter of the war's early years.

Berlin began work on the prototype, known as Curtiss Design 75, on November 1, 1934. Seeing that engines are the pacing element in aircraft design and development, he planned from the beginning an aircraft large enough in size and wing area to accommodate future growth in power-plant size. Berlin wanted to "provide the ultimate in performance, stability, maneuverability, controllability and maintenance, and . . . a structure which would lend itself to quantity production."[4]

The resulting pursuit had a generous 236-square-foot area wing, into which the landing wheels retracted by folding backward and rotating 90 degrees to present a clean undersurface. When test pilot H. Lloyd Child made the first flight on May 13, 1935, an air-cooled 700-hp Wright XR-1510 was used, but this experimental radial engine was soon replaced by a 775-hp Wright XR-1670. (These military designations indicate the engine's size in cubic inches, so the higher the number, the larger the power plant. The XR stood for experimental radial engine, its cylinders arranged in a circle and cooled by the airstream.)

Neither of these power plants was accepted for Air Corps production, so another air-cooled radial, the 750-hp Pratt & Whitney R-1535, accepted by the Army for attack and observation planes, powered the Curtiss Design 75 when it appeared on August 7 for the army competition. To their surprise, a rival Seversky pursuit turned up on August 15 with a big 850-hp R-1820 Cyclone, the single-row radial used by Army bombers.

Alexander de Seversky was born in Tiflis (then part of Russia, but now Tbilisi in the Georgian S.S.R.) on June 7, 1894, graduated from the Imperial Naval Academy, and was taking a postgraduate course in aeronautical engineering when the war began. Sascha, as he was called, lost a leg in 1915, when he was shot down while attacking a German

Four different air-cooled engines were tried on the first prototype for the Curtiss P-36; here, in 1935, it has a Wright R-1670. *Smithsonian*

destroyer, but resumed flying for the czar's navy in the Baltic. Sent to the United States in 1917 to buy aircraft until the revolution took Russia out of the war, he remained in America as an aeronautical engineer, became a U.S. citizen in 1927, and married a woman from a prominent Texas family.[5]

He became the president, designer, and test pilot of his own airplane company, along with the chief engineer Alexander Kartveli, also a fellow immigrant, who was born in Tiflis on September 9, 1896. In 1933, Seversky built an advanced all-metal low-

wing monoplane on twin floats. Piloting it himself, he set a new world's speed record for amphibians and then reworked his craft as a landplane to win the Army's first contract for a monoplane basic trainer.

Using the same 220-square-foot one-piece semi-elliptical wing, Seversky completed a second prototype in June 1935 as a two-seater fighter with streamlined landing

gear. When he realized the Army wanted single-seaters, he replaced the rear seat with a baggage compartment, put in a larger engine, and retracted the wheels backward into fairings under the wings.

The resulting Sev-1 demonstrated a 289-mph top speed with the 850-hp Cyclone and won the favor of the evaluation board. But Curtiss protested that the competition was unfair, since, among other things, the Seversky had arrived late after changing to

Alexander Seversky and his P-35 prototype with a Pratt & Whitney R-1830. With this plane, he snatched a production contract from Curtiss in 1936. The landing gear folded back into fairings. *Smithsonian*

the larger engine. Army officials were not entirely happy with the result, either.

For one thing, only 2 of the 16 companies interested in fighter design had actually provided prototypes. (Northrop's promising little 3A design had disappeared on a test flight off the coast.) General Frank M. Andrews, GHQ Air Force commander, complained that the selection board did very little test flying and recommended more thorough suitability trials.[6]

Howard Hughes's new world speed record of 352 mph, set on September 13, 1935, with his own beautifully streamlined monoplane, suggested the speeds possible for single-seat fighters of similar layout. The little racer couldn't carry the weight of a combat type, of course, and had used special 100-octane fuel. General Echols asked that the Hughes plane visit Dayton for inspection, but Hughes did not accept the invitation.

Assistant Secretary of War Harry H. Woodring set a new date, April 15, 1936, for pursuit proposals, giving the builders a chance to improve their craft. Four builders responded with sample aircraft. Consolidated sent the seventh PB-2A (P-30A) modified as a single-seater with a 700-hp Curtiss V-1570-61, the only in-line engine in the competition. But they used old technology, with an airframe too big for the power, and the price, $44,000 each for 25, was too high for the Air Corps.

Chance Vought had purchased Northrop's fighter design and it first flew on March 29, 1936, as the V-141 with a 750-hp R-1535. Smallest of the contenders, it suffered from tail vibrations. After the Army rejected the Vought, an improved example was sold to the Japanese army in July 1937. Its similarity in layout to the Zero caused some wartime comment, but the Zero was a carrier-based fighter with a different mission concept.

Don Berlin's Hawk 75 reappeared on April 4, 1936, powered by an 850-hp single-row Wright XR-1820-39 Cyclone, but Seversky again stepped up to a Pratt & Whitney Twin Wasp R-1830-9 twin-row radial. While the power was the same, the smaller diameter of the Twin Wasp reduced drag and improved visibility. Curtiss estimated the top speed of their Hawk as 294 mph with the Cyclone, or 297 mph if provided with a Twin Wasp, but only 285 mph was actually obtained during the tests.

As it turned out, the Air Corps decided to standardize on the Twin Wasp for production pursuits, and on the Cyclone, because of its lower fuel consumption, for bombers. Seversky won a contract, approved June 30, 1936, for 77 P-35 pursuits, while Curtiss had to be content, for the time being, with three Y1P-36s on a service test contract approved August 7.[7] To raise capital and get factory space in Farmingdale, Long Island, Seversky sold stock in his company. These investors would take control away from him in less than three years.

But fiscal 1938 funds would allow purchase of about 220 new pursuits, and both companies tried again with bids to be opened April 2, 1937. The first Y1P-36, number 37-068, was delivered to Wright Field with an R-1830-13 radial on March 4, 1937, and soon followed by its two service test companions. Curtiss also introduced the Allison in-line engine in the XP-37 flown to Wright on April 20. This was actually the original Hawk 75 rebuilt to use the liquid-cooled V-1710-11 with its streamlined nose and the pilot's cockpit moved back to the tail.[8]

Where will a pursuit plane fight: near to the ground or far above it? This must be answered by the kind of engine supercharging. As you go higher the air gets thinner and power decreases; an unsupercharged engine will lose a third of its power at 10,000 feet and 60 percent by 20,000 feet. A supercharger compresses the air and keeps engine power up to the unit's critical altitude, where power starts to fall off. Since thinner air at higher altitudes means less drag, the aircraft can go about 1 percent faster with every 1,000 feet of height and is fastest near its critical altitude.

The most common supercharger type was the gear-driven blower built into the back of the R-1830-13 on early P-36s. Yielding

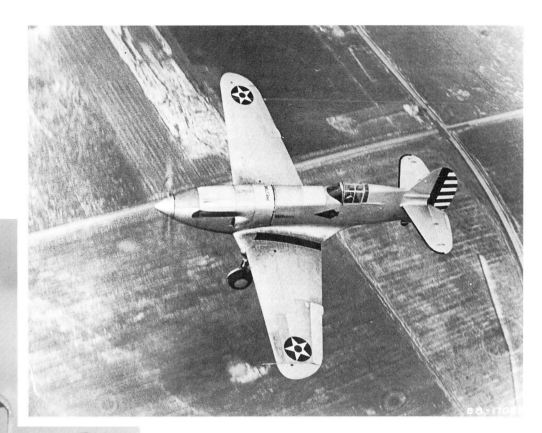

The Curtiss XP-37 was the first fighter with the Allison engine. Radiators were inside the fuselage behind the engine and a turbosupercharger was underneath. *Smithsonian*

Air Corps pursuit specialist Ben Kelsey with the second P-36A, whose wheels rotated 90 degrees to fit inside the wing. *USAF*

900 hp at 12,000 feet, it gave the Y1P-36 a top speed of 295 mph at 10,000 feet. The Allison V-1710-11 used an external exhaust-driven turbosupercharger developed by General Electric, which offered 1,000 hp at 20,000 feet, enabling the XP-37 to reach 340 mph at that altitude.

Since these turbosuperchargers were an American development unequaled in Europe, it was tempting to see them as a kind of magic for high-altitude speed, and the devices were not allowed to be exported before 1941. But they did have significant disadvantages. Turbosuperchargers were heavy, had to be placed outside the engine cowling to obtain enough cooling, and generated so much heat and pressure that explosions of their rotor blades and in-flight fires were frequent. Prewar models lacked an automatic regulator, so the need to control them was a distraction for already-preoccupied fighter pilots. With such problems, designers preferred the simpler gear-driven internal supercharger unless high-altitude speed was absolutely demanded.[9]

Seversky challenged Curtiss again when he flew his AP-1, a preproduction P-35, to Wright in March 1937. But this time Curtiss got the contract, while Seversky had trouble with his P-35. The wheel fairings and windshield had to be modified, dihedral added to the wing, and only four P-35s had been accepted by the end of 1937, while Seversky lost money on the contract. His unsold prototypes were used for air racing, gaining much publicity, and a few two-seater "Convoy Fighters" for bomber escort were sold to the Soviet Union and the Japanese navy in 1938.

Curtiss won the largest fighter contract since 1918, for 210 P-36s on July 30, 1937. Thirteen Curtiss YP-37s were also ordered on December 11, to service-test an Allison-powered pursuit. The first production P-36A, 38-001, was flown on April 20, 1938. It had the same Twin Wasp as the Y1P-36, and the usual two nose guns of American fighters, while no bomb racks were provided.

When the fourth P-36A, 38-004, was delivered on September 9, it had a new R-1830-17 with a carburetor for 100-octane fuel. This delivered 1,050 hp at altitude, improving performance, so the P-36A did 313 mph at 10,000 feet and its service ceiling was 33,000 feet.[10] (This aircraft was flown back to Buffalo on October 26, where it would be converted to the XP-42. Lieutenant Kelsey covered the 360 miles at full throttle in 61 minutes, helped by a good tail wind.)

While the P-36 was a fine fighter, the Air Corps knew its performance was modest compared to developments abroad. The Messerschmitt Bf 109 had shifted from its original 670-hp Jumo to a 1,100-hp Daimler-Benz in the Bf 109E-1 production model. Top speed was 354 mph at 12,300 feet, and four 7.9-mm (.30-caliber) guns were used. The Supermarine Spitfire I, which entered RAF squadron service in August 1938 powered by a Rolls-Royce Merlin II with 1,030 hp, also on 87-octane fuel, had a top speed of 362 mph at 19,000 feet with eight .30-caliber guns in the wings.

American cross-country tests in 1941 would reveal the Spitfire's limitations: its short range, which required frequent landings, and its marginal stability, which added to its superb maneuverability but became tiring and uncomfortable on long flights. "The plane that was superior in all respects in its own country would not have met our standards or been accepted . . . by our evaluating boards," asserted Ben Kelsey.[11]

To overcome this speed and firepower lead, the Air Corps had to push its experimental programs into production aircraft. From a power-plant viewpoint, this meant better supercharging and replacing the built-in drag of the air-cooled radials with the streamlined nose allowed by the P-37's new liquid-cooled in-line Allison engine.

Two guns in the nose had armed American single-seat fighters in 1918 and still did 20 years later. The first American-designed fighter to reach quantity production, the Boeing-built MB-3A of 1922, had a .30-caliber Browning on one side of the engine cowl and another on the other side, which could be replaced by a .50-caliber gun. Curtiss P-36A Hawks of 1938 had the same firepower.

Export Hawk 75s built for China and Argentina in 1937 and '38 added another .30-caliber gun in each wing, as did H75A Hawks built for France; "this seemingly simple modification involved changing 150 assembly templates and the fabrication of 350 new ones."[12] After this four-gun combination had been tried in a single P-36C in December 1938, a January 26, 1939, order specified four guns for the last 30 aircraft on the Army contract completed in May. Retainers were added under the P-36C wing guns to prevent used cartridges from damaging other aircraft in a stacked formation! (When would fighters be shooting in stacked formation?)

But the most important step was the Interceptor Pursuit concept, which resulted in the most effective fighter designs available when World War II began in 1939. A heavy armament of a cannon and four machine guns and Allisons turbosupercharged for high altitude were requested. Power could be doubled by using two engines.

THE INTERCEPTOR PURSUIT COMPETITION

On January 8, 1937, five companies were secretly invited to participate in a design competition for an experimental twin-en-

Lockheed's Kelly Johnson, the genius behind the radical P-38. *SDAM*

gine interceptor pursuit. The specification, X-608 Interceptor Pursuit (twin-engine), called for a top speed of 360 to 400 mph at 20,000 feet and a climb to that altitude in six minutes. Lockheed submitted its Model-22 specification, signed by Clarence L. Johnson, on April 13, 1937.

"Kelly" Johnson would become the best-known American fighter designer, and his Model 22 became the famous P-38 Lightning. Since a book-length biography about him is available, only brief mention need be

made here. Born February 27, 1910, in Ish-
peming, Michigan, of Swedish immigrant
parents, he won his aeronautical engineering degree at the University of Michigan.
While doing graduate work there, he was
hired in 1933 by Lockheed and spent his
entire illustrious career there.

Experience with Lockheed's twin-engine
designs, including the Electra transport, the
XC-35 high-altitude test plane, and a preliminary proposal for an XFM-2, prepared
the way for the boldest single-seat fighter
proposal of the time. The engines were the
same as those of the P-37 (V-1710-11 and
V-1710-15, with opposite rotation), but the
superchargers, radiators, main landing gear,
and rudders were carried on twin booms. A
center pod contained the pilot, armament,
and the nose wheel for the first tricycle
landing gear on a fighter. This permitted
faster landings, and therefore a higher wing
loading, than had been safe for other fighter
types, while an elaborate system of extended flaps kept stalling speed within reason.[13]

After evaluating competitive designs offered by Curtiss, Hughes, and Vultee, the
Air Corps awarded Lockheed the contract
on June 23, 1937, for one XP-38 prototype.
At the same time the P-38 was being developed, the Air Corps sponsored development
of a single-engine interceptor pursuit with
specification X-609, issued March 19, 1937.
Like the preceding requirement, it also
called for a top speed of 360 to 400 mph at
20,000 feet and included cannon armament
and nose-wheel gear as desired features.

Bell Aircraft submitted two design proposals using an Allison engine with an extended drive shaft to the nose, allowing
room for a cannon and two machine guns.

In Model 3, the pilot sat behind the engine,
but the Model-4 pilot sat in front of the
engine, with much better visibility. Along
with the model specification, dated June 3,
1937, a 30-minute film was prepared for the
seven officers on the selection board, perhaps the first use of this sales pitch in fighter
procurement. The Army ordered a Bell XP-
39, based on the Model 4, on October 7,
1937.[14]

Robert J. Woods, Bell's chief engineer
and P-39 designer, was born on June 21,
1904, of a poor family in Youngstown,
Ohio. Like Kelly Johnson, he earned his
aeronautical engineering degree at the University of Michigan. A six-foot, 200-pound
young man, he attracted Larry Bell's attention in 1931 with his work on the YP-24,
which led to the impressive Consolidated
P-30 mentioned earlier. After designing the
big "Airacuda" multiplace fighter for Bell,
he turned to the Airacobra, as the P-39 was
named.[15]

Bob Woods described the advantages of
a rear-engine installation: better streamlining and forward vision and more room in
the nose for heavy-caliber armament and
the retracted nose wheel. The 10-foot drive
shaft extending to the propeller added only
51 pounds to the airframe weight.[16]

The XP-39 was designed to accommodate
a single 37-mm T-9 with automatic loading
pointed through the propeller hub, along
with two synchronized .50-caliber guns, according to a December 2, 1938, directive.
But the Bell Airacobra prototype itself was
never fitted with guns.

Lockheed's XP-38 was the first Interceptor Pursuit to fly, on January 27, 1939, at
March Field, California. Since Lockheed
had no company pilot familiar with fighters,

The prototype XP-40 was a P-36A with single-stage Allison and radiator behind the wing. *Smithsonian*

Lieutenant Ben Kelsey did the test, narrowly escaping disaster when the flaps failed. The secrecy that surrounded the project was lifted for a transcontinental speed dash on February 11, an attempt to break the record set by Howard Hughes in his racer. After seven hours, two minutes flying time, the XP-38 was demolished in a crash landing at Mitchel Field, but Lieutenant Kelsey was unhurt.

Bell's XP-39 went by train to Wright Field for its first flight by James Taylor on April 6, 1939. Its Allison V-1710-17 was turbosupercharged to give 1,000 hp at 20,-000 feet, where a 390-mph top speed was expected. It was the first single-engine American fighter to have tricycle landing gear and the engine behind the pilot, today the standard layout for jet fighters like the F-16, while the P-38's twin-engine, twin-tail layout is seen today in the F-15.

While the promised performance of the experimental Interceptor Pursuit types was attractive, some engineers were skeptical of their exhaust-driven turbosuperchargers, while Army leaders considered that a 15,000-foot critical altitude available from built-in geared blowers would be sufficient for most fighters. Don Berlin complained that the P-37's "supercharger simply was

not working, and we didn't have time to develop that, too."

Instead, Berlin proposed on March 3, 1938, to fit a P-36 with an Allison using a single-stage, geared supercharger, adding medium-altitude speed without the turbo's disadvantages. The Air Corps quickly responded on April 26 with a contract to modify the tenth P-36A (38-10) to the XP-40. Powered by a V-1710-19 rated at 1,000 hp at 10,000 feet, it was first flown on October 14, 1938, by Eddie Elliott.[17]

The P-40 had arrived at just the right time, for President Roosevelt was asking Congress to expand the Air Corps from 2,300 to 5,500 planes. He understood the influence of German air power on the Munich crisis and that American air power needed to be rapidly increased.

The Air Corps called for bids on a pursuit proposal, CP38-390, to be opened on January 25, 1939, and on the same day issued new specifications for more advanced designs. Sensing that funding would soon be available, Curtiss and Seversky sent their prototypes to Wright Field. These included the YP-37 and XP-40 with Allison in-line engines, and the XP-41, XP-42, and AP-9 with advanced Pratt & Whitney Twin Wasp radials with gear-driven superchargers. Turbosuperchargers were used on the H75R and AP-4 Wasp-powered prototypes, as well as on the unconventional Bell XP-39.

Only the P-40 was nearly ready for production, while the best of the others would need service tests. Although Curtiss was the low bidder and had guaranteed a 360-mph top speed at 15,000 feet, only 342 mph at 12,200 feet had been attained in tests. By March 28, General Arnold suggested sending the XP-40 to the National Advisory Committee for Aeronautics (NACA) for tests in that government agency's full-scale wind tunnel, where several ways of cleaning up the design's streamlining were developed.[18] Then the XP-40 was returned to the company on April 11 for reworking.

The Military Appropriations Act for fis-

cal 1940, providing funds to begin Air Corps expansion, was signed by the president on April 26, 1939, and on the same day, 524 Curtiss P-40 low-altitude pursuits were ordered for $12,872,398, the largest Air Corps contract to that date. The next day 13 Lockheed YP-38s, at $2,180,728, and 13 Bell YP-39s, at $1,073,445, were added for service tests of high-altitude interceptors. All these planes had Allison engines and were to have two .50-caliber and two .30-caliber guns,

but a 37-mm cannon and turbosupercharging were to be added to the interceptors. One thing was settled: the Allison would be the only American-designed liquid-cooled engine available in World War II, as none of the liquid-cooled projects begun by four other companies would reach mass production.

Air-cooled engines were not entirely forgotten. Seversky's turbosupercharged private venture, the AP-4, had been destroyed by a midair turbo fire on March 22, 1939, but on May 12, 13 YP-43 similar high-altitude pursuits were ordered. Powered by an R-1830-35 of 1,200 hp at 25,000 feet, they were armed with two .50-caliber guns in the nose and two .30-caliber guns in the wings, like the P-36C and P-40. By this time, Seversky had lost control of his company to stockholders, who picked a new president, retained Alexander Kartveli as chief designer and engineer, and changed its name to Republic Aircraft.

The problem of streamlining the air-cooled radial remained. Pratt & Whitney did develop a special 1,200-hp Wasp with an extended propeller shaft that could be enclosed behind a large spinner, and this was tried in the Curtiss XP-42. Actually the fourth P-36A rebuilt, it was flown to Wright Field on March 5, 1939, but the problem of satisfactory engine cooling wasn't overcome.

That same type of engine was used by the Vultee Vanguard, designed by Richard W. Palmer, who had engineered the Hughes racer. The most highly streamlined air-

The first Vultee Vanguard was probably the most streamlined air-cooled fighter ever built. *SDAM*

cooled fighter ever built in America, with a completely enclosed engine and small wings, it was first flown on September 8, 1939, by Vance Breese.

Although designed for mass production, with many parts in common with the Vultee basic and advanced trainers then being offered the Army, it failed to win an Air Corps contract in the August 1939 competition for CP 39-770 pursuits. The Army also objected when company advertising called the Vanguard the P-48, since this might suggest Air Corps acceptance. After the scoop under the nose proved insufficient to cool the engine, the prototype was changed to use a standard R-1830-33 radial with a conventional cowling and got its only export contract in February 1940: 144 planes for Sweden.

Originally, the Bell YP-39 was to have the same turbosupercharged V-1710-17 used by the XP-39 and to reach 375 mph at 20,000 feet. On June 6, 1939, the prototype was sent to Langley Field for full-scale tests in NACA's wind tunnel. These led to several changes in configuration: the front wheel would no longer protrude from the nose, smaller main wheels could be enclosed in the wings, the cockpit hood lowered, cooling ducts moved to the wings, and the turbosupercharger replaced by a single-stage gear-driven system, like that of the P-40.[19]

On August 30, Larry Bell told the Materiel Division that the P-39 could attain 400 mph at 15,000 feet with 1,150 hp, if these changes were made. This proposal was accepted, and the prototype returned to the factory for rebuilding. It was flown again on November 25, 1939, as the XP-39B with the Allison V-1710-37, delivering

1,090 hp at 13,300 feet, the power plant then chosen for the YP-39s. Wrote Bell, in thanking NACA for their assistance, "We have eliminated a million and one problems by the removal of the turbo-supercharger. . . ."[20]

Looking forward to fiscal 1941 contracts, the Air Corps prepared specifications C-615, -616, and -618 for three different fighter types to be ready on January 25, 1939. Circular Proposals (CP) were issued March 11, 1939, for these types:

a. 39-770 Interceptor
           Pursuit
           (single-engine) specification C-616
b. 39-775 Interceptor
           Pursuit
           (twin-Engine)   specification C-615
c. 39-780 Multiplace
           Fighter   specification C-618

While the multiplace fighter concept was abandoned, the Interceptor Pursuit requirements expressed Air Corps desires for the ideal single-seat fighter. Originally, the C-616 Interceptor's top speed was to be 360 to 420 mph at 20,000 feet, and landing speed was limited to 70 mph. Fuel for one hour at 75-percent power plus one hour at full throttle was needed. Among the desired features were a 37-mm T-9 cannon, two .50- and two .30-caliber guns, and a nose-wheel landing gear, all to be seen only on the P-39.[21]

The purpose of CP 39-770 was to provide the 1940 development program with three pursuit interceptor types "having substantially better performance than the P-39, P-40, and P-43 airplanes."[22] Future production plans were foreshadowed when CP-

770 was amended on May 25, 1939, to cover lots of 110 to 300 aircraft and for "war production quantities" on June 10. Only designs were requested; the Army could not wait for sample aircraft.

By May 10, 1939, the Materiel Division was considering less restrictive requirements, deleting the mandatory tricycle gear and 37-mm cannon, and permitting designers more flexibility in supercharging and armament.[23] On June 29, CP-770 replaced specification C-616 with C-619, dated June 24, 1939. This pursuit specification allowed top speed and rate of climb to be measured at any critical altitude from 15,000 feet to 20,000 feet, and opened the contest to more conventional designs. At the same time, the due date for company responses to CP-770 was moved from July 6, 1939, to August 7.[24]

Taking advantage of the liberalized requirements, Republic won first place in this competition with the AP-4J design by Alexander Kartveli, a heavier P-43 using an air-cooled 1,400 hp Pratt & Whitney R-2180 and armed with two .50- and four .30-caliber guns. It won a contract, dated September 13, 1939, and approved October 12, for 80 P-44 pursuits. Kartveli had also utilized tests of the XP-41 in NACA's full-scale tunnel to improve the streamlining possible with an air-cooled radial engine.

Second place was given to the Bell 4-F, a YP-39 with an internally supercharged 1,150-hp V-1710-35. The 80 ordered were originally designated the Bell P-45 "interceptor pursuit," but were renamed P-39C before their delivery began in January 1941.

Curtiss offered a successor to the P-40 powered by a new version of the Allison, the V-1710-39 rated at 1,150 at 11,800 feet. As the third-place choice, it was considered worth a contract for two XP-46 prototypes. This same engine was also planned for the fourth-place Seversky AP-10, a drastically stripped interceptor that was ordered as the Republic XP-47.

The Douglas DB312 design received a "phase development only" contract for a mock-up and wind-tunnel model of a lightweight pursuit to be designated XP-48. This was expected to have an air-cooled, in-line, 525-hp Ranger SGV-770 and weigh only 3,400 pounds gross, with two machine guns. By February 1940 the XP-48 design had been abandoned, because its speed was so low that further development was unwarranted.

Looking forward to fiscal 1941, the Materiel Division's new chief, General George H. Brett, had suggested on February 24, 1939, another circular proposal for twin-engine interceptor pursuit designs. This was CP39-775, issued March 11, with bids due on July 6, 1939.[25] Lockheed responded with Model 222, a design similar to the YP-38, in report 1462, dated June 16, 1939. When powered by Allisons turbosupercharged to give 1,150 hp at 20,000 feet, Lockheed guaranteed 425 mph at 20,000 feet, or 411 mph at 15,000 feet, if gear-driven superchargers were used.[26]

The board of officers appointed on July 10 to evaluate the bids consisted of Lt. Col. Carl Spaatz, Lt. Col. Earl Maiden, and Major George Kenney. Of the four companies bidding on the contract, they chose Lockheed as the winner, with 763.3 merit points, compared to 611.6 points for a Grumman entry.

General Arnold asked the assistant secretary of war on August 9 to purchase 66 Lockheed P-38s, which the company had promised it could complete in 15 months.

The Air Corps planned to have these fighters delivered to the First Pursuit Group at Selfridge Field, Michigan, by December 30, 1940, replacing their P-35 and P-36s. Arnold also proposed investing in an advanced prototype with improved engines that became the Lockheed XP-49, and in the XP-50, the only fighter Grumman ever built for the Army.

But power-plant problems would prevent success for either interceptor. Grumman's XP-50, ordered November 29, 1939, was based on the Navy XF5F-1 design, with the addition of tricycle gear and turbosuperchargers for the Wright R-1820 Cyclones. Since these were the same power plants in production for the B-17, the XP-50 was ready first. Flight tests began February 18, 1941, but ended May 14 with a supercharger explosion that destroyed the aircraft and halted the project.

An authority for purchase (AFP) for the XP-49 was issued October 14, and a contract was approved January 22, 1940. Lockheed had originally promised delivery in 14 months, but engine development failures were to frustrate this hope. The engine first chosen was the Pratt & Whitney X-1800 (the Army's H-2600-5), but this radical liquid-cooled project was to be canceled on October 7, 1940, because Pratt & Whitney wanted to concentrate on their successful air-cooled Wasps.

By August 15, 1940, two Continental IV-1430-5 (IV for Inverted In-line) engines were to be substituted; this engine was supposed to offer (according to April 22, 1940, estimates) 1,600 hp at 15,000 feet, with 27 percent less frontal drag than the Allison. Lockheed got a new contract (September 9), now scheduling delivery in 16 months. But

this power plant was a long time coming and would be a disappointment when it finally arrived.

By 1941, the Air Force saw the XP-49 only as a test bed for the Continental engines, while the P-38 would continue to utilize any improvements in the Allison. A mock-up inspection of the XP-49 was held on August 25 and 26, 1941, but not until April 22, 1942, could Continental ship two engines to Lockheed. On November 11, 1942, 33 months after the original contract, the XP-49 made its first flight, but its actual performance was inferior to that of the regular production P-38s.[27]

Before the end of 1939, and before developmental problems became known, it appeared the American fighter performance was becoming superior to that in Europe. The Air Corps had on order 789 single-seat fighters of 4 different production types, as well as 6 prototypes: a pair each of Curtiss XP-46 and Republic XP-47 low-altitude fighters and the twin-engine XP-49 and XP-50 high-altitude experimentals.

Four design teams, led by Don Berlin, Kelly Johnson, Alexander Kartveli, and Bob Wood had provided the Air Corps with what then seemed a strong fighter program. Since the P-40 was so similar to the P-36, Curtiss was able to have the first production example within a year. Flown on April 4, 1940, this P-40 had a V-1710-33 rated at 1,040 hp at 14,300 feet and had a top speed of 357 mph at that altitude.

Lockheed had a more difficult production task with its radical twin-engine aircraft, which were expected to reach 405 mph at 20,000 feet, powered by 1,150-hp V-1710-27/29 Allisons. Not until September 1940 was the first YP-38 airborne, and the last

Curtiss designer Don Berlin with the first production P-40, whose radiator intake was placed under the nose. *Smithsonian*

YP-38 would not be accepted until June 1941, about 10 months late. The first Bell YP-39 and Republic YP-43 were also accepted in September 1940.

Although widely published pictures of the P-38, P-39, P-40, and P-43 prototypes impressed the public with American technology, Air Corps leaders aware of foreign progress were not complacent. Air Corps Chief Major General Arnold wrote the GHQ Air Force commander on November 14 to prepare a study of pursuit training and of pursuit plane and tactical development. He cited the feeling of officers that pursuits were less important than bombers, could not defeat large bomber forces, and did not offer the best career opportunities for ambitious officers.

The resulting report, dated January 11, 1940, did focus on personnel problems, but fighter design was the central concern.[28] "For a number of years, thought has been centered principally on bombardment. Pursuit has been sort of a stepchild." But air operations abroad showed that the bomber "cannot defend itself adequately against pursuit attack."

Armament, said the report, "should be the first consideration" in designing pursuit planes. Pilots and fuel tanks of all combat planes needed protection from enemy gunfire. It had become clear that neither the fighting planes on hand nor those on order for the Air Corps were ready for the real world of combat. The best fighter had yet to be designed, but could that challenge be met by American fighter designers in time for World War II?

These designers had to follow the directions of the Army Air Corps, which would have to answer the fundamental questions: What will the fighter do? Will it fight only

enemies in the air or support ground forces, too? Where will it fight, near the ground or far above it, and near or far from its base? What will it cost, and how many can be had, and when will they be ready?

Choosing designs by formal competition

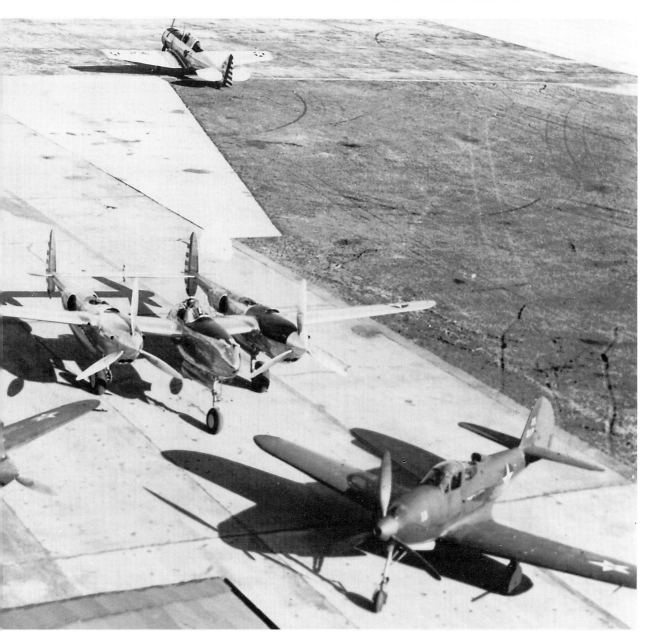

was clearly not the fastest or most effective system. While the five years before the war had seen great improvements in performance, from the P-30 to the P-50 designs, 1940 would bring radical changes in military requirements.

The three Allison-engine fighters ordered together in April 1939; the Curtiss P-40, Lockheed YP-38, and Bell YP-39. *USAF*

CHAPTER TWO

The Making of a Designer:
Ed Schmued and North American Aviation

Production of the YO-27 at Dundalk on November 1, 1932, contrasts with busy lines seen later. Fokker transports are in the background. *SDAM*

By the beginning of 1940, the designs of Curtiss, Lockheed, Bell, Republic, and Vultee seemed to have filled the fighter market. No one could have known that the Air Corps' best fighter had yet to be conceived by a company and a designer that had never offered a first-line fighter before.

The company was North American Aviation, which had opened its factory in California late in 1935. The designer was an immigrant from Germany, Edgar Schmued, whose aeronautical engineering was self-taught but who would take full advantage of the new design climate created by World War II.

"I was born December 30, 1899," wrote Schmued, "in a small town near Zweibrücken and the border with Lorraine. It was Hornbach, with about 1,200 inhabitants. My father, who was a dentist, thought it was too small a place to develop a practice. So he moved east of Berlin to Landsberg on the Warthe, a community of about 35,000, which, due to the last war, is now in Poland and called Grozow."[1]

Edgar's father, Heinrich August Schmued, was born in Salzburg, Austria, and his mother, Anna Barbara Hass, was born in Stuttgart, Germany. Edgar was the fourth of six children. Dr. Schmued retained his Austrian citizenship, which passed on to his sons. Edgar and his two brothers also kept their Austrian citizenship until after they crossed the Atlantic, although Edgar has always been referred to as German in American publications.[2]

Although Edgar attended Mittel und Gewerbe Shule (Middle and Business School), he credited his real education to his father: "I grew up and went to school in Landsberg. My father did very much to interest me in all technical matters. We belonged to a library and I always brought technical books home—the latest inventions, miscellaneous developments, descriptions of machinery. These interested me very much and practically consumed all the free time I had, and then some.

"I constantly had all the volumes of one particular edition of a technical encyclopedia at home, which didn't sit too well with the library. They wanted me to bring the books back regularly and then take them out again. This I didn't do, but I was learning how paper was made and how spinning machines worked.

"Now this was, to a large degree, responsible for my rather poor record in school. I was not a good student, because my interests were not in homework and schoolwork, but in technical developments. One of my early interests, of course, was aviation. It so happened that one day when my family was on an outing near the city, I heard a noise that was very uncommon, because it came from above. And there it was: a Wright airplane being flown by a Russian

Edgar Schmued as a student in Landsberg. *CS*

pilot named Abramovitch! He was flying from Berlin to Russia. It was my first sight of an airplane. I was just eight years old and it made such a tremendous impression on me that I decided, right then and there, that this was for me. This was going to be my life.

"So I took a great amount of interest in all the literature that was available in the field of aviation. My father was always willing to buy me any book that I wanted pertaining to aviation or any other field. He was really exceptional, and I owe him a great deal. The time he spent with me to explain the technical features of a machine or of a development started me on the right track. For this, I could never repay him. He was always supporting me and answering all the ques-

tions that he could. It was a very good introduction to technical life for me.

"My father's interest in me was really
outstanding. He was also technically very
apt and could do many things that you
wouldn't ordinarily expect of a dentist. He
had a number of inventions, but since he
was not a good businessman, he did not sell
them. Many ideas were very good. One was
a terminal for electric wiring, which was
rather unique and he built that into many of
the devices he developed.

"While he was very practical in technical
things, the family sometimes suffered from
his not being a good businessman. There
were nights when we went to bed hungry,
because money was scarce and we were a
large family of six children.

"When the time came for me to go to a
university or technical school, we found
that there was no money available. He just
could not afford to send me to any of those
schools, so he bought me all the books I
needed. I then decided I would educate myself technically and started studying and
educating myself to become an engineer.
Necessarily, an engineer without formal
training is just a self-educated man, and
under the circumstances, it was a good
choice. Although it was difficult, very difficult, it strengthened my character and I
succeeded in gathering enough knowledge
to step out and eventually become an airplane designer."

APPRENTICESHIP

Since he had not graduated from his school,
Edgar Schmued started as an apprentice in
a small engine factory. "There were two
types of apprentices in Germany: those that

just wanted to become a mechanic, and the
others who were planning to be engineers.
Those who planned to be engineers served
only two years and were called volunteers.
The others, who took three years to finish,
were called apprentices.

"I was a volunteer in an engine factory
and my father was able to impress the
owner of the factory with the necessity of
giving me the best training possible. I was
started on the bench and did quite a bit and
then I changed over to machines. I was
working on a lathe, a milling machine, a
shaper, and on a large lathe, and was also
learning hand forging. I became quite adept
in this art and ultimately the owner gave me
a project to build one of his engines completely from scratch. It turned out to be a
very nice project, and at the completion of
my two years, I had also completed this engine.

"I was very, very proud of that. Now I
was at least started properly. I was free and
I did quite a bit of work at home. I was
studying books on all fields, anything technical interested me, particularly aviation. I
had some very fine books, including one by
Eiffel, the man who built the Eiffel Tower.
His book, called *The Resistance of the Air,* was
a classic. I was one of the first ones to buy
and study it. I learned quite a few things
this way and it gave me a good grasp of
aircraft engineering problems. I studied the
structural and aerodynamic requirements
and whatever the state of the art could offer
at that time, which was not very much, but
it was fairly well worth it."

In March 1917, the German and Austrian
empires were deep into World War I, and
17-year-old Edgar avoided German con-
scription by serving in the Austro-Hungar-

ian Flying Service. His wartime experience, apparently as a mechanic, was brief—the Austrian empire surrendered by November 3, 1918—and he does not refer to it in any of his writings.

Returning to his family in Landsberg after the war, Edgar threw himself into a project to make a home-built airplane and began construction of a sports biplane in his father's library. His father bought a three-cylinder Anzani engine of Belgian origin for him. To remove the half-finished fuselage and wings from the home, part of the wall had to be removed, much to his little sister Else's astonishment.

The would-be builder had reckoned without the Versailles Treaty, which discouraged the manufacture of aircraft in Germany and required the return of any property taken when Germany occupied other countries. When members of the Allied Control Commission found out about his engine, which was alleged to have been taken away from firms in occupied Belgium, they decided to confiscate it. "This ended my attempt to build an airplane, since I couldn't afford to buy another engine." However, he continued, Else remembers, drawing airplanes.

By 1921, Edgar had left his Landsberg home to live in Bergedorf, a Hamburg suburb. There he was employed by a developer of automobile equipment who encouraged the young inventor. Before long, five German patents were registered in Edgar's name, from a *ventilvergaser* (carburetor valve), dated May 6, 1920, to a *brennstofffordervorrichtung* (fuel device) dated December 30, 1922, his 23rd birthday.[3]

But business enterprise in Germany at that time was being destroyed by a massive inflation that wiped out savings and therefore made investment capital nearly impossible to find. Costly legal complications also appeared.

In Schmued's own words: "I designed a vacuum tank, feeding gasoline to the engine, and a floatless carburetor for automobiles. This was quite an interesting undertaking, but we ran into trouble with patent lawsuits and had to quit building it. If we would have had the money to fight the lawsuit, we probably could have won. The risk was too great, so we abandoned it."

EMIGRATION

Germany in 1925 did not present good prospects for an ambitious young man. Inflation, unemployment, and political instability threatened the young Weimar Republic. Very few airplanes were being built. Edgar now had a wife, Luisa, a divorcée from Hanover who was nine years his senior. They had a son, Rolf Dietrich Schmued, born June 14, 1921.

Schmued's oldest brother, Erwin, became a dentist like their father and emigrated to Brazil, to practice his profession in São Paulo. Eventually, younger brother Erich, also a dentist, followed him to the substantial German community in the same city. The three Schmued sisters remained in Germany, where one, Elfriede Pauscher, was in Alzey, and the youngest, who became Else Opitz, still lived in Taunus in 1988.

Edgar decided to follow his brothers to Brazil in 1925 in the hope of "interesting people there in airplane ventures, and possibly starting an airplane outfit." His family was to remain in Germany until he was successful.

"In São Paulo, Brazil, I met a young man—a student and the son of a very rich textile manufacturer. The son was very interested in aviation and suggested that I make a presentation of my plans to his father. He listened patiently to my story and at the end asked me how much money he could make on his capital.

"I told him that with a well-organized and -managed company, he could make as much as 25 percent. He said, 'Young man, I can't support your venture, because I would be losing too much. I now make a 100-percent profit, and your plan would be losing money.' That was the end of my attempt to find capital for an aircraft venture in Brazil.

"While in Brazil, I was living with my brother, but I had to find some way of making a living. I hired out as an automobile mechanic in a General Motors automobile agency and there I met a General Motors executive, who was so impressed with the devices I had built for improving the serviceability of their automobiles that he asked me to join him at General Motors of Brazil, which I did.

"I headed the organization for field service units and agencies. This was quite a major step, because I was put in charge of organizing dealers' outlets. Many of my ideas I discussed with the field service manager of General Motors, who was very favorably inclined toward me, and suggested I go to the United States so I could utilize my ideas and develop them properly. I applied for a visa and received it in 1930."

TO AMERICA

Edgar's job with General Motors in Brazil had finally brought him the opening he had hoped for in the aviation industry. After Lindbergh's famous flight to Paris stimulated a boom in airplane construction, the automobile industry decided to move into the aviation business in a big way. Its first instrument was a holding company called North American Aviation, which bought shares of stock in selected airline and aircraft manufacturing companies. In May 1929, General Motors purchased a controlling interest in the Fokker Aircraft Corporation of America, whose founder, Anthony Fokker, of World War I fame, remained as chief engineer.

Edgar got a new passport from the Austrian consul in São Paulo, issued to him as a *flugzeug konstructeur* (airplane designer). The American vice-consul provided a Quota Immigration Visa #1788, dated December 2, 1929. In President Hoover's day, the law limited immigration to 153,000 persons per year, divided among the countries according to the national origin quotas established by the 1920 census. Edgar was one of 764 persons admitted that year as part of the Austrian quota.

By February 1930, Edgar had arrived at the Fokker factory at Teterboro Airport, Hasbrouck Heights, New Jersey, just a few miles from his entry to America in New York City. The 30-year-old engineer was 5 feet 7 inches tall, with brown hair and eyes, a trim mustache, and what his passport described as an "oval" visage.

Factory rules were strict at Fokker, for "our work must be clean, neat and exact." All workers had to sign a copy of the regulations, which should be observed "in order that you may qualify for regular promotions and increased income." Employees were exhorted to "take a constant interest in your daily and training work for your own sake. Promotion is sure for those who merit it." Workmen wore white uniforms with the Fokker trademark and number badges "always worn above the right breast pocket," while engineers wore suits and ties. Women were employed in the office and on certain assembly-line jobs, such as sewing fabric. Since "men and girls must work together, all men will conduct themselves as gentlemen and all girls as ladies." Today, one would expect a somewhat different wording! Wages began at 25 cents an hour for new apprentices.[4]

Edgar's fellow workers seemed to be mostly Dutch and German immigrants, which made adjustment to his new situation easier, but he needed to learn English rapidly. Nearby in Hackensack was the Broadway Evening School for the Foreign Born, where Edgar took a course in American and English literature taught by Grace L. Sturdevant. His class certificate states that his "quality of work was commendable" in the 91 two-hour sessions he took from October 1930 to May 1931. This was the only document on his education that he kept until he died.

In 1930, Fokker Aircraft was a busy place, despite the previous October's stock-market crash. Single-engine Fokker Universal, three-engine F-10, and even four-engine F-32 transports were on the assembly line. The engineers were working on prototypes of the XO-27 observation and the XA-7 attack planes for the Army. Since all these Fokker types were monoplanes, when most American firms were still building biplanes, it seemed that Schmued was on the cutting edge of new technology. "I felt," Schmued remarked, "that the companies in America

didn't have the proper organization by not having preliminary design departments, so I started the first preliminary design department in the U.S. as part of Fokker Aircraft, and as such, I did a great deal of design work for new models."

MOVING TO MARYLAND

Behind the scenes, however, decisions were made by corporate executives. On May 24, 1930, the General Aviation Corporation (GAC) was formed by General Motors to operate the Fokker Aircraft Corporation of America, which was dissolved on June 18. North American Aviation (NAA) held all GAC shares, but Anthony Fokker continued as chief engineer. NAA also bought a majority interest in the small Berliner-Joyce Aircraft Corporation near Baltimore, Maryland.

The pressure of the Depression was already beginning to dry up civilian plane sales when disaster hit a Fokker transport. On April 1, 1931, newspapers headlined the death in that crash of Knute Rockne, popular Notre Dame football coach, later made even more famous by a movie with Pat O'Brien and Ronald Reagan. Fokker's wooden wings were blamed for the crash, perhaps unfairly, and transport sales came to a halt. The first Fokker all-metal type, the XA-7, was completed in April, but the Army awarded the production attack contract to the Curtiss A-8 Shrike.

With the company in trouble, Fokker resigned, and the Hasbrouck Heights plant closed. All General Aviation operations moved by October 1931 to a Dundalk, Maryland, factory, about five miles from the Berliner-Joyce plant at Baltimore's Logan Airport. Schmued, whose wife and

The General Aviation YO-27, the Army's first three-place observation monoplane. Edgar Schmued is at the left of the men shown on May 13, 1932. *SDAM*

son had since come to America, also moved to Dundalk and felt prosperous enough to have a red sports car and join the National Geographic Society.

Activity at Dundalk included building the last American Fokker transports, flying boats for the Coast Guard, and a little XFA-1 fighter for the Navy, but the most interesting project was the Army's O-27. Previous observation planes had been two-

seat single-engine biplanes, but the first XO-27 completed by August 30, 1930, was the Army's first three-place, twin-engine monoplane with retractable landing gear for greater speed.

The Army was impressed enough to order 12 improved YO-27s for service tests from General Aviation on April 11, 1931. Edgar Schmued became the project engineer and was photographed with the first example finished at Dundalk on May 13, 1932. After the contract was completed, the YO-27 general specification report prepared by Schmued on October 9, 1933, calculated the top speed as 184 mph. This performance

YO-27
FRONT VIEW
MAY 13 1932

contrasts with that of the Douglas two-seat O-25C biplanes then in use; with the same 600-hp Curtiss engine, the O-25C did only 161 mph top and had only half the endurance.

Despite this advantage, no additional orders were placed. As a typical Fokker design with a welded steel-tube, fabric-covered fuselage and wooden wing, Edgar considered the plane "technically deficient." Later he wrote: "The only advantage for me was that I learned how to use wood in aircraft construction. This came in handy later on in World War II, when North American had to build rear fuselages in wood for the T-6

trainer to save aluminum for higher-priority purposes."

Schmued became project engineer of a Virginius Clark airliner design, the GA-43 single-engine, all-metal, low-wing monoplane. "Although it was not a very striking piece of design, it gave me at least a chance to organize and run a project." Since the airlines no longer wanted single-engine passenger planes, only five were built.

Every effort by the company to sell more aircraft had failed, and things looked grim. The Dundalk plant closed, and the remaining workers were transferred to Baltimore, where the Berliner-Joyce facility was finishing a few Navy observation planes. By June 1934, only 200 of 1,300 premerger employees were left. Old promises of regular promotion would have to be forgotten, and even survival through the Depression seemed doubtful.

THE RISE OF NORTH AMERICAN AVIATION

Rather suddenly, there was a great improvement in the prospects of Schmued's employer. The company that controlled their stock, North American Aviation, had to change from a stockholding to an operating company.

This was required when the Air Mail Act, passed on June 12, 1934, made it unlawful for the owners of airplane manufacturing firms to also hold interests in airlines carrying mail. The purpose was to open up competition so that airlines would not be limited to buying planes from a builder controlled by their own stockholders and so that builders could seek customers in any direction. This new market opening would make it possible for Douglas to sell its successful DC series to most of the airlines.

By January 1, 1935, General Aviation took the name of North American Aviation. Just as important was the company's new leadership. James Howard Kindelberger, formerly vice-president and chief engineer of Douglas, had become president of General Aviation on July 13, 1934. He brought with him more Douglas men: John Leland "Lee" Atwood, then only 30 years old, was to be the vice-president and chief engineer, while 28-year-old James S. "Stan" Smithson came to handle production.

Kindelberger, then 39, had been born in Wheeling, West Virginia, the son of an iron molder of Pennsylvania German ancestry. He was called "Dutch," a name he acquired while a student at Carnegie Tech. Apparently, there had been another student there, a "Dutch" Kindl, he once explained. "When he left, they just had to have another to hang [the name] on. Due, I think, to the similarity of our last names they hung it on me." Even the ordinary workmen in his factory called their boss Dutch.[5]

Kindelberger soon junked the General Aviation airliner under construction and decided to specialize on Army Air Corps business. Preliminary freehand drawings were made of a three-place observation plane, then called the GA-15, and a smaller two-place trainer. Since an Army basic trainer competition was coming up soon, the smaller plane had to be built first, and in a hurry. The general order for the NA-16 basic trainer was released; "to be built in nine weeks," says one report.

In those days of mass unemployment, the NRA (National Recovery Administration) desperately attempted to spread jobs

around by limiting each worker to a 40-hour week instead of the 52 hours then common in the industry. There were not enough funds to hire more workmen, but the prototype NA-16 moved along ahead of schedule anyway. Kindelberger's biographers say that one night he returned to the old plant after supper to find yelling and singing men completing the plane. The

story goes that after ringing out their eight hours on the time clock, the men liked to get some beer and then come back and have fun finishing the plane. After all, there was no law against having fun, and it was off the clock.[6]

Finished and photographed on April 5, 1935, the NA-16, with its low-wing design emphasizing easy maintenance and economical production, arrived at Wright Field on April 22 and defeated the rival Seversky BT-8 for the Army basic trainer contract. Both cockpits were originally open, but then a low sliding cover was added, along with the new company logo on the tail.

President J. H. "Dutch" Kindelberger and vice-president Lee Atwood, who led the growth of North American Aviation. *NAA*

North American's first NA-16 trainer, as originally seen on April 5, 1935, with open cockpits. *NAA*

Above, the NAA logo Edgar designed appears on tail of NA-20, an export demonstrator with the enclosed canopy of production BT-9 basic trainers. *NAA; Below,* shown in Army colors on June 26, 1935, the GA-15 became the XO-47 observation plane. *NAA*

This North American Aviation logo was chosen in a contest won by Edgar Schmued with his drawing of a flying eagle on a triangle. Schmued got a $25 prize. "Big bucks in those days," says fellow engineer Carl J. Hansen, who got $15 for second place.[7]

Schmued was pleased with the new leadership and described Dutch Kindelberger as bringing "new initiative and vigor" to the organization. It was brillant leadership, he said. "Dutch was very inspiring and spent a good deal of time with me on new ideas. He let me develop his ideas of the XO-47 observation plane for the Army."[8]

Completed in June 1935, this was a three-place monoplane, as was the O-27, but the XO-47 was an all-metal single-engine aircraft whose landing gear retracted into the wings. It was said to be the first plane designed around the observer, who sat between the pilot and gunner and below the wing, with his own field of vision. While 238 O-47s would be built in California from 1938 to 1940, the Army's tactical concept was unsound, for the O-47 could not be made fast enough to survive fighter interception in enemy airspace.

CALIFORNIA, HERE WE COME!

From his experience at Douglas, Dutch believed that the future of the aircraft industry was in California. That same year, Reuben Fleet had moved Consolidated Aircraft to San Diego. Good flying weather, lower heating and real-estate costs, an expanding economy, and a chance to begin a new up-to-date factory, were attractive advantages for North American, but could the best workers be convinced? "There were rumors about hostile Indians west of Pittsburgh, so

I fed them beer and crab cakes and lectured them on the marvels of the west," Dutch said later.[9]

When the Army approved the first contract for 42 BT-9s (the NA-16 basic trainer), the move to California was on. September 24, 1935, was the starting date of the lease, and the rent was $600 a year on the 20-acre site on the east side of Mines Field, which later was designated Los Angeles Municipal Airport. A brand-new factory designed to be expanded for mass production was begun November 1 at the corner of Imperial Highway and Aviation Boulevard, providing Inglewood, a suburb of Los Angeles, with a major employer. The aircraft industry became the major factor in doubling the population of the Los Angeles area in a few years.

Of 250 workers at the new factory by the end of 1935, about 75 had come to California from Baltimore, but Schmued was not the first to arrive. His wife, Luisa, already feeling far away from their native country, didn't want to move so far. Instead, Edgar decided to try working at Bellanca Aircraft, at New Castle, Delaware, in September 1935. Meanwhile, he had qualified for American citizenship, which he received on October 21, 1935.

After only a few weeks, Edgar realized that Bellanca's old-fashioned construction techniques and lack of good sales prospects did not offer a promising future. Seeing him unhappy and knowing how much his work meant to him, Luisa relented, and the little family loaded up their car for the long drive west, becoming part of the continuing movement of America's population.

They had reached California on old Route 60 and were four miles east of Indio when Schmued's car was hit head-on by the car of an elderly Kansas couple. Luisa Schmued, then 45, died Wednesday afternoon, November 12, 1935. Their son, Rolf, 14, asleep in the backseat, was cut and bruised but not seriously hurt, while Edgar suffered a concussion, a badly broken leg, and needed 10 stitches for a torn eye. He remained at Coachella Valley Hospital until January 1936.

His closest friend, Richard "Dick" Thaiss, who had also arrived in Inglewood with his wife, Liesel, in November 1935, came to his aid. A German immigrant himself, Dick had been hired by Fokker as a tinsmith in 1927, and later became shop foreman of sheet metal and subassembly in the new plant's experimental department. He would set a record of his own when he retired in 1965 after 37 years of consecutive employment, then the longest ever at North American.[10]

After the accident, Rolf lived with Dick, Liesel, and their six-year-old daughter, Elisabeth, and that Christmas, Dick and other workers cheered the boy up with the gift of a bike. Edgar came to the Thaiss home, too, after he left the hospital. Neither father nor son spoke of the tragic crash. Although downhearted since the accident, Edgar gradually recovered with the help of Liesel's *blutwurst* and the Thaisses' cozy conversations in German. Like many American-born children of immigrants, Elisabeth Thaiss had to begin school before she knew English. Liesel remembered that while Edgar and Dick picked up English rapidly at work and Rolf and Elisabeth learned it at school, the wives, who were usually confined at home, learned the language much more slowly.

Not until February 1936 was Edgar able to begin at North American and move to 9600 Redfern Avenue, Inglewood, where he lived until March 1940. Schmued was one of those men who submerge private pain in intense work, and work was something the company now had plenty of.

Design had just begun on the NA-21 twin-engine bomber, featuring heavy armament, with a larger bomb capacity than the B-17, five .30-caliber machine-gun positions, and the first hydraulic power-driven turret on an Air Corps plane. Edgar designed the power-driven nose turret and the lower rear gun installation.

"Tommy" Tomlinson of TWA was selected as the test pilot, because of his expe-

rience with supercharging and twin-engine planes. He began the test flights on December 22, 1936, but described the tests as a "nightmare" when the new turbosupercharged Pratt & Whitney R-2180s suffered several critical failures.[11] The bulky aircraft was too slow, a mistake not made with the later B-25 design. When bids were submitted in an Army bomber competition in

Edgar Schmued in 1936, shortly after he returned to work. *CS*

The NA-21 bomber, with a front turret that Edgar Schmued designed, became the XB-21 after Air Corps tests. *NAA*

A BC-1 with retractable wheels was the forerunner of the Harvard and AT-6, the world's most widely used advanced trainers. *NAA*

March 1937, the more conventional Douglas B-18 won with a far lower price. However, the Army did purchase the NA-21 prototype and designate it the XB-21.

North American's trainer development was the company's first success story. The first production BT-9, flown on April 15, 1936, by company pilot Paul Balfour, was followed by a growing number of similar basic trainers for the Army and several foreign countries. It developed into an advanced trainer with retractable wheels and larger engine, the BC-1 for the Army, first flown on February 11, 1938.[12] This type also won the company a contract, its largest then, on June 22, 1938, from Britain for 200 examples called the Harvard I by the Royal Air Force.

The Army's BC (Basic Combat) designation had been chosen to imply to congressional budget committees that this was a combat type instead of a mere trainer. It was not, in fact, a combat plane, although a heavier all-metal light bomber version for export, the NA-44, was flying in July 1938. This all-metal fuselage became the company standard, and by 1940 the Army's BC series became the AT-6, the most famous advanced trainer of World War II.

North American got its first chance to build a fighter when Peru, anticipating a border conflict with Ecuador, asked for a low-cost single-seater based on the BC-1 advanced trainer and NA-44 light bomber designs. On Monday, August 1, 1938, the NA-50 design began. The preliminary design department then originally occupied a second-floor office at the plant's southeast corner, facing Imperial Highway.

Ed Horkey, who was hired as an aerodynamicist after he graduated from Cal Tech in 1938, described the process. "I think Ed had a young mind that never grew old; he was always open-minded and enthusiastic. When I started there, I was in his office with Alex Burton, Paul Balfour, Schmued. It was a relatively small office, four desks and a drafting table for Ed. Ed would lay out a three-view and an inboard profile. Kindel-berger would come up and they'd talk about it for a while, and they'd decide pretty much how to go.

"Harold Raynor would usually come in and do the weight work, and then I would start figuring the performance estimates and doing the aerodynamics. Nobel Shropshire would get into the contracts, and the first thing you know we'd have a proposal out and shortly thereafter a contract. We would go ahead and build some airplanes in short time and low cost. Ed had the preliminary design group and was at the starting point of so many projects."[13]

The resulting NA-50 was a businesslike, all-metal fighter using an 840-hp Wright R-1820-G3 Cyclone. Its 270-mph top speed

and two .30-caliber guns didn't put it into the same league with P-40s or Spitfires, but it was useful for a low-budget air force. After seven were delivered to Peru in April, Thailand ordered six in November 1939. By the time those were ready for delivery, they were requisitioned by the U.S. Army Air Corps on March 4, 1941, designated P-64, and used at training bases.

Horkey remembers his coworkers' humor. "I was a little inclined to wear flashy clothes in those days, so I showed up one day in a wild shirt and tie and was sitting there working a slide rule, when some guy in a white gown shows up and puts a dumb

The first North American fighter, the NA-50 for Peru. *NAA*

"The head office sent me down to check the noise level on your suit. . . . It's off the scale!" Ed Horkey's cartoon of an office practical joke.

instrument in front of me on my desk. And he's fiddling with these damn knobs and taking readings and I finally get off of my slide rule and ask him what are you doing? He said, 'Well, Mr. Schmued told me to come up here and check you out with this *noise meter.*' And of course, those other three guys just cracked up."

That small shop setting would change over the years. "Up to the year 1930," Dutch, their boss, said later, "I could carry in my head practically all you had to know.

Now we have subdivided specialties."[14] The company's rapidly expanding sales soon transformed the old intimate atmosphere. Company president Kindelberger and vice-president and assistant general manager Atwood were now absorbed by all the details of running a great corporation, although their engineering origins guided them well in choosing among projects. Raymond Rice was now chief engineer and carefully assigned leadership tasks to design engineer Ed Schmued, and project engineers like Ken Bowen and Carl Hansen.

Said one magazine writer, "Personalities are ruthlessly submerged in the company headed by J. H. Kindelberger. . . . North

American is an example of man dominated by organization. However, it is a domination that brings out all that is best in the machine."[15] When Charles Lindbergh went through the factory on May 8, 1939, he described it as "a very efficient establishment—in many ways the most efficient I have yet seen."[16]

"Inspection of the huge plant reveals straightforward working," continued the above-mentioned magazine article. "There are no tangents, no missteps. From the 200 men working in the drafting room on the second floor . . . to the new planes ready for delivery, there is no wasted motion. Under the saw-toothed skylights a double assembly line works and raw material at the starting end takes on new additions every few minutes as the plane is built in a manner that reminds one of a striptease dancer in reverse."

Kindelberger had visited Britain and Germany in 1938 and noticed the difference between the factory techniques used to produce their rival Spitfire and Messerschmitt fighters. The German design was planned around simple tooling and mass production, with straight-lined wings instead of the compound curves of the Spitfire's wing. It was apparent that the German production program would be larger in numbers.

Dutch set an example for his men with his "extraordinary capacity for work"; he went without a formal vacation for many years, claimed no hobbies, and ate dinner at home with his family only four times in one three-month period. "My one thought is to sell enough of our products to keep the organization going without any layoffs. There are a lot of these men to whom a layoff is little short of a tragedy. They are raising families and need every dollar they can make. I hope to be able to keep them constantly employed and earning, for that's what makes good American citizens."

Such work-centered attitudes earned the loyalty of Edgar Schmued and his other engineers. Although the company's success with trainer contracts had already brought steady growth, Air Corps expansion offered sales opportunities with larger aircraft.

When the Army requested bids on medium bomber and on observation types in July 1939, North American responded with several design proposals. The winner was the NA-62, which won an order for 184 bombers designated the B-25. Schmued participated in the B-25 preliminary design and "also developed the bomb racks and rack controls." His patent application for the bomb control mechanism was filed September 18, 1939.[17]

Carl "Red" Hansen became the B-25's project engineer and carried through the start of mass production on the most important American medium bomber of the war. Before the end of 1939, North American added orders for sales for 600 more Harvards, 230 more basic trainers for France, 251 Army BT-14s, and a complicated XB-28 experimental project.

Near the end of 1936, NAA had delivered the first 82 basic trainers, employed 991 people, and had 117 aircraft, worth $5,230,-721, on order. Three years later, deliveries during 1939 amounted to 793 planes, with 4,639 employees at year's end, and a backlog of 1,543 planes, worth $50,599,802. The company was on the way to becoming the largest wartime airplane producer in America.

Company appetites remained high

enough to reinstate an earlier project, the NA-35 primary trainer. Edgar was put in charge, and an all-metal prototype was designed and built in only 39 days.[18] First flown by Vance Breese on December 9, 1939, and powered by a 150-hp Menasco, this two-place low-wing monoplane was clearly planned with mass production in mind. Except for the open cockpits and fixed landing gear, its clean-cut lines foreshadowed the Mustang.

The NA-35 had a 29-foot 9-inch wing span, 25-foot 6-inch length, and 148-square-foot wing area. It weighed 1,218 pounds empty and 1,760 pounds gross with 24 gallons of fuel. Top speed was 150 mph at sea level, cruising speed 124 mph at 3,000 feet, landing speed with flaps 46 mph, and cruising range 305 miles.[19]

In an article describing his design, Ed wrote how the airfoil he selected, the slotted flap, the shock strut design, and the aluminum-alloy engine mount contributed to a superior trainer.[20] But the NA-35 never entered production, for North American would soon be preoccupied with production of Schmued's most famous design, the Mustang. Lockheed's Vega Division purchased the NA-35 prototype and design rights in 1940, only to be blocked by a government decision to avoid primary trainers with all-metal construction because of a feared aluminum shortage.

Breese, a Chinese colonel, Schmued, and the NA-35. *NAA*

The NA-35 primary trainer piloted by Vance
Breese, with Edgar Schmued in rear cockpit.
NAA

CHAPTER THREE

Birth of the Mustang, 1940

NA-73X on its back after the crash. *NAA*

BRITAIN NEEDS FIGHTERS

Before the war began, the British were not especially interested in buying American fighters, for their own Rolls-Royce–powered Hurricanes and Spitfires seemed far superior in both speed and firepower. Instead, Royal Air Force purchases were for advanced trainers and patrol bombers.

France, however, did need fighters and by the end of 1939 had made new contracts with Curtiss that resulted in the completion in 1940 of 420 Hawk H75A and 259 H81A fighters, although most of these would be finished too late to help France itself. The H81As were an export version of the Army's P-40, with French equipment, six guns, and pilot armor; the RAF would call them Tomahawks. For 1941, the French hoped the U.S. Army would let them have P-38s and P-39s.

As the war entered its fifth month, Britain began to realize its own need for American fighters. Not for Fighter Command, for there was no American production match for a Spitfire, but for the empire's valuable colonies in the Middle and Far East, threatened by Germany's Axis partners. While not as fast as Spitfires, the greater range of American types would make them suitable guards against the Italian and Japanese aircraft likely to attack Egypt or Singapore. By the end of January 1940, the Brewster Buffalo was on order, although its converted automobile factory would supply only 170

to Britain in 1941. Most would go to the Far East, with their pilots still unaware of the Mitsubishi Zero's performance.

Over a thousand fighters would be needed in 1941, both for the Middle East and for Army Cooperation Command squadrons in Britain, which needed to replace their slow two-seaters with single-seaters that were fast at low altitudes. Since Fighter Command at home had first priority on Spitfires and Hurricanes, the most likely future supplier was Curtiss. Tests of the XP-40 in Canada in May 1940 indicated that while less capable than the Spitfire, it could comfortably handle roles in which high-altitude performance wasn't the main factor—providing the Curtiss was properly armed and fitted with leak-proof (self-sealing) fuel tanks. All the Curtiss and Brewster fighters for Britain and France would have armor, but the Air Corps fighters on order had none.

On March 4, 1940, the Army had held the mock-up inspection of the XP-46 project that Curtiss hoped would replace the P-40 on production lines in 1941. This design would have the new 1,150-hp Allison "F" engine (called V-1710-39 by the Army), six guns, and leak-proof fuel tanks. *The New York Times* reported on March 14 that the United States was planning to release P-40 deliveries for export to make way for its replacement, the "over-400-mph" XP-46.

In fact, that very day, British and French

officials meeting with the president's Liaison Committee insisted that they had to have the P-38 and P-39, as well as the P-46, in 1941. Air Corps leaders had resisted these requests before, but now they realized that the 789 pursuits the Army had ordered in 1939 had no armor, self-sealing tanks, or enough firepower. Letting the Allies buy into the fighter program was a way of funding these crucial modernizations.[1]

On March 25, the government's new Release of Aircraft Policy was completed. The Allies would be allowed to buy certain modern types, providing that their manufacturers would offer a more advanced design to the Army and the Allies would provide information about their own combat experience. By April 10 (the day after the invasion of Norway), the Anglo-French Purchasing Commission was told they could complete contracts for 2,440 American fighters.

Bell Aircraft won the first new Foreign Release Agreement for a fighter on April 4, 1940. That company had been facing a cash-flow crisis because the Army then paid only after the planes it ordered were delivered. Knowing that the Allies paid a sizable advance, Larry Bell hurried to the commission's New York offices at 15 Broad Street to see Sir Henry Self, the tall, aristocratic buyer of aircraft.[2] Bell was offering the Model 14, an export P-39. Sales brochures promised that this Airacobra would do 400 mph at 15,000 feet with an 1,150-hp Allison.

His offer was accepted and 170 Model 14s were ordered in May for the French, adding a lot of weight in armor, self-sealing fuel tanks, and four wing guns. These changes were also to be incorporated in the Army's

P-39D (Bell Model 15), to be built concurrently in 1941. And the French also decided to replace the 37-mm cannon with the 20-mm Hispano gun that was being ordered into production in America. In exchange for the Army's permission to sell the Airacobra, Bell would design its radical Model 16 with a Continental pusher engine, which became the Air Corps' XP-52 project.

Turbosuperchargers, used on the Lockheed P-38 and Republic P-43, were considered by Secretary of War Harry Woodring to be too secret and too scarce for export.[3] But Lockheed offered an export version of the P-38 on March 21, 1940, called the Model 322-61, using the same 1,090-hp Allison C-15 model engine as the P-40 Tomahawks. Promised top speed was 404 mph at 15,000 feet, compared to the 405 mph at 25,000 feet guaranteed for the army's turbosupercharged YP-38.

A Foreign Release Agreement for Model 322 was made between Lockheed and the Air Corps on April 12 and approved by the War Department on April 17, 1940. This agreement provided that the Army's P-38s would "include substantially the same type of pilot protection and gas tank protection incorporated in airplanes proposed to be exported . . . without any additional cost or expense to the Government." Lockheed was also required to deliver another prototype, "one- or two-place," to be designated XP-58 and delivered in 16 months, without cost to the government. (Presumably, the company expected to pass these costs on to the British contract.) At least 18 Air Corps P-38s were to be delivered prior to any exports.[4]

Although their own deliveries could not come until late in 1941, the Anglo-French

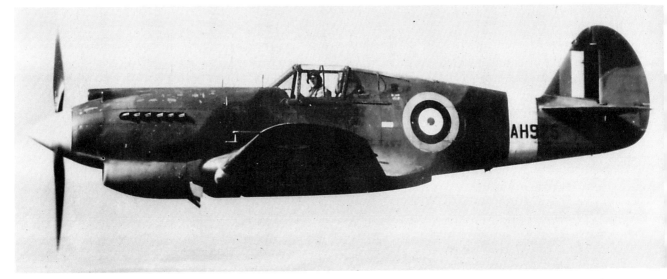

The first American fighter in production for the RAF was the Curtiss H81A Tomahawk, a P-40 originally ordered for France. *SDAM*

Purchasing Commission ordered 667 export models with armor, self-sealing tanks, and the 20-mm gun. This very expensive commitment would later be regretted by the RAF, which inherited the Lockheed and Bell contracts on June 17, 1940, after France decided to capitulate to Germany.

Curtiss could offer earlier deliveries of its P-40s, since the first production model for the Army was in the air by April 4, 1940. A Foreign Release Agreement made with the Army on April 18, 1940, halted P-40 deliveries at 200 planes and released the advanced P-46 for export.

This allowed Curtiss to concentrate on the export P-40, the H81A Tomahawk, for the rest of 1940, and promise P-46s to the Allies in 1941. In return, Curtiss would replace the deferred 324 P-40s with 324 P-46s, beginning in March 1941, and would build a new design for the Army, designated

the XP-53 with a Continental engine that eventually became the XP-60.

But changing to the very different P-46 would interrupt production in 1941, just when fighters might be most needed. On May 24, 1940, the Curtiss Company proposed discarding P-46 production and substituting a redesigned P-40 with the same 1,150-hp Allison F3R engine, heavier armament, armor, and gas-tank protection.

This version was the H87A, named the Kittyhawk by the British and produced concurrently for the Air Corps as the P-40D. Expecting to get a better airplane at an earlier date, the Army accepted the change on its contract and the RAF also bought 471 1,090-hp H81A-2 Tomahawks and 560 1,150-hp H87A Kittyhawks.

NORTH AMERICAN ENTERS THE FIGHTER FIELD

The RAF would need more fighters than Curtiss alone could build and was looking for a second source for P-40 production even before the Kittyhawk program was established. North American Aviation, with its successful mass-production skills, was an obvious choice, and as early as February 25, 1940, Dutch Kindelberger was asked to consider building P-40s.

But Edgar Schmued, now the chief designer, was driven by "a burning ambition to build the best fighter. I made many sketches without knowing what it might end up as, but when the time came I was ready."[5] Among the ideas he had considered offering France was a light low-wing monoplane with a Ranger SGV-770, a 525-hp air-cooled, inverted in-line engine. Four wing guns were the suggested armament for this proposal, which would be quickly replaced by a more powerful design.

North American's chief structures engineer, Richard Schleicher, said of Schmued's preliminary designs: "Working alone, he prepared the designs of future aircraft. Ed went about his work quietly and methodically and cast a spell of friendliness on those with whom he came in contact. These characteristics prevailed in Ed's life to the very end. As far back as 1934–35, Ed was designing the various installations that later would be found in NAA aircraft—particularly the P-51. He had layouts of the 'ideal' cockpit, engine, and gun installations, etc., that were lacking only a wing, fuselage, and tail to make a new airplane. Once the performance requirements were known, Ed needed only a few days to evolve a new three-view.

"Aided by his copy of *Huette* [a German engineer's handbook] and his little notebook of technical formulae, he could idealize any required type. His weight and performance estimates were uncannily accurate. Ed could find a solution for nearly any problem and would exude confidence and enthusiasm with those who worked with him. Ed could be disturbed, but never aggravated to anger."[6]

As Schmued told the story later: "We desperately wanted to build a fighter. It started very peculiarly. First there were rumors of NAA building the Curtiss P-40 to ensure quick delivery to the British, and rumors that a batch of drawings from Curtiss-Wright (P-40) were at North American Aviation, but I have never seen any of them and I firmly believe there weren't any.[7]

"One afternoon in March, Dutch Kindelberger came to my office and said, 'Ed, do we want to build P-40s here?' From the tone of his voice, I knew what kind of answer he expected. I said, 'Well, Dutch, don't let us build an obsolete airplane, let's build a new one. We can design a better one and build a better one.' And that's exactly what he wanted to hear. So he said, 'Ed, I'm going to England in about two weeks and I need an inboard profile, three-view drawing, performance estimate, weight estimate, specifications, and some detail drawings on the gun installation to take along. Then I would like to sell that new model airplane that you develop.' That was the order I got from Dutch Kindelberger.

"He said that the rules for the design were simple. Make it the fastest airplane you can and build it around a man that is 5 feet 10 inches tall and weighs 140 pounds. It should have two 20-mm cannons in each wing and should meet all design requirements of the United States Air Force. Now with this specification [NAA SC-1050, issued March 15], as skimpy as it was, I started working along. We looked around to

Edgar Schmued's first light fighter design. *NAA*

find an engineer or somebody in our organization that weighed 140 pounds and was 5 feet 10 inches.

"Right in our Engineering Department we found a man that fitted that specification. It was Art Chester, a famous race pilot who joined North American because there was no air racing anymore during the war. He was a well-thought-of man and we were

very happy to have him. He later became our project engineer on the power plant of the P-51, and we used his size to build an airplane around him. That was the beginning of the P-51," wrote Schmued, who had hired Chester the day he turned up at North American in 1939 and put him to work on the NA-35 engine installation.

"Meanwhile, I had prepared the three-view drawings and reports of the new fighter that Dutch had requested. He was on his way to England, joined by Lee Atwood.

When he came back about two weeks later, we had no contract, but we started then on our own mock-up of the airplane. In three days we had it built, using paper, plaster of paris, whatever was suitable. Meanwhile, the British apparently looked at this proposal carefully and concluded that on the strength of North American's past performance with the Harvard trainer, which was delivered in large quantities, we could be trusted to come through with a good airplane. About two to three weeks after Dutch Kindelberger had returned, we received a contract for 400 P-51s."

NAA vice-president Lee Atwood was then in New York handling negotiations with the British, who were told of the plan to build a new fighter around the Allison engine. At this point, since no detailed drawings had been completed, the type was referred to as an extension of 1939's NA-50A design.

Germany's invasion of Norway on April 9, 1940, may have stimulated prompt action on the rather vague promise for superior performance. On Thursday, April 11 (the day after the Allies were given permission by the president to order many fighters), Sir Henry Self, director of the Anglo-French Purchasing Commission, signed a letter of intent to purchase "400 NA-50B" fighters to NAA Spec 1592 as amended. An Englishman had just launched production of the greatest American fighter of the war.[8]

The promised plane was to have an Allison engine and was not to exceed $40,000 in cost; affordability was a British concern before the days of lend-lease. By Wednesday, April 24, company General Order NA-73 was issued for construction of one "Allison-engined pursuit." A week later, on May

1, a Lee Atwood letter to the commission promised 320 aircraft to be delivered from January to September 30, 1941, and 50 per month afterward. Eight guns and armor protection would bring estimated gross weight to 7,765 pounds, and the price was estimated at $37,590.45 per plane.

Since Sir Henry's authorization from London had been to buy P-40s, he told Atwood to get XP-40 test data from Curtiss so he could tell London that North American was utilizing P-40 experience. After Atwood made a quick train trip to Buffalo, Curtiss agreed to sell him a box of data. Atwood's letter on May 1 said that the Cur-

Sir Henry Self, the first to order the Mustang into production, on a visit to the North American factory on May 6, 1941. *NAA*

tiss people "are furnishing data covering a series of wind tunnel, cooling and performance tests of a *similar airplane,* which data will assist us. . . ."[9]

Most of these tests referred to the XP-40, as the XP-46 was then only a mock-up, but their mention would cause a dispute that would complicate history, as we will see later. George Gehrkens believed this box was never opened in California, since the NA-73 concept was already settled and the project engineers never saw the Curtiss data.[10] But aerodynamicist Ed Horkey does remember seeing a wind-tunnel report on a P-46 model. "We ran a quick study and said that this was just a rehashed P-40, and we don't see where it's all that great, and we'd do better starting from scratch."[11]

North American signed a Foreign Release Agreement on Saturday, May 4, with the United States Army Air Corps, who was to get the 4th and 10th production articles of the proposed aircraft. On May 29, 1940, a contract was made with the Royal Air Force for 320 NA-73s, to be numbered AG345 to AG664. By the time final approval by officials in London was secured on July 20, France had surrendered and the opening phase of the Battle of Britain had begun.[12]

Schleicher said: "Faced with the challenge of producing a new fighter aircraft and the advent of the laminar airfoil, Ed soon joined all the facets of his previously prepared idealized concepts and there emerged the NA-73. His charge to me as chief structures engineer was: 'I want smooth surfaces—right up to limit load and a tail that will stay with the airplane.' From these instructions evolved the minimum skin thickness of 0.040 inches and a tail strong enough to withstand the high Mach

number moment and drag coefficients shown by wind-tunnel tests to be asymptotic at Mach 1.0."[13]

How this fighter was designed is described by Edgar Schmued: "One Saturday afternoon early in May, our preliminary design group began work on a general arrangement drawing. This drawing and a preliminary weight study were rushed to New York for approval by the British Purchasing Commission. When the drawing and weight study received official approval a few days later, the real job began.

"We made a number of small changes. Then, as you might say, 'hell broke loose.' The detailed design work had to be coordinated by the preliminary design group, with assistance from each specialized engineering group—power plant, aerodynamics, armament, hydraulics, landing gear, electrical, etc. The design engineers worked so closely with the experimental shop that the airplane took shape almost as soon as the drawings came out of the blueprint machine. We organized a small engineering group and Dutch Kindelberger gave me the right to pick any man in engineering for this project. Project engineers or group leaders, it didn't make any difference."

Some 2,800 drawings and 41,880 engineering man-hours would be needed just for the first article to make its first flight. Julius Villepique, the top layout draftsman, began the drawing-board task. Born in Topeka, Kansas, the 31-year-old Villepique had joined NAA in September 1939. His tall, 6-foot 1-inch frame, usually topped by a jaunty tam-o'-shanter, contrasted with Schmued's stolid 5-foot 7-inch height and his appearance, but they became close co-workers and friends.

Schmued's account of the engineering continues: "I finally started with about eight design engineers and had scheduled to build up to 37 in two to three weeks. We made a very careful time study of this project. Each man who led a group, like the wing group, fuselage group, power plant, or landing gear, was called in and he made his own estimate of the time he thought he needed to get his drawings and data out to the Experimental Department. Engineering was, of course, preceded by an estimate of the time required to complete the engineering and work in the shop to build the airplane.

"The time required to build the airplane we estimated to be about 100 days, and the requirement to have this airplane in production within a year's time, which the British required and North American accepted, made it necessary to get the airplane out as fast as possible. In this period of time, one year, we had to build the experimental airplane, flight-test it, make the necessary changes which may show up during flight testing, and tool up for production so that the airplane could be produced within a year's time. This was a very stringent requirement.

"We had planned to use an NACA-23 series airfoil. But when we heard that the NACA had developed a laminar-flow, low-drag airfoil, we decided to use it on the P-51 Mustang. This airfoil was specifically adapted by Ed Horkey, our first and only aerodynamicist, and his assistants, who developed the ordinates of the laminar-flow airfoil that was used on the P-51. Dutch asked me, 'But suppose that wing doesn't work?' I said we'd build him a new wing in one month. Impossible, of course, but that

was the spirit of the time."

Ed Horkey fills in the details of the crucial shift in airfoil design: "Russ Robinson was an NACA aerodynamicist of considerable technical capability and persuasive merits. He came by with Ed Hartman, who was the local engineering representative and coordinator for NACA, and also a recognized engineer, particularly on propellers. They said that NACA had tested in a wind tunnel what was called a laminar-flow low-drag airfoil. It was somewhere around 20-percent thick and showed wonderful characteristics.

"Our concern was that we didn't get all of the great laminar flow projected, since 20 percent would be too thick an airfoil, even in those days. It was decided to lay out new airfoils, which were around 16-percent thick at the root and 11-percent thick at the tip. There were various equations available like those from Laplace, Theodorsen, and Joukowski, etc., that could be used. In other words, what we did is pick the pressure distribution we wanted. Then we drew an airfoil shape, and with the above equations, we could check our pressure distributions. If it didn't match, we could make a change to the airfoil contour. Then go back and recalculate the pressure distribution.

"This is called a reiteration process, which was so time-consuming that North American had to assign quite a few people to help me. I remember in particular, Irving Ashkenas, George Mellinger, Cecil Davis, Harvey Hogue, and Nevin Palley from aerodynamics and stress, and with a bunch of electric calculators, we sat there and went through this process to lay out the P-51 airfoil. Then after this was done, we brought in Bob Davie, who was head of the wind-tunnel model design, and had him build some models of the wings."[14]

Two alternative scale models of the wing, identical in area and plan form, were brought to Dr. Clark B. Millikan, of the Guggenheim Aeronautical Laboratories, California Institute of Technology (GAL-CIT) at Pasadena, for comparative wind-tunnel tests. This wing shape would remain the same all through the Mustang's lifetime; a 37.03-foot span and 233.42-square-foot area, with chord tapering from 104 inches at the root to 50 inches at the tips.

One model, however, had conventional NACA 23000 family airfoil sections, while the other had modified 45-100 family laminar-flow sections, an airfoil permitting a smoother air flow over the wing surface.[15] (The first digit of the NACA designation gives the maximum height of the camber line in percent chord, and the second the location of this maximum height in tenths of chord aft of the leading edge.)

When the tests were made in the 10-foot diameter GALCIT wind tunnel on May 21 and 22, the low-drag effect of the newer airfoil section was in evidence. But Schmued wrote that the results were unsatisfactory, because "the slight surface turbulence adjacent to the tunnel walls was affecting the airfoil characteristics at the wing tips."

Realizing that this tunnel was too small for complete data, the designers rushed the new wing model to the larger, 8-by-12-foot tunnel of the University of Washington at Seattle. There the tests worked fine, allowing the first application of a laminar airfoil in the design of an airplane.

"There was some concern," reports Horkey, "that the wing tips of the model were too close to the GALCIT tunnel walls and maybe we weren't getting correct data, particularly for maximum lift. We had started with a Spitfire elliptical type, but Ed had proposed more of a blunter tip, as it ended up on the final P-51. I got on a DC-3 and went up to Seattle with the model tucked away in the back of the airplane. We tested for both maximum lift, drag, and stall characteristics, and they came out great, so that was our shape from then on."

The laminar-flow wing has its greatest thickness about halfway back from the leading edge, instead of about a quarter way back as on the older airfoils, and is of equal contour about the chord line. This airfoil allows the air to separate and flow smoothly over the long incline and over the point of greatest thickness, after which it continues to the trailing edge, breaking down into the turbulent flow that causes increased drag. Moving the greatest wing thickness back reduced drag. "The P-51's performance proved that it was the best airfoil we could have used."

Ed Horkey remembers a 1954 book by Theodore Von Karman that "mentioned Sir George Cayley in Britain back in 1837, who had taken a trout fish, cut it into sections, and taken the ordinates of the periphery and divided them by three. When you took the ordinates of the laminar airfoil and then put the trout numbers as X's, you found they were identical. God had invented the laminar airfoil way before us! Did that ever make us humble!"[16]

A one-quarter-scale mahogany model of the NA-73, lacquered and rubbed down to a high polish and practically identical with the future prototype, was brought to Cal Tech by Ed Horkey. Dr. Millikan had prepared corrections for tunnel-wall interference, and wind-tunnel tests were made from June 28 to July 26, 1940. They showed a high airfoil efficiency factor and low radiator drag.[17]

According to Schmued's account: "At the outset, an airplane has to be designed in such a manner that the air can flow evenly around the body. There is one simple way of really designing smooth curves. That way is to use conic sections to produce the surfaces that are used on all parts except the wing and tail. This means primarily the fuselage, so all curves on that fuselage were designed by conic sections. Conic sections are very simple. If you take a cone and section crosswise, you get a circle. You make a section that is under an angle and you get a parabola. All these curves are smooth, which can be calculated and then precisely shaped, and the air likes that.

"This is the kind of shape the air likes to touch. The drag is at a minimum and it was the first time that a complete airplane, with the exception of the lifting surfaces, was designed with second-degree curves. I laid out the lines myself and it was a first."

In the words of technical historian James Hansen, this was indeed "the first case of an aircraft's actual construction matching its design specifications without adding thickness in building the metal skin. The idea of the Mustang designer, a German perfectionist named Edgar Schmued, was to produce an airplane whose aerodynamic shape was the same as that decided upon by the aerodynamicist, not that shape plus an overcoat of lapped aluminium alloy that in places might add up to four sheets of thickness."[18]

DETAIL DESIGN WORK ON THE MUSTANG

Schmued told some of the difficulties confronting the project: "Now, whenever you start a project of this order, the scheduling method, the timing which is given to the respective engineering designers, must be very carefully weighed so that it makes a good integrated picture. Most engineers are optimistic about what they can produce, especially when they are as enthusiastic as our people were. I knew from experience that most people, under such conditions, would be optimistic with their timing.

"I gave every man responsible for a part of this airplane complete freedom in setting up the time he required to do his assigned job. I discussed all these things with these individuals and, for instance, the wing man came to me after a day or two and said he needed about 4,000 hours to design the wing. I knew that was just about an impossible schedule, so I gave him 6,000 hours, knowing that he would have to work like a slave to make this time period.

"And so it went with every group and every man in every group. I set loose enough schedules for them to be able to make it. This schedule, despite the fact that I gave them more than they asked, was very tight. It requires a good deal of planning, and at that period, the people working on this airplane were top engineers.

"Dutch Kindelberger had given me free rein in selecting any and all engineers, and I made the very best of this freedom and picked the best people I could find. We had about 14 or 15 people two weeks after we started and planned on growth up to 49 people in a period of a few weeks, and then drop down to 10 to 12. As we made this schedule, we needed 100 days to design and build the airplane. How well this schedule was developed is proven by the fact that the airplane was completed by engineering and the shop in 102 days, just 2 days more than anticipated."

SCHEDULING DESIGN

"Now, when we started to lay out our schedule, we used a most practical method. We had a system of planning for a three-month period of time. The board was on a piece of pasteboard (drywall) with the sheets large enough for this three-month schedule. We had vertical columns, one for each day, and horizontal columns for each item, leaving little squares on the board. The top line of squares was for the date, there was 1, 2, 3, 4, 5 . . . for each day, and then a nail in the middle of that square, where we would hang a dateline rod.

"That was a piece of eighth-inch welding rod, painted black with an eye on the top that we could move from day to day. We scheduled all items this way that were required for a certain design part. It would have a red pin for each due date, and when that piece was finished, we would remove the pin and put a black pin in. All pins on the left side of the dateline should be black and all on the right side should be red.

"This was a very flexible and accurate system. We could simply change pins when we changed dates. All I had to do was walk through the engineering group and check the board on the wall to see if the [pins on the] left-hand side of the datelines were black and those on the right side were red. This did not always occur as planned; some-

times there were black pins on the right side because the fellow was producing faster than he anticipated, or there were red points on the left side, because he didn't quite make the schedule. This always gave me an indication for action.

"If too many red pins appeared on the left side, obviously the man either needed help, or there was a lack of information, and I could step in and find out why he could not meet the planned schedule. I would either give him extra help—an engineer—or provide the information that he was missing. It was the best scheduling system that I could think of and proved to be a good working system, enabling us to quickly receive data on the airplane.

"Let's take the wing, for instance. The man starts working on some line drawings, which really don't represent anything special. There are just a few loose lines which mean a lot to him but very little to anyone else. This usually started a rush because he felt he was falling behind schedule. All things start with a handful of lines, which, when eventually filled in, became a design. Now under the circumstances, we had very good luck with the system. It was excellent and it was not felt as a whip by the people who used it. There was no feeling of pressure on my side, nor on those who designed the details.

"Now the preliminary design which I had made of the airplane, including the line drawing, was quite specific. Everything that was contained in the airplane was shown in such a manner that it took very little for a designer to pick up the part and start on detail design, which is very important. If you want a good product, number-one item is that you have a good concept and must be in the right ball park with your ideas. Second, you have to have good detail, for if you have a good concept and good details, you've got a world beater; like the P-51.

"The handling of the whole project was extremely simple, thanks to the scheduling system I used. I needed no pressure whatsoever, for they all worked so willingly that it was a pleasure. There was one case where one man after about three weeks' time got a little dizzy on a Sunday afternoon and I took him home. He was back on Monday morning. The schedule worked so well that I would recommend it to anyone that has a project of similar proportion."

Art Chester was in charge of the powerplant design group at Ed Schmued's request, despite Ray Rice's skepticism about "backyard engineers." Chester designed an engine mount using a riveted aluminum-box beam structure, instead of the usual welded steel-tube framework. He and Marc Malsby worked overtime in the evenings on the assembly drawings.

"Sometime each evening," wrote Malsby, "Ed Schmued would drop around to check our progress. Ed never pressured us, but was concerned that our work was being performed in a timely manner." The resulting mount was outstanding for rigidity, lightness, and accessibility. Chester later started his own company to fabricate all of the propeller spinners for the P-51B/D and F-82 fighters.[19]

The wide landing gear, wheels 11 feet 10 inches apart, made the Mustang easier to handle than the narrow-treaded Spitfire (only 5 feet 8 inches), and Messerschmitt (6 feet 6 inches), or the 8-foot 2-inch spread of the P-40. Hydraulic pressure folded the wheels inwardly into the wing roots. The wing was built in two panels and bolted together beneath the fuselage, forming the cockpit floor. Fuel tanks and guns were installed between the two wing spars, and flaps and ailerons were hinged to the rear spar.

SOLVING DESIGN PROBLEMS

Airplane pilots are fond of telling stories about their adventures, stories that are difficult to document. Engineers also like to entertain their listeners with accounts of their experiences, as some of Ed Schmued's favorite anecdotes illustrate.

"Like all things, there are problems that are sometimes affected by simple human errors, which are quite possible and very likely ever-present. As an example, one of the difficult pieces to get in the shop was an enormously large magnesium casting which we had proposed. When the drawing of this casting was sent to the Aluminum Company of America, they simply laughed at us about the big size.

"We went back to look for someone who might be willing to try to pour the casting. Since it was something like 30 pounds, with dimensions of roughly 22-by-8-by-20 inches, it was extremely difficult to find someone to even look at the drawings. Finally, we found a small foundry that made little bits and pieces of magnesium castings. The firm's name was Osbrink and they made small castings of approximately 2 to 3 ounces in weight. When they saw the drawing, their boss nearly collapsed. 'Oh, my God, I have never made a casting of that size.' We talked with him, encouraged him, and said, 'Look, if you succeed, you get the business of all the castings,' so he then agreed to try it.

"I sent one of our designers to stay with the pattern as long as necessary until the casting was made. He stayed with the project three days and finally there came a happy cry. They made a casting that met all the requirements, then the biggest magnesium casting anybody could think of. The man that I had sent there took the hot casting and put it in the rumble seat of his car. When he delivered the casting, he noticed it had burned a hole in the rumble seat's floor covering.

"We started work immediately in the shop. The fitting to hold the landing gear in that casting was a forged piece [the trunnion of the landing gear]. It was very difficult at that time to get that kind of priority to get the work done. By the grace of God, we found someone who, under the war-production pressure, made us a hand forging. Finally we got the forging for the landing gear machined, but then discovered a human error!

"The trunnion of the landing gear had to fit in the magnesium casting, which had a nominal dimension of 5 inches diameter, so the trunnion itself had a dimension of 4.9975 inches, leaving $2\frac{1}{2}$-thousandths of an inch clearance. The man that made the drawing made a very human mistake by writing the dimension of 4.975 inches, causing the landing-gear trunnion to rattle in the casting. That man came to me and said, 'Ed, I ruined your schedule, because we won't have a landing gear.' A human error has been made, but let's not worry about who made the mistake; let's see what we can do to fix it, was my reply.

"Then it occurred to me that if we chrome-plated the steel pinion up to the proper dimension, we could save it, because we knew we wouldn't have a chance to get a second forged gear in time. This became a first of national quality control, because it saved the government millions and millions of dollars. It was a method of bringing undersized dimensions of steel parts up to dimensions by chrome plating, and became an international method, not only in America, but in the whole world. It was a first of great potential. By doing this, we saved the landing gear, which otherwise would have been lost. This was just one of many problems we faced. When you rush a design through like this, you are inviting mistakes and they do happen. I feel we had great teamwork.

"Their great effort in getting things in order, after a mistake had been made, saved us time and money. Engineering went along and we had some problems with manpower. After you build up the number of people in a group to a peak period of roughly 49 people, it then drifts down to a very small group, which is called maintenance engineering.

"This is the group that sees that final dimensional corrections are made before the airplane is really finished. This group is usually smaller than your original group. We had started with a group of 8 people, built it to 49, and it went down to the average design team manpower of 38. It was the best team I could have ever asked for. They were good, cooperative, and hardworking people. There aren't enough words of praise for them, they were magnificent. When the 102 days were over, practically everyone collapsed. They all took a few days off, because they really deserved it."

Interviewed in 1984, Schmued remarked

that "We could never build another plane today in 100 days as we did then. Today they just don't have what it takes. There are too many levels of authority within the building companies. They have a president, a vice-president, another vice-president, still another vice-president, and many other levels."[20]

More details are given in Schmued's manuscript: "We discovered that when the wing was very thin, the aileron control system had to be extremely well designed to fit into the small space that was available. We used some rather unorthodox systems for the aileron control by using a wobble plate. That is a term for a special form of mechanism which we used that was very successful.

"Then there were some other features of the airplane that are essential. For instance, the radiator of the airplane; if it is a ducted radiator (surrounded by cowling), it has a tendency to spill air. The air that is coming into the opening cannot all go through the core of the radiator itself and spills around the edges. Here it is very important to locate the radiator in a position where it cannot interfere with either wing or main-fuselage drag, because any spillage is turbulent air, producing drag. To keep that to a minimum, I moved the radiator as far aft as I could, and as far below the wing as I could. With the radiator located in this position, we really got an optimum.

"Since the radiator was far enough aft, it interfered as little as possible with fuselage drag and with wing characteristics. We had a world beater! We also found out, later on, that the heat from the engine actually produced thrust in the radiator by increasing the velocity of the air flowing through.

"That horsepower gained by the radiator was only discovered by wind-tunnel investigation. We were contractually required to wind-tunnel test the P-51, and long after the first airplane flew, we got around to test a model which had an electric motor to drive a three-bladed propeller. We found from wind-tunnel data that the P-51 should not be as fast as it was actually clocked. Our chief thermodynamicist, Joe Beerer, studied the problem and noticed the favorable effect of the radiator." This added thrust is called the Meredith effect, after the British engineer F. W. Meredith, who described it in a paper published in 1935.

The distribution of power is approximately as follows: 100 percent energy in fuel is put into the engine, but about 30 percent of this has to be radiated into the air to cool the engine. Another 30 percent of the energy is lost in the exhaust heat of the engine. Then 25 percent is usually used on the propeller. This amount of power drives the airplane, overcoming the drag, so 15 percent of the fuel energy is lost in mechanical friction. This indicates that an airplane, or any other heat machine, is not a particularly economical device.

"The British Air Ministry was extremely helpful. Among others, they sent us Dr. B. S. Shenstone [who arrived February 25, 1941], to assist us in some of the airflow problems into the radiator. The radiator, as we had it, consisted primarily of a fairing, which started at the bottom of the fuselage and enclosed the radiator. Dr. Shenstone advised us to provide an upper lip on the radiator housing, which was about 1½ inches below the fuselage contour. By doing this, we got a much better pressure distribution in the air scoop.

"Previously, air would go in at the bottom of the scoop and spill out on top. By providing this lip and the gap between the fuselage and the radiator lip, we actually equalized the pressure distribution in the duct and got a much better cooling system. We reduced some of the loss due to spilling, which is always detrimental and will produce a certain amount of drag. It is always a problem with any kind of a ducted radiator installation, so this all helped to reduce the spillage."

Aerodynamicist Ed Horkey fills in the details. "The back was the greatest place in the world to put [the radiator]. However, we started out with an opening to the radiator duct, the top line of which was the bottom line of the fuselage. The problem was that being so far back in the fuselage caused the boundary-layer buildup and the airflow wasn't doing the job of furnishing enough [air] to the radiator to give efficiency or enough cooling.

"Meredith had brought forth the theory or proposal to take in air at a high velocity and slow it down, which, of course, builds up pressure. As it goes through the radiator core, the pressure helps some, but primarily you have more dwell time. Then with the increased pressure and temperature, you squeeze the air down again as it goes out the back and you actually get some thrust from this, or what can be called negative radiator drag. It was great, but with the problems we had at the inlet, we weren't achieving cooling or a drag reduction.

"Ed certainly looks at it from a different viewpoint than we in aerodynamics did at that time. Actually, with the one-quarter scale model at Cal Tech, Irving Ashkenas, who had been working with me, was doing the night shift and I was doing the day shift. He was over one night and came up with the idea of why not put a boundary bleed in. In other words, take that top line of the radiator duct and bring it down from the bottom line of the fuselage and let the turbulent boundary layer that built up under the fuselage go by the entrance and therefore you would get more efficient air into the duct. He went ahead one night and did this on the model and the results were great. Other people may have come up with that later on. I want to give full credit to Irving Ashkenas as really being the developer of the boundary-layer bleed. This is in full use yet today. For instance, one can look at the F-16 and see the tremendous boundary-layer gutter that they use."[21]

Perfection of the cooling system was an ongoing process, requiring the input of Horkey's department, wind-tunnel model work, and, above all, continuous flight testing. And most of it would have to be redone in 1943 and 1944 when the Mustang shifted to the more powerful Merlin engine.

Writes Horkey: "The boundary-layer bleed wasn't all that simple. If you drop the radiator inlet down far enough to get rid of all of the turbulent boundary layer, the drag would be too high; so it ended where it was a compromise of the bleed depth to get an acceptable cooling performance with minimum drag.

"It so happened that later on when we started the P-51B project, we got the boundary-layer bleed a little too small. What would happen was that it caused a duct rumble. Chilton described it to us as somebody pounding on a locker. The boundary layer would build up, and airflow would go around the duct inlet, and then it would all of a sudden go inside again, and this would create a large impact load. We did two things. We got the model out again and started checking the bleed. We also took an actual P-51B up to Ames Aeronautical Lab and cut the wing span down a little and mounted in the 16-foot high-speed wind tunnel.

"I took the first ride, and when we got up to 500 mph in the tunnel, we got the rumble. It was quite a thrill. Smith J. DeFrance of NACA at Ames, Manley Hood, and Bill Harper all worked with us. We lowered the top inlet of the radiator duct a small amount and also went to the cutback, or slanted, inlet shape and solved the problem on the P-51B. Later on, on other airplanes like the P-51H, we had to make an eighth of an inch change, and again make sure we had this problem in hand.

"I am absolutely certain, having been there, that the boundary-layer-bleed solution credit should be given to Irving Ashkenas. He later went on to Northrop and participated in the development of the P-61 and their flying wings. He still has a company that does aerodynamic consulting on drag, stability, and control, etc."

PRODUCTION ENGINEERING

Not only must a warplane be good, it must be easy to build. Designing a fighter for the best performance is one thing, engineering it for mass production is something else. While prototypes were built by the veteran craftsmen who came from the east, the production line had to be moved by largely inexperienced and unskilled labor.

Before the war, a long period of time usually passed between preliminary design and production engineering, but in this case, the process was nearly simultaneous. Even before the prototype was completed, production engineering and tooling had to push forward. Mass production meant that the making of each part had to be broken down into simple operations by comparatively unskilled workers. Parts went into subassemblies, and subassemblies became assemblies as the production line moved on. While correcting mistakes in a part for the prototype was easy, changing parts already on the production line was much more serious. This process is the project engineer's responsibility.

Engineering hours on the first production plane began in July 1940 and had reached 77,700 hours when the initial drawings were released in November. By the time of the first production airplane's initial flight on April 25, they reached 154,076 hours, and 272,426 hours had been expended by the completion of the NA-73 project in January 1943.

Kenneth P. Bowen was the first project engineer, assisted by 25-year-old George Gehrkens. Ken was born in England in 1904 and came to America in 1929, joining the company back in the Berliner-Joyce plant in Maryland. He had been the project engineer on export trainers (NA-16) and then on the British Harvards, with George, a recent UCLA graduate, as assistant project engineer. Their work had so satisfied the customers that this pair was put in as production project engineer and assistant project engineer of the NA-73.

When Bowen left early in 1941 to take charge of engineering in the new Dallas plant, Herb Baldwin took his place. Baldwin was outwardly a cheerful type, and his sudden suicide in July 1941 stunned coworkers. George Gehrkens then became production project engineer. Arthur G. Patch was in charge of making the unorthodox thin wing section producible, while John F. Steppe had to translate the fuselage's compound curves and flush skin joints into production drawings. Richard L. Schleicher was the structural engineer responsible for getting the right combination of strength and weight.

First Flights

"We had formed an exceptional group of engineers. There was an enthusiasm in this group that was unequaled anywhere. We worked every day until midnight. On Sundays we quit at 6:00 P.M., so we knew we had a 'weekend.' The airplane was scheduled to be completed in engineering and in the Experimental Department in 100 days. How well this schedule was developed is proven by the fact that the airplane was completed by engineering and the shop in 102 days, just two days more than anticipated. Unfortunately, we had no engine be-

The 1,150-hp Allison V-1710-39 used on the NA-73, XP-46, and P-40 Kittyhawk. *USAF*

cause the Allison people responsible for delivering it told us that since nobody ever designed a fighter in 100 days, 'Why would you need an engine in 100 days?' So subsequently, we had to roll the airplane out of the hangar, without an engine, and it was sitting on the ramp waiting for the Allison for another 18 days.[22]

"The NA-73 airframe was completed by September 9. Without a real engine, the wooden mock-up engine was used with a real propeller and AT-6 landing wheels, and then the plane was photographed. "Copies of the photos were sent to the Allison Division without comments; without words, these pictures said we could fly if we had an engine.[23]

"Only prodding by our power-plant group at the Allison factory in Indianapolis made it possible. One of our power-plant engineers was parked at Allison's front door with the order: 'Don't come home without an engine.' We waited until we finally got the engine, but then we discovered that Allison had changed the wiring harness on the engine, which now did not fit our engine mount. We hadn't been informed, so in the next 18 days we had to make a new engine mount to fit the changes.

"Now the airplane was given to the Flight Division to test and produce the instrumentation and all the necessary work that is required to ready the airplane for flight testing. Flight testing of the NA-73X started after the Flight-test Department completed the necessary instrumentation."

On October 11, 1940, mechanic Olaf Anderson did the first run-up of the new Allison F3R (Air Corps designation V-1710-39) on the NA-73X. While the older Allison V-1710 C-series engines used on the first

The first NA-73X as it came out of the factory. *NAA*

Warming up for taxi tests. *NAA*

P-40s had epicyclic reduction gear, the 1,150-hp V-1710 F series had spur reduction gears, changing the improved P-40 Kittyhawk's shape to a shorter nose with a propeller shaft that was 10 inches higher. This F-model engine was also some 30 pounds lighter and had 10 percent less frontal area.[24]

Since the Mustang was designed for this engine from the beginning, the fuselage cross section was more slender and compact than the Curtiss fighter, which had originally been designed around an air-cooled radial engine. With the V-1710-39 engine and a three-bladed 10-foot 6-inch Curtiss electric propeller installed, the NA-73X was ready.

All metal except for the fabric-covered control surfaces on the tail, the gleaming new prototype was rolled out on Mines Field for its maiden flight. The only markings were the black NX19998 license numbers on the wings. Contract test pilot Vance Breese began October 15 with the first taxi run. The first two flights, of 5 and 10 minutes, were made on Saturday, October 26, 1940.

Six functional checkout flights followed on October 31 and on November 4, 8, 11, 12, and 13, making a total of 3 hours and 20 minutes. After Vance Breese completed his job for North American Aviation, he was replaced as contract test pilot by Paul Balfour. A high-speed test run was scheduled for November 20.[25]

"Before this flight, I asked Balfour to get into the jacked-up airplane and go through the routine of a takeoff and flight. He responded that one airplane is like the other and he would not need the routine checkout. The high-speed run was scheduled the next morning at 7:10 A.M. He made two high-speed passes over the Mines Field airport, and on the third pass for a high-speed checkout, he forgot to put the fuel valve on 'reserve' fuel and subsequently ran out of gas after 15 minutes." (Accident reports made to the CAA indicate that 32 gallons remained in the right fuel tank, and there were no fuel-line or engine failures. Balfour stated that he "exited the aircraft without difficulty.")

"He had to make an emergency landing on a freshly plowed field with the wheels digging into the soft ground, flipping the airplane upside down. Fortunately, he was not injured. We decided not to wait until

the badly damaged airplane was rebuilt and prepared the second airplane, which was actually the first production aircraft, for test flying.

"Flight testing had to be done in a relatively short time because the schedule of finishing the first production airplane in one year was pressing very hard. Time was running out, and a good deal of flying had to be done to get all the information we needed to produce the airplane. Relatively little was changed, of minor importance, because the plane performed so well."

A close-up after the crash showing the original radiator intake. *NAA*

Vance Breese in the cockpit. *NAA*

CHAPTER FOUR

The War's Impact on Fighter Production, 1941-1942

Four 20-mm cannon armed P-51 serial number
137324. *NAA*

No American fighter planes were in the Battle of Britain, which, like no other event, focused world attention on the fight for air superiority. For the first time, a nation's fate was decided by its fighter pilots and their planes. When Britain stood nearly alone, Hurricanes and Spitfires defeated the Luftwaffe's air offensive.

In the month ending September 16, 1940, the day after the greatest air battle over London, the United States Army Air Corps prepared to expand its fighter force by ordering 610 more Lockheed P-38s, 623 more Bell P-39s, and 540 more Curtiss P-40s, all with Allison engines. These were to be built in 1941 and 1942, side by side with the aircraft already sold to the British. Republic, who had no RAF orders, got the largest Army fighter contract, for 820 air-cooled fighters of the yet unseen P-47 type.

North American Aviation wasn't on the Air Corps fighter production program, but before the first NA-73 was flown, Britain had ordered 300 more on September 24, 1940, bringing the total to 620. The official name, given by the British in a December 9 letter to the company, was Mustang I. An additional two aircraft were inserted by the Army contract, approved September 20, for two XP-51s for Air Corps tests. While the original delivery schedule had called for the first Mustang in January 1941, and the next five in February, engine deliveries fell too far behind to meet that schedule.

Meanwhile, the original NA-73X prototype (NX 19998) had been repaired and Vance Breese resumed flight tests on January 13, 1941. Louis Wait, the company's chief test pilot, took over in February until the NA-73X was returned to the shop for

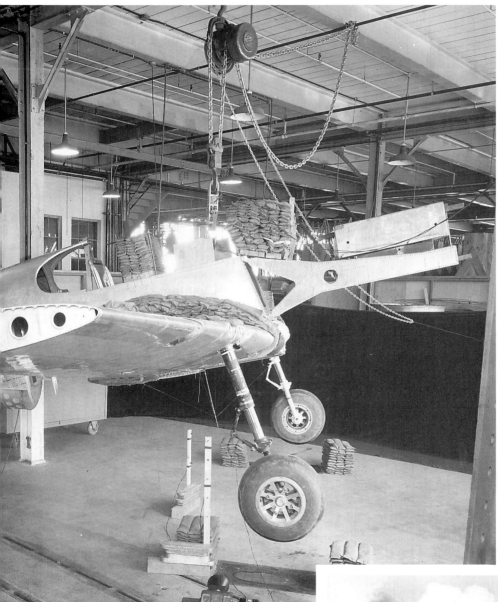

Drop test of landing gear made on March 8, 1941, after original engine was removed. *NAA*

The NA-73X prototype flew again in 1941, but the Army tail stripes were added by a photo retoucher. *NAA*

drop tests on the landing gear and a new production engine. When it returned to fight status, Air Corps Captain M. J. Lee made seven flights beginning March 16, but no record of his impressions has been found.

Robert C. "Bob" Chilton was hired by the company as the engineering test pilot, and it later became his "responsibility to perform the flights leading to proof of the Contract Specifications requirements." He began familiarization flights with NX19998 on April 4, 1941. By the time the prototype finished its last flight on July 15, it had accumulated 40 test hours on 45 flights.[1]

The first production NA-73 was flown by Louis Wait on April 23, 1941. Bearing the RAF serial number AG345 and the company construction number (c/n) 73-3098, this aircraft was unpainted at first, but was later given the camouflage then usual on British aircraft: dark earth and dark green (called "sand and spinach") with sky gray undersides. Chilton began his work on AG345 with a radiator and scoop test on

The first NA-73 production ship, AG345, before any colors. *NAA*

May 1 and had made 17 various test flights by May 23.[2]

Instead of the prototype's curved windshield, there was a flat panel of 1½-inch laminated armor glass. Additional protection specified by the British included self-sealing for the two 90-gallon rubberized fuel tanks in the wing roots, an armor plate (¼-inch) firewall in front of the pilot, and a semicircle ¼-inch plate behind the propeller hub to cover the coolant header tank. Behind the cockpit, 5/16-inch armor protected the pilot's back, and 7/16-inch his head.

Originally, the British had requested four 20-mm cannons with belt feed in the wings, but since these weapons would not be available in sufficent quantity until 1942, eight machine guns had been provided. These included two synchronized .50-caliber guns below the engine, firing through the propeller, and another in each wing, inboard of

two .30-caliber guns. RAF ammunition allotments called for 300 rounds for each .50-caliber gun, 932 for each inboard .30-caliber wing gun, and 814 rounds for each outboard .30-caliber wing gun.[3]

Since the commitment to provide the Army Air Corps with an example was now two months behind schedule, an Allison engine belonging to the Air Corps had been rushed to the plant and installed on the fourth production airframe (c/n 73-3101). (Exact data is given here, to correct errors published elsewhere.) It became the second NA-73 to fly when Bob Chilton made the first test on May 20, a power calibration and aileron trial.

As an official Air Corps type, the plane bore the designation XP-51 and serial num-

AG345 in flight with British markings and extended nose intake. *NAA*

ber 41-038. Some of the parts were hand-made, not yet standard production pieces, and some AT-6 components were still used. Chilton flew 21 more tests on the XP-51 from May 24 to July 2.

The assembly line had the second RAF Mustang, AG346 (c/n 73-3099), ready for Chilton's first functional check flight on July 3, and the third, AG347, had its first check flight on July 30. By August 1, Chilton had completed company tests on AG346 and it was now ready for British acceptance.

Squadron Leader (later, Wing Commander) Michael N. Crossley, an RAF ace

The Mustang I's clean lines are displayed by AG345. *NAA*

who had downed nine German planes while flying Hurricanes during the Battle of Britain, arrived from England to perform the acceptance test flights. Wing Commander Christopher Clarkson, who was responsible for producing the pilot's handbooks on all the American aircraft built for the RAF, also flew the Mustang.

Schmued describes Crossley: "He was a very pleasant Britisher, 6 feet 2 inches tall, but the cockpit was designed for a 5-foot 10-inch pilot. When he sat in the Mustang cockpit, his knees were just about under his chin, but he didn't complain. After he made his routine flights, which were most satisfactory, he had one more test to do: firing the guns out over the Pacific Ocean.

"Such gun firing had to have Coast Guard permission, which was a few weeks coming. The impatient officer complained to me: 'I don't understand you Americans; we in England just fire into the countryside, and you would be surprised how few people get killed,' and out he went, complaining about the delays." Fortunately, the Navy later made their firing range at North Island available for ground firing tests.

AG346 was finally accepted in August and became the first Mustang to be crated and shipped to England, leaving Long Beach harbor for the long voyage down through the Panama Canal and across the Atlantic. The XP-51 was also accepted, and an Army pilot flew it to Wright Field on August 24, 1941. Mustangs AG345 and AG347, however, remained with the company for developmental testing through March of 1942.

Six more Mustangs were accepted in September, beginning with AG348 (c/n 73-

3102), on which Chilton began production functional tests on September 19, 1941. This was the last Mustang completed with a short nose intake and some hand-tooled parts; the rest were straight production ships. To improve the ram air delivery to the carburetor, the air intake was extended forward to directly behind the propeller, like that on the P-40, and this change was made to all the production ships. AG348 also had the distinction of being the first Mustang later shipped to the U.S.S.R. by Britain.

RAF Squadron Leader Michael Crossley about to fly a Mustang. *NAA*

The fifth NA-73, AG348, still had a short intake on August 9, 1941, and eventually went to the U.S.S.R. *NAA*

Afterward, deliveries accelerated rapidly, with 138 Mustangs accepted by year's end and another 84 NA-73s in January 1942. February 13 saw the initial production functional flight of AL958, first of the 300 aircraft on the second order. They had the contract order number NA-83, although identical to the NA-73, and also had the Mustang I name. By July 1942, the last of 620 Mustang Is had been accepted.

AG346 arrived in Liverpool on October 24, and made the first Mustang flight in Britain on November 11. At Liverpool's Spekes Airport, the British press was shown the Mustang, along with the Curtiss Kittyhawk, on December 5, 1941. Mustangs were distributed to 15 RAF Army Cooperation Command squadrons in Britain by the end of 1942, while the Curtiss Kittyhawks received at the same time were deployed to fighter squadrons in the Middle and Far East. Older Curtiss Tomahawks had been used by these squadrons until the Mustangs and Kittyhawks arrived.[4]

Of the Mustangs shipped to England, 12 were lost when a U-boat torpedoed the *Ocean Venture,* a new California-built British ship, in the North Atlantic on February 8, 1942. Eight more went down on another

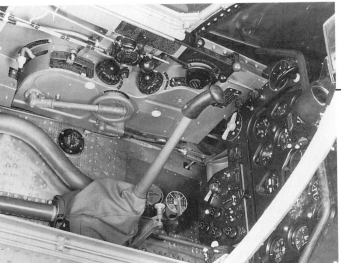

The cockpit of an NA-73 Mustang. *NAA*

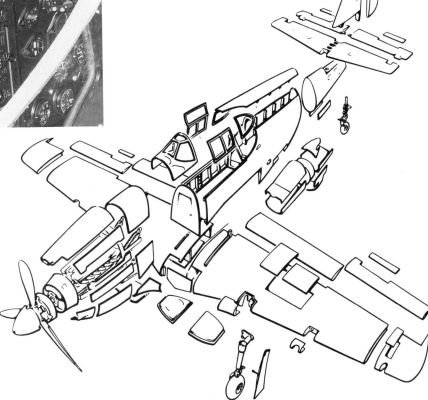

An exploded view of NA-73 structure. *NAA*

ship a few days later.[5] Four were sent to the Soviet Union in May 1942: AG348, 352, 353, and 354. The former was tested at the Soviet Air Force Research Institute, and the others went to a regiment opposing the Finnish air force.[6]

No. 26 Squadron became the first to receive Mustangs in January 1942. A camera facing left was added behind the pilot's head, for the primary purpose of Army Co-operation units was armed reconnaissance. Their missions consisted of low-level cross-Channel dashes to France, machine-gunning and photographing enemy troops, trains, and rivercraft. The first sortie was by AG418 of No. 26 Squadron on May 10, 1942. Enemy fighters were to be avoided,

Early RAF Mustang I sorties were often flown in pairs. Here AG550 and AM112 of No. 2 Squadron fly together in 1942. *IWM*

when possible, but because of low flying, frequent collisions, and flak, their operations were very dangerous. Of 10 Mustangs lost in July 1942, only one loss was blamed on enemy fighters.

By the time the Mustang entered action, RAF tests had gotten a very favorable response from British pilots. Considered "definitely the best American fighter that has reached England," it was faster than the Spitfire VB up to 25,000 feet, had twice the range (up to four hours at an economical throttle setting), and could easily outdive the Spitfire. The British plane had better climb, ceiling, and faster turns, and since its high-altitude superiority was due to the Rolls-Royce engine, it was recommended that later Mustangs be "speedily equipped" with the Merlin-61 engine used in the newest Spitfire IX.[7]

The commander of the Air Fighting Development Unit (AFDU) considered the Mustang "an excellent low- and medium-altitude fighter . . . pleasant to fly . . . extremely stable . . . far smoother in all maneuvers" than the Spitfire.[8]

Tests on AG351, fully loaded to 8,300 pounds and painted, recorded a 370-mph top speed at 15,000 feet, a 30,000-foot service ceiling, and 990-mile range at 180 mph.[9] "One man in the Air Ministry later confessed to me," said Schmued later, "that he had taken our performance guarantee of 370 mph and knocked it down to 300 mph because he supposed that all American manufacturers lied about performance. When he found out our quotation was correct, it opened up new possibilities for our plane."[10]

THE ARMY TESTS THE MUSTANG

After the first XP-51 was flown to Wright Field on August 24, official performance tests, delayed by weather and low priorities, were conducted from October 8 to December 22. The second XP-51, accepted and flown to Wright on December 16, also used the standard V-1710-39 with 8.80:1 supercharger gear ratio, rated at 1,150 hp for takeoff and at 11,800 feet. Weighing 6,275 pounds empty, the XP-51 was tested with eight guns, 200 rounds for each .50-caliber gun, and 500 for each .30-caliber gun, and

with 170 gallons of fuel. Top speed was measured at 382 mph at 13,000 feet and a gross weight of 7,934 pounds. Range was 750 miles at a 325-mph cruising speed. Performance guarantees of 375 mph had been exceeded.[11]

Curtiss, meanwhile, had not been idle. More than a year after the Army had approved the contract, the XP-46 was first flown on February 15, 1941, nearly five months after the Mustang prototype. On September 11, 1941, the first Curtiss XP-46 was delivered to Wright, and the second on September 22. Regular performance tests were delayed for the same reasons as those of the XP-51, and, the results were very disappointing.

With six guns and without the self-sealing planned for the fuel tanks, the XP-46 weighed 5,625 pounds empty. Although using the same 1,150-hp V-1710-39 engine as the XP-51, the smaller Curtiss did only 355 mph at 12,200 feet, weighing 7,081 pounds. With the full fuel capacity of 156 gallons, range was 717 miles at 305 mph.

Since the contract had called for 410 mph, the Army fined Curtiss $14,995 for failure to achieve performance guarantees, reducing the costs for both prototypes to $407,-949. The superior XP-51s cost the Army only $35,175 each, since they were actually production aircraft.[12] Although a Curtiss engineer would later claim, on October 28, 1943, that XP-46 performance was "strikingly similar" to the Mustang, this is not confirmed by the data.[13]

Fortunately the P-46 had been dismissed in favor of the improved P-40E, called the Kittyhawk in the RAF, with the same 1,150-hp Allison. Curtiss did fly the first H87A-1 Kittyhawk on May 22, 1941, and

Second XP-51 in flight with Wright Field arrowhead insignia. *AAF*

A close-up of the XP-51's engine mount and nose gun. *NAA*

The first Army Air Force XP-51. *NAA*

The Curtiss H87A (P-40E) Kittyhawk was the principal American fighter built in 1941 for RAF overseas squadrons. *SDAM*

While the Curtiss XP-46 had the same engine as the XP-51, it was much slower. *SDAM*

RAF acceptances began August 27. Production accelerated rapidly, and during 1941 Curtiss completed the last 926 Tomahawks and 1,320 of the newer Kittyhawks, dividing deliveries between the AAF and the RAF.

North American's fighter also faced competition from four other builders whose 1941 acceptances included 926 Bell P-39 Airacobras, as well as 205 of Lockheed's exotic twin-engine P-38 Lightning. There were also 160 Republic P-43 Lancers, an interim type until the P-47 could be available, and 71 Vultee P-66 Vanguards, both on lend-lease contracts for China. Table One compares the characteristics of models

TABLE ONE
AAF Fighters, December 1941

	P-38E	P-39D	P-40E	P-43A1	XP-46	XP-51	P-66
	LIGHTNING	*AIRACOBRA*	*WARHAWK*	*LANCER*		*MUSTANG*	*VANGUARD*
Gross Wt. (lbs.)	15,000	7500	8280	7935	7322	7965	7100
Wg. Area (sq. ft.)	327.5	213	236	223	208	233	197
Wing loading (lb./sq. ft.)	44.04	35.21	35.08	33.34	35.20	34.18	36.04
Horsepower	2300	1150	1150	1200	1150	1150	1050
Crit. Alt. (ft.)	25,000	11,800	11,800	20,000	11,800	11,800	13,100
Power loading (lb./hp.)	6.52	6.52	7.20	6.21	6.37	6.93	6.76
Vmax (mph)	390	368	354	356	355	382	340
@ Alt. (ft.)	25,000	13,800	15,000	20,000	12,200	13,000	15,100
Ser. Clg. (ft.)	39,000	32,100	29,000	36,000	29,500	30,800	28,200
Climb (ft.)	20,000	15,000	15,000	15,000	12,300	15,000	19,700
in minutes	8	5.7	7.6	6	5	7	9.2
Int. Fuel (gal.)	300	120	148	218	156	170	185
Range (miles)	500	800	700	650	717	750	850
@ Vcruis (mph)	300	213	258	280	305	325	290

Aircraft data from *Army Aircraft Characteristics* May 1946: 31–36, and test reports.

In December 1941, the most-produced Air Force fighter was the Curtiss P-40E, with six .50-caliber wing guns and a drop tank.

being produced in December 1941 along with the XP-46. Pilots would have to develop tactics making the best use of each type.

With two turbosupercharged engines, the P-38E interceptor had the highest speed and ceiling, although its size and heavy wing loading meant it was the least maneuverable. At lower altitudes, the Lockheed Lightning was less agile. Bob Chilton remembers being challenged on a test flight by a P-38, but he just opened up his Mustang's throt-

Lockheed's P-38E was the fastest Air Force fighter in 1941. *MFR*

tle and pulled away from the twin-boomed Lockheed.

The Bell P-39D had better performance than the less streamlined P-40E, but the XP-51 was still faster, and lower wing loading gave it a maneuverability edge. Of the two radial-engine types, the P-43A-1 had the best ceiling due to its supercharger and low wing loading, while the P-66 was inferior in all respects except maneuverability. Neither of these fighters for China had self-sealing fuel tanks, unlike the Air Force types, and were not used in combat by American pilots.

Four .50-caliber guns and a 20-mm cannon in the nose concentrated the P-38's firepower. The P-39D had two .50-caliber

guns in the nose with a cannon: 20-mm for the export version, or 37-mm for the Air Force, plus four .30-caliber guns in the wings. Mixing the ballistics of three different weapons did not help accurate firing.

The P-40E's six .50-caliber wing guns later became also the standard for Mustangs. Both the P-39D and P-40E could carry a drop tank or a 500-pound bomb underneath the fuselage. Two .50-caliber and two .30-caliber guns armed the P-43A-1, while the P-66 also had two .50-caliber guns in the nose, plus four .30-caliber guns in the wings.

Bell delivered the first of 675 Airacobras (P-400) for the RAF on June 2, 1941. But when the RAF tested it fully loaded and painted, top speed was rated at only 355 mph at 13,000 feet and service ceiling at 27,000 feet. The only RAF squadron to use them was disappointed in their performance and serviceability, and the British kept only 32 Airacobras, relinquishing the remainder of their order to the Soviet Air Force or to the AAF.[14]

Parallel with the P-38E, Lockheed was producing Model 322s for Britain, the first 143 without turbosuperchargers. These had been requisitioned by the AAF in December 1941, but three were forwarded to England in March 1942. Their performance at high altitudes was considered so limited that the RAF was glad to cancel its expensive contract, and its remaining aircraft were absorbed into the P-38F program.

MUSTANGS FOR THE AIR FORCE

Shortly before 1942, North American's fighter prospects didn't seem promising. When lend-lease funds had become available in April 1941, contracts were made for 1,500 P-40E-1, 344 P-39D-1, and 125 P-43A-1 fighters, but only 150 P-51s (NA-91) were begun on July 7 to replenish the RAF squadrons. (As lend-lease aircraft were considered U.S. government property, all were given Army Air Force designations and serial numbers, as well as RAF or other user identifiers.)

Since that contract would extend Mustang production only to September 1942, the company needed to win Air Force contracts. But when Bob Chilton came to Wright Field on October 21, 1941, to check out a Spitfire V and a Hurricane II and make comparisons with the Mustang, he noticed the XP-51 sitting with only one hour added to its logbook since it had arrived. Other projects, he was told, were considered more important, and the P-51 wasn't under an Army production contract. These other projects included the more powerful Republic P-47 and Curtiss P-60, both scheduled for 1942 production, so the Army didn't seem to need another fighter type. Only a very junior second lieutenant, Winthrop Towner, was the P-51 project officer.

Air Force indifference to the XP-51 at that time was indicated by the report made to the AAF chief on *The Future Development of Pursuit Aircraft.* The Pursuit Board met from October 11 to 30, 1941, to "make a thorough study of our current . . . program for pursuit aircraft." Eight production and 18 experimental types were discussed, but the XP-51 was not included.[15]

The board's report did face the questions of where and what the pursuit would fight and concluded that a truly "all-purpose" fighter could not be built to fight anywhere and anything. Instead, the fighter should be made for "its primary mission of destroying hostile bombers. It must be able to overcome or to evade such hostile pursuit as it may encounter."

Destroying enemy bombers would require interceptors of both high- and low-altitude types, as well as a specialized night fighter. Heavy armament was needed and the .30-caliber gun was no longer useful. But the mission of "convoy defender" to protect American bombers penetrating deeply into enemy territory was seen as requiring a large multiplace aircraft whose development "may not be possible now." Extension of existing fighter range by drop tanks was not mentioned.

The Army overlooked the Mustang in favor of its own ambitious fighter development program. At the same time that North American began the first NA-73, the Army planned to use the newest engines and laminar flow airfoils to get advanced performance. On February 20, 1940, Request for Data R40-C had been sent to 13 selected companies, and 9 responded with preliminary experimental fighter proposals.

The Board of Review met on May 15 to appraise these designs, and on May 29, the same day Britain ordered the Mustang I, the board's recommendations went to General Arnold. The three winners were all pusher-type aircraft with tricycle gear. First was Richard Palmer's Vultee XP-54 with twin tail booms, which was promised to do 510 mph at 20,000 feet. Second was the Curtiss-Wright XP-55, a swept-wing canard; third was the tailless Northrop XP-56.

Contracts for preliminary engineering data and wind-tunnel models were approved June 22, 1940, for all three of the R40-C aircraft, with options for prototype construction. Additional experimental prototypes were ordered from more conventional builders. Curtiss pushed ahead with its P-60, big P-62, and even bigger XP-71, while Bell engineers worked on the XP-39E, XP-59, and the XP-63, and Republic planned the XP-47E and XP-69. Lockheed XP-49 and XP-58 twin-engine types and a McDonnell XP-67 were in the works.

It's not surprising, then, that the Air Corps thought it would not need the P-51. But of all the experimental types discussed in detail by the board in October 1941, only the heavy Northrop P-61 night fighter would ever fly into combat with American pilots. The war that began on December 7, 1941, would have to be fought with the basic fighters already ordered into production.

Looking at the two types then in large-quantity production, the P-40E and P-39D, the Pursuit Board did recognize that their performance was handicapped both by the overweight of armament and protection added to the basic design and by the low critical altitude of the Allison engine. This situation would be improved with 1942 deliveries of the P-40F, powered by the 1,300-hp Merlin XX being made in the United States by Packard.

But the Army's main hope for fighter superiority was in the turbosupercharged high-altitude P-38 and P-47 types, along with a new successor to the P-40, the Curtiss P-60A, just ordered in October. These three types might provide the upper defense layer needed.

AFTER PEARL HARBOR

The Pearl Harbor attack sharply increased U.S. Army needs for fighters, so Airacobras,

Right, the Republic P-43 was the only air-cooled fighter produced for the Air Corps in 1941. *USAF*

Below, Vultee's P-66 Vanguards started out on a Swedish contract, briefly wore British markings, but were lend-leased to China. *SDAM*

This Bell Airacobra I built for RAF was turned back to the Air Force. *SDAM*

Lightnings, and P-66s awaiting shipment abroad were requisitioned for the Air Force. Mustang and Kittyhawk deliveries to Britain, however, went uninterrupted, at least when shipping was available. On December 29, Chilton took an opportunity to fly Mustang AG434 to nearby March Field to familiarize Army pilots there with the type.

The aerodynamic efficiency of the XP-51 was also demonstrated when both prototypes were sent to Langley Field to be flown by NACA pilots. One of them, John P. Reeder, later wrote that of 22 propeller-driven fighters he tested, "the P-51s were my favorite." The shape of the laminar flow airfoil reduced peak airflow velocities over the wing, thus postponing and minimizing the "compressibility" effects that plagued

other contemporary fighters above a Mach number of about 0.7. Special flight-test instrumentation and motion-picture cameras were added to record the effects of gradually increasing dive speeds.

In the words of historian Richard Hallion, "This modified XP-51 was, in fact, the ancestor of all postwar 'X-series' research aircraft. Besides acquiring valuable information on flight above Mach 0.7, it also demonstrated that, with a cautious, well-planned test program, the lives of test pilots need not be risked recklessly. It was with the NACA XP-51 that test pilots first saw the streaming of shock waves from the wings as the airflow over the wings exceeded the speed of sound."[16]

A series of tests were made in 1942 of roll capability, during which aileron deflection was increased from 10 to 20 percent. Deflections of 15 percent were chosen for the

P-51B and later production models. Another test series examined dive recovery characteristics at high speeds.

THE A-36 DIVE-BOMBER

Before long, Air Force interest in the Mustang did increase. As it happened, the Army felt its most immediate need was for close support aircraft to help the ground troops. Douglas A-24 dive-bombers had been obtained from the Navy in 1941, but combat experience in the southwest Pacific indicated that type was too slow to operate without fighter escort.

As early as February 4, 1942, Colonel K. B. Wolfe, Chief of the Production Engineering Section, reported that "we will not have a useful dive-bomber before March 1943." He recommended that the AAF cancel the Vultee Vengeance two-seaters on order and obtain "a suitable dive-bomber, low-altitude attack fighter in its place."

Soon North American was asked to develop a dive-bomber version of the Mustang, designated A-36 by the Army. Company work on that project, the NA-97, began on April 16, 1942. Army requirements meant the addition of an external rack under each wing for a 500-pound bomb or a 75-gallon drop tank for ferry flights, and dive brakes to limit acceleration. A contract for 500 A-36A dive-bombers, serialed 42-83663/84162, was not finally approved until August 21, but work was well under way.

George Gehrkens went over to Northrop to look at the dive brakes on the Vengeance dive-bomber for the RAF, which became the A-35 for the AAF. He suggested a simi-

After America entered the war, U.S. markings were painted on Mustang Is retained in California for tests, like AL958, the first NA-83. *NAA*

An A-36 (NA-97) with dive brakes retracted.
NAA

lar system of horizontal wing spoilers for the Mustang. AM-118 was fitted with the additions planned for the A-36, and Bob Chilton began testing the dive brakes on May 30 and the outside wing tanks on July 4. By July 18, he was performing dive-bombing tests.

Meanwhile, work went ahead on the lend-lease contract for the P-51, which had the four 20-mm cannons in the wing that the British had wanted to replace the eight machine guns. Unlike the 20-mm guns on the export P-39s, which had just 60 rounds in a drum, these were belt-fed with 125 rounds per gun. As early as October 30, 1941, Chilton had flown cannon drag tests with dummy guns on AG347, and cannon firing tests were made on June 8, 1942, with real guns installed on AM190.

By the time the first P-51, 41-37320, was flown by Chilton on May 30, 1942, the

The fifth P-51 in flight, but the aerial number has been censored. *NAA*

Army decided some were needed for its tactical reconnaissance squadrons and requisitioned the first 20 accepted off the line in July 1942. The RAF got 93 of the 150 as the Mustang IA (serials in the FD418-567 range), two were set aside for the NA-101 Merlin project, and another 35 were added to the AAF batch by the end of deliveries in September. P-51 41-37324 was modified at the factory to have two K-24 cameras, one behind the pilot's head, pointing to the left, and one on the floor near the tail, aimed straight down. The other 54 Army aircraft were so modified at depots and redesignated F-6A for photo reconnaissance, until reverting to a P51-2 designation in October 1942.

Increasing Air Force interest in the Mustang led the company to originate the NA-99 on June 23, 1942. This was a straight Air Force fighter with improved engine, drop tanks, and all .50-caliber armament (the AAF was dropping .30-caliber guns on fighters), which won a 1,200-plane contract approved August 24, 1942, for production of the P-51A in 1943. While the names Apache and Invader were suggested for the AAF P-51 and A-36 in 1942, the Air Force wisely decided to stick with Mustang as the official title.

The first A-36A flight was on September 27, 1942, on 42-83663. Chilton performed this test, as well as later terminal-velocity dives with brakes open and closed. Extensive bomb-drop tests were performed at dive angles up to 85 degrees with brakes open. Hydraulically operated, the four aluminum horizontal lattice brakes extended from each wing's top and bottom surfaces. These brakes were best opened before entering the dive, in which both 500-pound bombs were dropped at once.

An Allison V-1710-87 boosted for low-altitude operation was rated at 1,325 hp at 3,000 feet. The two synchronized .50-caliber guns in the nose, which had been omitted on the P-51s, were restored, and four more were mounted within the wings. When carrying bombs, the A-36A had a top speed of 310 mph at 5,000 feet, a range of 550 miles, and a 25,100-foot service ceiling. When the bombs were gone, the A-36A could reach 366 mph at 1,000 feet and 368 at 14,000 feet, with a 27,000-foot service ceiling. Above 10,000 feet, its speed was less than that of the XP-51, whose engine was rated for medium altitudes.

After 500 A-36As were accepted between October 1942 and March 1943, deliveries began on the last Allison-powered Mustang, the P-51A. Bob Chilton made the first flight on February 3, 1943, on 43-6003. The power plant was a V-1710-81 with automatic boost control, 9.6:1 supercharger gear ratio, 1,200 hp for takeoff, 1,125 hp at 14,600 feet, and 1,360-hp war emergency power. Top speed ranged from 340 mph at 5,000 feet to 390 mph at 20,000 feet, and service ceiling was 31,350 feet on a P-51A at 8,633-pound gross. Four .50-caliber wing guns with 1,260 rounds and underwing racks for two 500-pound bombs or 75-gallon drop tanks were provided, but synchronized guns were not included.[17]

TESTING THE P-51A

Five P-51A-10s were delivered to the AAF School of Applied Tactics (AAFSAT) at Orlando, Florida, for tactical employment trials. After comparative tests and mock combat with the P-38G, P-39N, stripped P-40M, and P-47C, it was reported that "below 22,000 feet, the P-51 is considered to have the best all-around fighting qualities of any present American fighter. Its main advantages are its fair rate of climb, quick acceleration, very high level speed and exceptionally high diving speed. Its main disadvantages are the poor search view and limited view over the nose."

Detailed comments concluded that:

The four-gun armament was the minimum acceptable, but armor protection for the pilot was good. The cockpit was rather small and uncomfortable.

Inset, **the only A-36 in RAF colors, with 500-pound bombs and dive brakes extended.** *IWM*

Four .50-caliber wing guns armed the P-51A, whose third example, 36005, is seen here. *NAA*

A P-51A-10 in flight. *USAF*

Landing and takeoff were easy and the run was shorter than most fighters; 1,675 feet to clear a 50-foot obstacle.

Flying characteristics were excellent, stalling characteristics good, and all maneuvers could be performed with ease.

Escort flying qualities were good because of long range and excellent fighting capabilities.

Top speed was about 410 mph (true) at 18,000 feet (presumably with war emergency power).

Combat range on internal fuel at 12,000 feet was 210 miles out in 45 minutes, allowing 15 minutes for combat, and 210 miles back.

Rate of climb was good, 22,000 feet in ten minutes.

The Mustang was the best U.S. fighter available, but when the earlier Mustang IA was compared by the RAF with the best German fighter, a captured Fw 190A, the picture was less optimistic. The Focke-Wulf had better climb, acceleration, and speed at altitudes over 20,000 feet.[18]

Production of Allison-engine Mustangs ended in May 1943, after 1,581 ships, including 310 P-51As, had been manufactured. The RAF received the 23rd A-36A (EW998) and 50 P-51As (as Mustang II, FR890/939) to make up for the lend-lease P-51s taken by the AAF. Thirty-five Army P-51As became F-6Bs when two cameras were added; most went to the 107th Tactical Reconnaissance Squadron based in England in 1943.

An unusual episode in Mustang trials was the testing of the third P-51A-2, 43-6005, with retractable skis for operating from snow or ice-covered surfaces. These tests began in July 1943 at Grenier Field, New Hampshire, and were completed at Ladd Field, Alaska, in February 1944. The three skis, made by the Luscombe Engineering Company in North Wales, Pennsylvania, had only a "negligible" effect on flight maneuverability and reduced indicated air speed by 10 to 25 mph. However, the Air Force did not find skis, also tested on the P-38, P-40, P-47, and P-63, necessary for World War II operations.[19]

MUSTANGS IN CLOSE SUPPORT

On August 19, 1942, the RAF provided fighter cover when the Dieppe hit-and-run landing challenged German fortifications on the French coast. Included were four Mustang squadrons and the AAF's 31st Fighter Group with Spitfires. The Luftwaffe responded with their best fighter pilots and planes: the Focke-Wulf Fw 190.

While the landing force was protected from air strikes, 106 Allied aircraft were lost, compared to 48 German fighters. The AAF Spitfires lost eight planes and won only one confirmed victory. On 72 RAF Mustang sorties, 10 planes were downed by flak and fighters. It was going to be a hard war for American planes and pilots, who had to take on a very experienced enemy. Nevertheless, the Mustang did score its first known victory when F/O Hollis H. Hills, a volunteer from Pasadena, California, flying AG470 with Canada's 414 Squadron, downed an Fw 190. Back home, newspapers reported the successes but didn't mention the losses. Hillis later flew Grumman Hellcats of VF-32 for the United States Navy.

Future Mustang I missions would most often be called "rhubarbs," that is, low-level strikes at ground targets, especially trains, with only infrequent encounters with enemy fighters. Photoreconnaissance sorties were called "populars." On October 21, 16 Mustangs of No. 2 Squadron demonstrated their range by being the first single-engine fighters to fly all the way from Britain to Germany, where they strafed barges on the Dortmund Canal and returned without loss.

Army Cooperation Command was disbanded in 1943, and its fighter squadrons were assigned to the 2nd Tactical Air Force, formed to support the coming invasion of occupied Europe. By the time of the D-day landings in June 1944, the Allison-powered Mustang had been eclipsed by newer models, but five RAF squadrons did support the invasion and two (No. 26 and No. 268) were still using these reliable mounts until the war in Europe ended.

MUSTANGS IN THE AAF

The first AAF P-51s in action, with their cameras and 20-mm guns, were those of the

The third P-51A with its experimental retractable skis. USAF

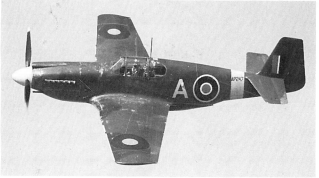

RAF Mustang I, AL247 of No. 4 Squadron. *IWM*

154th Observation Squadron in North Africa. On April 9, 1943, Lieutenant Alfred Schwab flew 41-37328 on the first Mustang photo sortie into Tunisia.[20] The 111th Reconnaissance Squadron joined the action with P-51s in July.

As the fastest low-altitude fighter around, the P-51 was judged "ideal" for tactical reconnaissance.[21] The only loss, in 198 sorties by September 30, was one downed by an Army AA gunner who mistook the P-51 for a Messerschmitt Bf 109. Yellow bands were then painted around the wings of Twelfth Air Force Mustangs to prevent such mistakes.

Next into action were two A-36A groups. After shifting during training from two-seater dive-bombers to the single-seat North Americans, the 27th and 86th Fighter-Bomber Groups were shipped to North African bases, from which attacks against targets in Italy began on June 6, 1943. On August 22, A-36s were used to escort medium bombers for the first time, setting a new round-trip record, of over 800 miles, for single-engine fighter missions. In 23,373 sorties by 1944, 8,014 tons of bombs were delivered, 177 A-36s lost, mainly to flak, and 84 enemy aircraft destroyed. Some A-36 pilots suggested the name "Invader" for their planes, to distinguish them from the fighter Mustangs, but that name had already been allotted to the Douglas A-26 bomber.

Mustangs entered combat against Japan on October 16, 1943, when the 311th Fighter-Bomber Group, with two A-36A squadrons and one of P-51As, began operations from India.[22] Thirty more P-51A fighters arrived with the First Air Commando Force of Colonel Philip G. Cochran

for special operations within Burma in March 1944.[23] The 54th Fighter Group at Bartow, Florida, got P-51As and served as a replacement training unit to supply pilots for overseas groups.

Allison-powered Mustangs had proven themselves excellent for tactical support of ground operations. An entirely new power plant, however, would be needed to transform the Mustang into the most successful destroyer of enemy aircraft the Air Force was to have. While North American had suggested development of a two-stage V-1710 model supercharged for higher altitudes, Allison had fallen behind British progress in that respect.

MORROW VICTORY TRAINER

It is remarkable that despite the constant Mustang design activity, Schmued found time for other projects, like the Morrow Victory trainer and the "low carbon steel" version of the AT-6 trainer. Both ideas were inspired by the shortage of strategic materials that worried wartime America. Like the huge "Spruce Goose" of Howard Hughes, these projects proved unnecessary to win the war, but at least the small trainer project didn't cost the taxpayers any money, since it was a purely private venture.

Howard B. Morrow, owner of a very successful candy business, was visiting Los Angeles in 1940 when he suddenly decided to go into the airplane business. "I knew absolutely nothing about airplanes!" he wrote in his good-humored autobiography, but that didn't keep him from starting the Morrow Aircraft Corporation. He moved his company from Van Nuys to San Bernardino in

Howard Morrow and his wife watch construction of his "Victory" trainer. *SDAM*

February 1941 and hoped to build a trainer and a small private-cabin type.[24]

Morrow first tried to work with pilot Harry Crosby, but a satisfactory engineering arrangement wasn't established. Big companies had scooped up all the good engineers, and Morrow was stalled until, by chance, he met Ray Rice, who recommended Schmued as a designer. Working in his spare time, Schmued prepared a two-place, low-wing monoplane trainer design to be built entirely out of wood, except for the engine mount and landing gear. Powered by a 175-hp Lycoming O-435A, the "Victory trainer" was covered by smooth plastic-bonded plywood and had retractable wheels and a cockpit enclosure.[25]

Wing span was 30 feet 4 inches, wing area 142.5 square feet, and length 25 feet 4 inches. Weight was 1,886 pounds empty and 2,450 pounds gross, with a fuel capacity of 27 gallons normal and 42 gallons maximum. Speeds were 180 mph top, 160 mph cruising, and 53 mph landing. Initial rate of climb was 900 feet per minute, service ceiling 17,500 feet, and range from 370 to 672 miles.[26]

After a trial flight of the prototype, NX33661, in November 1941, an official test flight was held before celebrities like General Arnold, Dutch Kindelberger, and Donald Douglas, with actress Carole Landis there to cut the ribbon. Unfortunately, inexperienced workmen had left many "bugs" in the aircraft, and test pilot Vance Breese cut short the flight. Student engineers were then hired to work out the difficulties and complete a second prototype.

The day after Pearl Harbor, the government took over Morrow's factory and airport, which is now Norton Air Force Base.

Since Morrow had no government contract or priorities, he was completely out of business. The Air Force had all the trainers it needed, and efforts to sell the Morrow to foreign powers failed.

The whole episode was a reminder that building successful airplanes required the skill and experience represented by the established companies. "Spud" Morrow continued as a successful candy man, remained friends with Schmued, and his autobiography is frank about his shortcomings as an airplane builder. "We should have been smart enough to give up building our own airplane—and to have made parts."[27]

A LOW CARBON STEEL AIRPLANE?

"The idea of someday seeing aircraft being produced on a production line using automotive materials and manufacturing practices always remained with Ed Schmued," wrote Richard Schleicher. Prospects began in 1934, when the Department of Commerce aviation director Eugene Vidal sponsored a design competition for a two-place light plane that could be built for the cost of a Buick sedan, then about $750. Many designers were intrigued by this challenge, especially when Vidal asserted that there was a potential market for 10,000 such aircraft.[28]

Back at the old General Aviation plant in Maryland, Ed quickly calculated that this price could not be met, given the cost of an engine and of aluminum airframe materials. But supposing cheaper materials were used?

One day Ed approached Richard Schleicher, the company's structural engineer, about the possibilities of using low carbon steel (the kind used in auto bodies) in an airframe. This less expensive metal had about the same strength as aluminum, but weighed more than twice as much. Ed thought that by using spot welding instead of riveting, some of this weight could be reduced. Still more weight could be saved by casting a 90-hp Ford V-8 engine in aluminum.

Schleicher was impressed by the concept and looked for financial backers, while encouraging Ed to prepare a simple intermediate design for a two-place aluminium sport plane with the V-8 cast in aluminum. No financial backing could be found, however, and the idea was put aside until the war brought a shortage of critical materials such as aluminum alloys and quality stainless steel.

A wartime materials substitution program inspired U.S. Steel to offer National Emergency (NE) steels, one of which attracted Schmued's attention and which he suggested to North American as a way of saving critical alloys in the AT-6 program. On March 31, 1941, Dutch Kindelberger directed research on low carbon steel and its use on sample test AT-6 wing panels. At that time, the company was preparing for

production of 9,331 NA-88 (AT-6C/SNJ-4) trainers in Texas for the Air Force, Navy, and lend-lease.

An experimental wing with spot welding was ready for static test, but failed at 90 percent of its design load—a real accomplishment for a first try. A second wing, using 4610 steel, was made by October 15 and successfully survived 105 percent of its required load increment. More parts were made, and Schmued and Schleicher took a sample tail fin by train to Pittsburgh to demonstrate their work to steel company officials, and to Wright Field for Air Force examination. The steel men were delighted by an opportunity to take business away from the Aluminum Company of America, and the Air Force endorsed the plan, but "the big bubble burst."

T. P. Wright, head of the War Materials Allocation Board, objected that the low carbon steel still contained 1.7 percent of scarce nickel, and rejected the plan.[29] North American had to be content with minor changes in the NA-88, including some steel parts and wooden fuselage side panels. For about a 150-pound increase in weight, 1,246 pounds of aluminum alloy was replaced, however.[30]

Morrow trainer taking off. *SDAM*

CHAPTER FIVE

A Push for Performance:
Merlin-powered Mustangs

So many Mustangs roll out of Inglewood that these P-51D-20s must await delivery pilots. *NAA*

here will a fighter fight, near or far from its base, near to the ground or far from it? For the Spitfire, the answer in 1939 was simple. It protected Britain's cities and, for first two years of the war, fought from home bases. For the Mustang in 1943, the task was protecting American bombers flying at high altitude deep within Germany. Like the Spitfire, none of the American fighters had the internal fuel capacity for such distances, and most of them lacked the Spitfire's high-altitude speed.

The use of external droppable fuel tanks to extend a fighter's range is now a long-standing practice, but that was not so for American fighters in 1940. Yet these drop tanks became essential to the air offensive necessary for the Air Force in World War II.

Back in 1932, tear-shaped 52-gallon external tanks had been standard on the Navy's Curtiss F11C-2 biplanes, while the Army's equivalent, the P-6E, had a shaped auxiliary tank under the fuselage. These Curtiss Hawks also had racks under the wings to carry 10 30- or 2 116-pound bombs instead of the tanks; the Navy ships, alternatively, could even release a 474-pound bomb in a dive.

Those features were not used on subsequent U.S. fighter types, which simply enlarged internal fuel capacity to extend range. No bombs or drop tanks were seen on Air Corps fighters from 1937 to 1940, be-

cause all bomb racks had been removed from Army pursuits by a June 23, 1936, technical order. This order was rescinded December 7, 1939, for new aircraft to be delivered in 1941, but it was emphasized that bomb provisions must not compromise fighter performance.

Curtiss president Burdette S. Wright proposed fitting a single-seat pursuit plane to carry a 500-pound bomb for ground attack or a 52-gallon auxiliary tank for "strategical moves or for accompanying bombers" in a letter to Army Air Corps chief, General H. H. "Hap" Arnold on May 16, 1940. His similar offer in July 1939 had been rejected, but the Army now had something to think about.[1]

The P-40C became the first new Air Corps fighter with a tear-shaped drop tank when deliveries began March 31, 1941; this 52-gallon tank was needed to replace the internal fuel capacity reduced by installing self-sealing tanks. The P-40D/E series, whose deliveries began on July 11, 1941, also had self-sealing to prevent fuel from leaking through bullet holes and had provision for a drop tank.

The same reasoning added a drop tank to the P-39D, for 170 gallons of internal fuel on the P-39C model had been reduced to 120 gallons by self-sealing. In February 1941, it was decided that 623 P-39Ds on order were to get belly fittings for a 75-gallon tank or 600-pound bomb, and the first P-39D was accepted in April.

On May 15, 1941, Lockheed offered to install drop tanks on P-38s for ferry missions, and the first test of two 75-gallon drop tanks on a P-38E was made January 15, 1942. Now the twin-engine Lockheeds could be flown across the Atlantic to save shipping space and time. Two P-38F groups were flown to the Eighth Air Force in Britain that summer with 150-gallon tanks, but both groups were sent to North Africa before they could be utilized for escort work.

There were no drop tanks with the Army fighters in the Philippines when the war started, but the use of drop tanks by the enemy was noted in a memo to President Roosevelt from General Arnold on March 23, 1942: "Japanese bombardment formations are often accompanied by Zero fighters, which carry a 'belly-tank' constructed of plywood and canvas. This materially increases their range. On going into action they drop these 'belly-tanks' to improve their maneuverability in combat."

These tactics had actually begun during the invasion of China. When unescorted Japanese bombers began raids on Nanking on August 15, 1937, Chinese fighters put half of these bombers out of action in only three days. But on September 19, the appearance over Nanking of Japanese fighters equipped with drop tanks reversed the battle, and their bombers operated with impunity.

Before the P-51 had attracted Air Force attention in 1942, mass-production plans centered on the P-39 and P-40. But the AAF soon realized that their performance was inadequate to meet German fighters such as the Bf 109G-2 and Fw 190A-3 at high altitudes. On May 6, 1942, the British agreed to provide Spitfires to the two AAF groups that had trained on P-39 Airacobras before coming to England to begin combat operations. While Lockheed P-38 squadrons pushed their combat training, Bell, Curtiss, and Republic were developing new designs to try to beat the competition.

THUNDERBOLTS

Republic Aviation had the most promising design for high-altitude operations. They had gotten a contract in 1939 for 80 P-44 fighters, intended to follow the P-43, but with a 1,400-hp R-2180 radial engine. The

Alexander Kartveli, designer of the Republic Thunderbolt. *NAA*

company was also encouraged to develop its first XP-47 design, ordered on the same day, with the same V-1710-39 engine and six-gun armament as the XP-46. Neither design was up to 1940's new demands on fighter capabilities.

Chief engineer Alexander Kartveli offered a new design on June 12, 1940, to replace the P-44. This proposal utilized the biggest engine available, the new Pratt & Whitney XR-2800-21 Double Wasp turbosupercharged to give 2,000 hp at 27,800 feet. On September 6, the prototype contract was revised to provide one XP-47B, and a September 13, 1940, contract ordered 171 P-47B and 602 P-47C Thunderbolts, with 54 P-43 and 80 P-43A Lancers to fill the gap until Double Wasps became available in quantity.

The P-47B models were used to train groups for overseas service, and deliveries began on September 14, 1942, of the P-47C,

The first P-47C Thunderbolts began supporting Eighth Air Force bombers in April 1943. *USAF*

the first version to enter combat. The heaviest single-engine fighter yet, it weighed more empty—9,900 pounds—than the P-51 did fully loaded, and its normal gross was 13,500 pounds. All eight of its wing guns were .50-caliber, with 267 rounds per gun.

The P-47 was a formidable child of American industry, combining the most horsepower with the heaviest firepower, and more (15,683) of these Thunderbolts would be built than any other American fighter. But there was an important disadvantage; its big radial engine swallowed fuel at a fearsome rate and had a greater built-in drag than any in-line engine.

With 2,000 hp for military power, top speed ranged from 352 mph at 5,000 feet to 420 mph at 30,000 feet. When 2,300-hp war emergency power with water injection became available in 1943, 433 mph was possible at 30,000 feet. Service ceiling was 42,000 feet, and climb to 15,000 feet took 7.2 minutes. The 305 gallons of fuel within the fuselage were burned up by the R-2800-21 so rapidly that endurance was just one hour when cruising at 350 mph, or 2.1 hours at

305 mph. A 75-gallon drop tank was added in August 1943 to extend range at reduced speed to 920 miles in four hours.

Thunderbolts replaced the short-range Spitfires as Eighth Air Force bomber escorts in the same month that P-51s began sorties in North Africa, and the barrel-shaped P-47s fought their first battle over France on April 15, 1943. Unfortunately, fighters tied to bomber formations cannot keep their most economical cruising speed, and the Thunderbolts usually had to leave the bombers before they had reached the most dangerous part of their mission. Even after a 108-gallon drop tank became available for the P-47D model, combat radius was 400 miles. While the P-47 performed better than the P-38, the drag of its radial engine handicapped its speed, compared to what might be had from a fighter with a better in-line engine than the Allison.

The Curtiss XP-60 was the first U.S. plane designed to use a Rolls-Royce Merlin engine. *USAF*

ENTER THE MERLINS

Much of the Spitfire's performance was due to its Rolls-Royce Merlin engine, so in 1940 the Packard Motor Car Company, which had built the famous Liberty engines of World War I, was assigned to produce the Merlin in Detroit. They began with the Mark XX model, designated V-1650-1 by the AAF, with a built-in single-stage supercharger. This engine was used by the Curtiss P-40F, delivered on parallel production lines along with the Allison-powered P-40E in 1942. While Allison-powered models were used against Japan, the Merlin-powered P-40F fought in North Africa.

Curtiss hopes centered on the XP-60, which combined the 1,300-hp V-1650-1 with a laminar wing and eight .50-caliber guns. Don Berlin had begun this design in April 1940 as the XP-53 with a Continental engine, but the Merlin had been substituted by January 29, 1941. First flown on September 18, 1941, with one of the first Packard Merlins, the XP-60 did 380 mph at 20,000 feet.

A production contract was approved on October 31 for 1,950 P-60As, each to be powered by a turbosupercharged 1,425-hp Allison V-1710-75. Although a top speed of 420 mph at 29,000 feet was promised, only one XP-60A was flown—on November 1, 1942. Unwilling to interrupt the P-40 production program when fighters were needed in a hurry, the AAF had dropped P-60A production plans on February 2, 1942, in favor of having Curtiss build 1,400 more P-40s and introduce the P-47 on their production line.

Other fighter projects initiated in 1942 included the XP-72 planned by Alexander Kartveli with a huge 3,000-hp R-4360 radial, while the XP-73 designation was considered in June 1942 for Howard Hughes's mysterious twin-engine D-2. No XP-74 is recorded, but the XP-75 marked Don Berlin's move from Curtiss to General Motors. He proposed developing a long-range fighter by matching the Allison V-3420 engine (actually two V-1710s joined together as a heavy bomber power plant) with a mixed bag of parts from three different production airplanes. Bell responded to the problem with the P-76, which was a P-39 with a new Allison and wing design, and the P-77, a light all-wood fighter with a Ranger engine.

None of these designs ever reached service, for the most logical response to the immediate problems of war was to put a better engine into an airframe already in production. The power plant most immediately available was British, an improved Merlin with a two-stage supercharger intended for the Spitfire IX. On January 29, 1942, the Curtiss XP-60 had been scheduled for installation of this two-stage Merlin 61 and redesignated XP-60D.

But this project was soon superseded by the recommendation of Major Thomas Hitchcock to develop the Mustang, "one of the best, if not the best, airframe that has been developed in the war . . . as a high-altitude fighter by cross-breeding it with the Merlin 61 engine." As assistant air attaché at the American embassy, he noted that "while the prospect of an English engine in an American airframe may appeal . . . to those individuals who are interested in furthering Anglo-American relationships . . . it does not fully satisfy important people on both sides of the Atlantic who seem more interested in pointing with pride to the development of a 100-percent national product, than they are concerned with the very difficult problem of developing a fighter plane that will be superior to anything the Germans have."[2]

He knew that Rolls-Royce test pilot Ron Harker had suggested that idea after flying a Mustang I on April 30, 1942, and Rolls-Royce decided to proceed with a prototype conversion on June 3. Harker had praised the Mustang and thought it resembled a Bf 109F, "probably due to its being designed by one of the Messerschmitt designers, who is now with North American."[3] (This error would often be repeated by British writers. However, Edgar Schmued never worked for Messerschmitt or for any other German aircraft company and never met Messerschmitt until that designer visited Northrop in 1953.)

On June 17, Rolls-Royce Director Ernest W. Hives saw a Merlin Mustang as "the best bet at the moment," but warned: "The risk, of course, that if we make the Mustang into a first-class machine the U.S. will want to collar them, because . . . their fighter position is not too clear."[4]

Left, the second Mustang X, AM208, achieved 433 mph on tests. *Via Bowers*

Below, **AL963, the fourth Mustang X.** *Via Bowers*

Rolls-Royce first fitted a Merlin to the Mustang X, AL975G; the *G* stood for the guard required on a secret aircraft. *NAA*

Allocating five Mustang Is to be reengined, Rolls-Royce made the first conversion, known as the Mustang X, from AL975, with a large air scoop under the special Merlin 65 for the supercharger's intercooler. It was flown on October 13, 1942, followed on November 13 by another, AM208. Top speed was measured at 433 mph at 22,000 feet.

Stimulated by this British effort, the Air Force had authorized its own Merlin project on June 12, 1942, and North American submitted Model Specification NA-101 on July 24. On July 31, a letter contract for an XP-78 design was issued, and on August 13, two P-51 airframes, 41-37352 and 37421, were released from the lend-lease contract. They were redesignated XP-51B in September.[5]

Among the engineers working on this project was young Sam Logan, who had been hired in 1942 and assigned to the Confidential Design Group. "I was thrilled by the ability of the men and the exciting new projects that were being designed in the small enclosed room of the newly completed engineering building. Even though I was just 20 years old, I was given small design projects to complete. There was no permanent organization structure in the approximately 30-man group—Ed was the only boss, and everyone greatly respected and admired him. Assignments were made to fit the jobs that needed to be done. Everyone was flexible, and Ed molded his men into efficient teams that produced designs that almost always resulted in hardware built in coordination with the experimental shop.

"One thing that really impressed me was that Ed came to each man in his group at least once a day to watch the progress, to

Chief technical engineer Larry Waite and chief engineer Ray Rice, looking at chief designer Ed Schmued's drawings. *NAA*

coordinate, and to answer questions. I was surprised when he stopped by my table on my first day, looked at my design, and complimented me on the quality of my drawing. This spurred me to even greater effort, and I was anxious to perform the very best that I could for him. . . . When the Rolls-Royce project began, I was assigned the design of the carburetor air intake duct, lower engine cowling, and engine throttle controls."[6]

In Schmued's own words: "The Rolls-Royce team in Derby actually took one of our NA-73s and modified it for a Merlin engine with a high critical altitude, and the airplane performed marvelously. As a matter of fact, the British invited Americans to witness the trials of this airplane. The U.S. Air Force was convinced that the airplane would make an excellent air superiority fighter if it had the Merlin engine. So it was agreed between the British Purchasing Commission and the United States Air Force to order the P-51B model, which was a redesign of the airplane."

The American-built Merlin V-1650-3 engine weighed 355 pounds more than the Allison and required an intercooler for its two-stage supercharger, which meant complete redesign of the cooling intakes under the fuselage. Eighteen major differences between the Merlin 61 and the Packard version caused the RAF to discard a plan to build P-51Bs to be completed in England with Rolls-Royce engines.

Packard's changes included a new carburetor, an automatic supercharger speed shift, a water-alcohol injection for emergency power, a more durable ball-bearing water pump, a new Delco magneto, and a centrifugal separator to prevent oil foaming. In a reciprocal interchange of information, Packard sent Rolls-Royce 9,000 drawings during the war.[7]

For the updraft carburetor, the engine air intake was moved down from the top of the nose to underneath, behind the propeller hub. This change makes it easy to recognize the Merlin-powered Mustangs. To balance the heavier 11-foot 2-inch four-bladed Hamilton propeller, 61 pounds of ballast was added in the tail.

The first Mustangs had a single Harrison radiator with the oil cooler in the center of the engine cooler. The Merlin Mustangs needed a separate oil cooler and separate supercharger intercooler system. Since the original radiator had some heavy copper, "We had the Trane Company design an aluminum radiator that weighed a great deal less, with ample cooling capability."

The four-bladed propeller was first flown on August 18, 1942, by Bob Chilton on Mustang AL958. Since the first Packard V-1650-3 failed ground tests, a second had to be shipped by air from Wright to NAA and was received November 18, 1942. It was rated at 1,380 hp for takeoff, 1,595-hp war emergency power at 17,000 feet, and 1,295-hp war emergency power at 28,800 feet.[8]

Since both XP-51Bs had begun as P-51s, they had provisions for four 20-mm guns, but production P-51Bs would have the .50-caliber wing guns standard on the A model. Bob Chilton took 41-37352 up for the first time on November 30, 1942. By then, the AAF had already decided to go ahead with mass production.

Design of a production version, the NA-102, was begun on August 26, and a contract for 400, designated P-51B-1NA, was approved by December 28, 1942. North American's Dallas factory began the similar NA-103 on October 8, 1942, and contracted December 28 to build 1,000, designated P-51C-NT. The old P-51A contract was changed to include 800 P-51B-5NA, and 90 P-51B-10NA, all as company number NA-104. General Arnold reported to President Roosevelt on November 12, 1942, that 2,290 Mustangs had been ordered.[9]

While much cleaner looking than the British conversions, the XP-51B suffered many problems with the new cooling system. "At the first flight," said Schmued, "we had about 50 of these P-51B airplanes on the line ready for delivery and waiting for tests of the new engine, radiator installation, and canopy design. The airplane went up and the pilot radioed in 15 minutes later that the engine was overheating. He had to come down. The engine was almost frozen because there was not enough cooling.

"We opened up the whole system, pulled the radiator out, opened the radiator header, and found that it was completely clogged up with corrosion particles that looked like popcorn. How did this happen? We did not know then that the Merlin engine had copper tubing embedded in [its] aluminum castings for the internal cooling circulation. Our aluminum radiator was not compatible with copper tubing. The cooling liquid provided an electrolite and set up a battery, causing a very severe corrosion, aggravated by the heat of the system. We were really in trouble, because here were 50 airplanes sitting on the line, ready for delivery, if we could only cool them.

"At that time, shortly before this happened, I went to the Bureau of Standards in Washington and discussed the possible help they might be able to give us if some unusual problems should arise. This was the unusual problem of the day. I called, on a Friday of course—doesn't every crisis happen on Friday afternoon?—and asked them to help us because we were in dire trouble. They said, 'Sure, send one of your men in with the problem and we will take a look and see what we can do.' They kept a man there over Saturday and Sunday to help us. I can't tell you how grateful I was that we had this help.

"When our man came back, he brought such an unusual solution for our very serious problem that you wouldn't believe it. The answer from the Bureau of Standards was: take your radiator and slosh it with Keg-Liner, which is a lacquer used in beer cans to isolate the liquid from the metal. We used this method, sloshing the radiator with Keg-Liner, and installed it. After that we never had any more cooling trouble. Everything performed perfectly and we could get rid of our 50 airplanes we had on the line.

The first XP-51B introduced the Merlin engine with the air intake under the nose. *NAA*

"It was a marvelous idea to invite the Bureau of Standards to help us solve our problems. I found that they are the most informed people on technical matters in the country. They really can help in problems that stump engineering departments. . . . I must say that they were most obliging and helpful and deserve a great deal of credit for being there when we needed them."

The Keg-Liner was a help, while the coolant system was redesigned by Bill Wheeler with a new Harrison radiator and a corrosion inhibitor, called MBT, developed by Union Carbide. Part of the problem had been that Rolls-Royce used a coolant mixture of 30 percent water and 70 percent glycol, while the Allison had used only glycol. "It took us a year," wrote Wheeler, "to convince Wright Field to change the glycol specification."[10]

By December 4, 1942, Chilton resumed functional tests on the first XP-51B, whose radiator intake had been modified to deal with the noticeable boundary-layer rumble. The second XP-51B was flown February 2, 1943, and Chilton flew the first production P-51B-1, 43-12093, for the first time on May 5, 1943. This aircraft was used to establish the official performance figures reported May 18, and then the first XP-51B was ferried to Wright on May 20.

The top speed of 441 mph at 29,800 feet was the best of any AAF fighter to date and was achieved with 1,275 hp. Empty weight was 7,038 pounds, gross weight was 8,350 pounds with a 1,312-pound load, or 8,840 pounds maximum. The rate of climb was 3,600 feet in 1 minute, 10,000 feet in 2.8, 20,000 feet in 5.05, and 30,000 feet in 9.8 minutes, with a service ceiling of 42,000 feet.

When three P-51B-1 Mustangs were sent to the Proving Ground Command (PGC) at Eglin Field for tactical employment trials, the design's success became evident. After comparative tests with the P-38J-5, P-39N, P-40N-1, and P-47D-10, the PGC reported: "No other American fighter . . . can equal the excellent overall flying characteristics and performance of the P-51B above 25,000 feet. The airplane handles beautifully and feels extremely good in all maneuvers.

"The P-51B-1 is by far the best climbing airplane of all current American fighter types," and its "diving characteristics are superior to those of any other fighter."

Its top speed was about 345 mph at sea level, and 400 mph or better from 11,000 feet to 40,000 feet, with the best speed of 440 mph at 30,000 feet. From sea level to 11,000 feet it "was slower than the P-51A, which is the fastest fighter below that altitude," but then gained an increasing advantage up to 30,000 feet. At 16,000 feet, the P-51B was about 10 mph faster than the P-38J and about 20 mph faster than the P-47D, and the advantage grew at altitudes over 30,000 feet.

The PGC rated the Packard V-1650-3's war emergency output at 1,670 hp at 15,500 feet in low blower and 1,480 hp at 27,000 feet with high blower. An internal fuel capacity of 184 gallons allowed 13 minutes for takeoff and climb, a 220-mile cruise-out, 30 minutes of full power combat, and 220-mile cruise-back.

When a pair of 75-gallon tanks were added under the wings, cruise-out distance increased to 600 miles. The two inboard .50-caliber wing guns had 350 rounds each and the two outboard .50-caliber guns had 280 rounds each, while a pair of 500-pound

A puzzling Mustang configuration; apparently an XP-51B with a four-blade propeller, but the normal carburetor air scoop is not visible. *NAA*

The second XP-51B, 137421, shows Merlin nose and four 20-mm cannon. *NAA*

The first production P-51B-1, 312093, had four .50-caliber guns. *NAA*

A P-51B-1 in flight over California. *NAA*

bombs could replace the drop tanks on the wing racks.[11]

A favorable evaluation also came from the RAF, whose AFDU had received a Mustang III, as they called the new model, on December 26, 1943. Their fighter, serialed FZ109, which weighed 10,000 pounds for operational load, was tested against a Spitfire IX using a similar engine.

The Mustang was described as "delightfully easy to handle" and "a much cleaner aircraft . . . than the Spitfire IX . . . and is always 20 to 30 mph faster . . . at all heights." Range was between 50 to 75 percent better. Because of its higher wing loading, the Mustang did not climb or turn as quickly as the Spitfire.

When it was compared to a captured Messerschmitt Bf 109G, the Mustang III was "faster at all heights" and "greatly superior" in turns, while climbing slightly better above 25,000 feet and worse below 10,000 feet. The Fw 190 was a more dangerous opponent with its unmatched rate of roll, but the Mustang turn was slightly better. This German type was "nearly 50 mph slower at all heights, rising to nearly 70 mph above 28,000 feet."[12]

North American rushed production of the P-51B, but some trouble remained. Said Schmued: "With the coming of the Merlin engine, we ran into a number of problems with the airplane. At one time, after we had P-51s in service with Merlins, we lost some tails. When we investigated, we found that the rule, which the Air Force had established for a special maneuver called a rolling pull-out, that the force distribution over the tail surfaces is just two to one, or three to one, was not so. It is more severe.

"After we beefed the tails up, we had no more problems. In this case, the requirements that the Air Force established for design criteria of the horizontal tail were not adequate for the speed of the P-51. We had to beef it up over and above the requirements to have a safe airplane."

It is noteworthy that Curtiss also had tail problems when they tried the same Merlin engine in their XP-60D. On May 6, 1943, the tail broke off while pulling out of a dive, and the pilot parachuted to safety. Since all Packard Merlins were now allocated to the Mustang, Curtiss had to concentrate on trying to make the air-cooled XP-60E and XP-

Mustang experts. Designer Edgar Schmued, project engineer George Gehrkens, and test pilot Bob Chilton at a "P-51 Love-In" held January 30, 1970. At the right sits Colonel Don Bochkay, Eighth Air Force, an ace of the top-scoring 357th Group, and racing pilot Clay Lacy is in the rear. *SDAM*

The problem with this installation was that the center of gravity moved backward, causing stability problems. The pilot was instructed to be very careful when flying the airplane until at least 30 gallons of that tank were used up. A bob weight was mounted to the front of the control stick to prevent the pilot from overcontrolling the airplane. "It was no particular problem, but it was just a nuisance for the pilot to fly the airplane for all the time it took. Eventually, we had no complaints on it. This mission of escorting bombers to Berlin turned the war into our favor."

Bob Chilton said, "I did the first long-distance test flight for our company on the P-51, before they finally approved the aft tank behind the seat. I ran out of gas before the airplane did. I was sitting there 7½ hours. It was horrible. Simulated a flight to Berlin by going to Phoenix and back over the ski resort in the Palm Springs area. Thirty thousand feet over San Jacinto, I

started to dogfight with myself, zooming around for five minutes at full bore. Back to 30,000 feet and cruise-back. I went up and down California a few times. Santa Barbara and then San Diego. Came back here and can't get it up yet. Santa Barbara and then back here. Seven and a half hours was brutal in an airplane."[19]

A mid-August 1943 report on the first 85-gallon tank in a P-51B said it would take about 75 days to reach production deliveries in the P-51B-10, but that current aircraft could have a tank added, although longitudinal stability might be marginal.[20] In the meantime, the Eighth had to rely on its four P-47 groups for escort. But the Thunderbolts, built to intercept enemy bombers, hadn't enough range to accompany American bombers very far; their practical radius was 400 miles with a 108-gallon drop tank.

THE MUSTANGS ARRIVE JUST IN TIME

On August 17, 1943, 60 of 183 American bombers were lost while striking Schweinfurt, beyond the range of friendly fighters. When 60 more were lost on October 14, it ended the idea that the bomber could go it alone. But neither the P-38 nor the P-47 could go all the way to Berlin and other distant targets.

On September 17, 1943, the first P-51Bs arrived in England. Originally they were assigned to two groups attached to the Ninth Air Force, which was organized to support the armies assembled to invade Europe. To deal with the complications delaying the Merlin-powered Mustang's introduction to combat, project engineer George Gehrkens was told to go to England in October. After a two-week wait in New York for decent weather, he flew over in a C-54.

Meeting with Ninth Air Force chief, Brig. Gen. E. R. Quesada, on November 9, he learned that about 130 P-51Bs for the AAF had arrived in England, plus another 50 for the RAF. The first 75 to be assembled were going to the 354th Fighter Group, commanded by Lt. Col. Kenneth R. Martin. His pilots had trained in the United States on P-39s and had no P-51 time. It was expected that these pilots might get about two hours practice on older Mustangs borrowed from the RAF and at least two hours on P-51Bs before going into operations. Kits to install the 85-gallon fuselage tanks were expected

to arrive by January, and numerous difficulties in the oil and coolant systems required work.[21]

After receiving its first P-51Bs on November 11, the 354th Fighter Group made its initial operational sorties on December 1, 1943, from Boxsted, Essex. That same day a second group, the 357th, which also trained on P-39s, arrived on the *Queen Elizabeth*. They got their first P-51B on December 19, had 15 by January 1, 1944, and flew their first sorties with the 354th on January 14.

These missions were flown under the actual control of the Eighth Air Force, whose new commander, General James Doolittle, had replaced General Eaker on January 6, 1944. General Doolittle had a more aggressive philosophy about fighter escort of bombers; he urged fighter units not to cling to the bomber formations, but to push

A P-51B-1 of 357th Fighter Group taking off; white nose and tail stripe were painted on so Mustang wouldn't be mistaken for a Messerschmitt. *USAF*

Mustang fuselages in mass production. *NAA*

ahead and strike enemy fighters before they could position themselves against the bombers.

On February 20, Doolittle launched AR-GUMENT, a week of heavy attacks on the German aircraft industry. Escorting the bombers that day were 668 P-47, 94 P-38, and 73 P-51 fighters. The proportion of Mustangs steadily increased and they were given the longest missions. On March 4, 121 Mustangs were included on the first mission to go all the way to Berlin.

Doolittle regarded the P-38 performance as only second-rate and all three of his P-38 groups had their Lockheeds replaced by P-51s by the end of the summer. The twin-tailed Lockheeds continued to be used for high-altitude photoreconnaissance. By late 1944, only one P-47 group remained in the

Here the wings have been added. *NAA*

104-0-8

The P-51B-15 added a built-in fuselage tank, and bare metal replaced the olive drab finish. *NAA*

VIII Fighter Command, the other Thunderbolts having been transferred to the Ninth Air Force to support the ground forces

MASS PRODUCTION

North American Aviation now had to produce enough fighters to meet the new situation, and to clear the way, B-25 production in California was closed down by July 1944,

continuing in Kansas City. From 20 P-51Bs accepted in June 1943, acceptances rose to 763 Mustangs in October 1944. The wartime high for Mustang monthly production occurred in January 1945, when 857 were accepted, including 286 P-51Ks from the Dallas factory.

While all of these planes had Merlin engines and essentially the same performance, considerable improvements were made in efficiency. The California plant completed 400 P-51B-1NA and 800 P-51B-5NA, which added a carburetor air filter and cold-weather provisions. These became the

An RAF Mustang III (P-51C) with Malcolm hood. *SDAM*

Drop tanks and a radio compass are seen on this Fourteenth Air Force P-51B at K'un-ming, China. *SDAM*

Fourth P-51C-1 from Dallas has perforated panel to bleed off air. *NAA*

P-51B-7NA when the 85-gallon fuselage tanks were installed at modification centers. These 85-gallon tanks were factory-installed on the 398 P-51B-10NA, beginning in December 1943, while starting in February 1944, the newer V-1650-7 with increased power at lower levels was used by the 390 P-51B-15NA ships. Altogether, 1,988 B models were completed.

In August 1943 the factory in Dallas, Texas, began deliveries on 350 P-51C-1NT, their version of the P-51B, which became the P-51C-3 when fuselage tanks were installed. Beginning in February 1944, the V-1650-7 powered 450 P-51C-5NT, and 950 P51C-10NT were delivered with the fuselage tanks. Altogether, there were 1,750 C models made in Texas. Weighing 9,800 pounds, the P-51C, with a V-1650-7, did 439 mph at 25,000 feet and climbed to 30,-000 feet in 12 minutes.

On September 25, 1943, General Arnold had requested that the RAF trade up 1,200 Merlin Mustangs expected in the future for P-47s.[22] Some adjustments to delivery plans were made, while No. 19 Squadron, which had been the first to use Spitfires, became the first to go operational with the Mustang III in February 1944. Actual assignments to the RAF included 293 P-51B and 636 P-51C models, both called Mustang III and used by some 19 squadrons.

An AAF photoreconnaissance modification was primarily made to assess the bomb damage inflicted on the enemy. There was an oblique installation of two K-24 cameras in the rear fuselage in 71 F-6B-1NA and 20 F-6C-1NT Mustangs, which originally had been listed as the P-51B-2NA and P-51C-2NT. Photo Mustangs retained their guns for self-defense.

Since the P-51B/C models had only four guns, they had only half the firepower of the P-47, and part of that was sometimes lost when guns jammed after violent maneuvers affected the feed system. The pilot's visibility to the rear was limited, a condition partially improved by the RAF's invention of the Malcolm Hood, a balloon-type sliding canopy of British manufacture that improved the pilot's visibility. A simple correction of feed cams helped the gun situation, but a canopy allowing the pilot all-around vision was-needed.

This led to the most widely used Mustang version, the P-51D. It began with installation of a bubble canopy on the 10th P-51B-1, 43-12102. Change Order NA-106, dated May 1, 1943, switched two P-51B-10 aircraft (42-106539/106540) to the P-51D-1 configuration with a full-blown, sliding canopy and six .50-caliber guns in the wings. The first was flown on November 17, 1943, by Bob Chilton, and the improved all-around vision was immediately apparent. Both examples were flown to Eglin Field for tactical tests.

A contract for 2,500 of a production version, the NA-109, had been approved July 21. Deliveries of 800 P-51D-5NA began late in March 1944 and were joined by 200 similar P-51D-5NT Mustangs from Dallas, beginning in June. They arrived in Eighth Air Force groups just before the massive Normandy invasion on June 6, 1944.

Powered by a V-1650-7 of 1,490 hp at takeoff and 1,505 war emergency power at 19,300 feet, the P-51D-5 had 269 gallons in the three internal tanks, with two 75-gallon or 110-gallon metal tanks, or the 108-gallon paper tanks supplied by a British firm, under the wings. The ammunition supply

Chilton over the Santa Monica mountains, flying the olive drab 10th P-51B-1, 43-12102, modified with bubble canopy. *NAA*

One of the last P-51C-10NTs with Chinese markings. *NAA*

A production P-51D-5 on factory flight.

Mustangs with invasion stripes added for the June 6, 1944, invasion of Normandy. The 486th Fighter Squadron, 352nd Fighter Group has a mixture of models, with a P-51D-5 in front of various P-51Bs. *USAF*

included 500 rounds for each inboard gun and 270 rounds for the other four. Two 500-pound bombs could be used, and fixtures for 10 five-inch rockets were added to the P-51D-20 and later models. Wing span was 37 feet, and length 32 feet 3 inches, while weight was 7,125 pounds empty and 11,600 pounds with maximum fuel load.

Top speed at 10,100 pounds was 395 mph at sea level, 413 mph at 15,000 feet, and 437 mph at 25,000 feet. Service ceiling was 41,900 feet. Tactical radius was 325 miles with internal fuel and 750 miles with the 108-gallon tanks—enough to go anywhere in

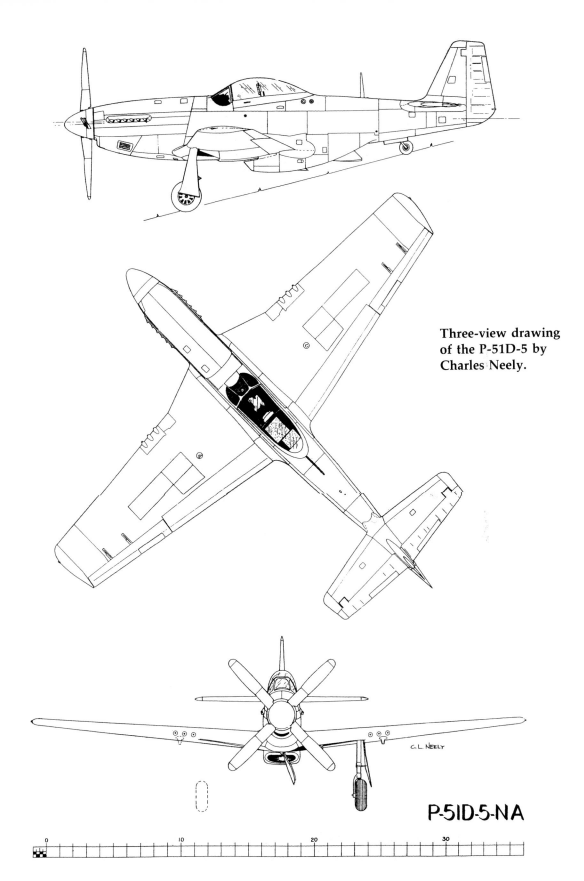

Three-view drawing of the P-51D-5 by Charles Neely.

C.L. NEELY

P-51D-5-NA

0   10   20   30

Europe. Ferry range with 489 gallons was 2,300 miles at 245 mph, and range with two 500-pound bombs was 950 miles at 362 mph. As in all fighters, dive speed had to be limited so accumulated forces would not cause structural failure during the pull-out. The P-51D was red-lined at 505 mph indicated airspeed, compared with 460 mph indicated for the P-38.

Table Two compares the P-51D-5 with the other AAF fighters in production when the Allies invaded France in June 1944, setting the stage for the war's last year in Europe. The P-38J-15 and P-47D-25 were

the important rivals in the war against Germany. While the P-63A was replacing the P-39 on Bell's production line, Curtiss was still delivering the P-40N, only slightly improved over 1941 models; both were primarily for lend-lease quotas. It will be seen that the Mustang was superior to all four in range and speed, while the P-38 retained the highest service ceiling.

Takeoff over a 50-foot obstacle required a distance of 2,500 feet for the P-51D, compared with 3,400 feet for the heavier P-47D. There are many situations in which a shorter takeoff is appreciated, but none

T A B L E T W O

AAF Fighters in Production, June 1944

	P-38J-15	P-40N-20	P-47D-25	P-51D-5	P-63A-9
	LIGHTNING	WARHAWK	THUNDERBOLT	MUSTANG	KINGCOBRA
Gross Wt. (lbs.)	17,500	8,350	14,500	10,100	8,800
Wg. Area (sq. ft.)	327.5	236.0	300.0	233.0	248.0
Wing loading (lb./sq. ft.)	53.44	35.38	48.33	43.35	35.48
Horsepower	3200	1125	2300	1505	1150
Crit. Alt. (ft.)	26,400	14,100	31,000	19,300	22,400
Power loading (lb./hp.)	5.47	7.42	6.30	6.71	7.65
Vmax (mph)	414	350	428	437	408
@ Alt. (ft.)	25,000	16,400	25,000	25,000	24,500
Ser. Clg. (ft.)	44,000	31,000	42,000	41,900	43,000
Climb (ft.)	20,000	14,000	20,000	20,000	25,000
in minutes	7	7.3	9	11.5	7.3
Int. Fuel (gal.)	416	159	370	269	136
Range (miles)	750	360	475	950	450

Aircraft data from *Army Aircraft Characteristics* May 1946: 31–36.

Three rival Air Force fighters of 1944; the **P-38J-15 Lightning,** *right;* **P-63A-9 Kingcobra,** *below;* **P-47D-25 Thunderbolt,** *below right.* See Table Two for comparative performance data. *SDAM*

Additional dorsal-fin area improved the stability of new P-51D-15. *NAA*

Compare this P-51D production line with the 1932 factory scene shown before. *SDAM*

more than that confronting Mustang pilot Jack Ilfrey, 94th Fighter Squadron, 20th Fighter Group, when he landed in enemy-occupied Holland to rescue a fellow pilot, Lieutenant Duane Kelso, who had just made a forced landing in his flak-damaged Mustang.

When he taxied up to his friend's aircraft, Ilfrey jumped out on his wing and dumped his parachute, making room for Kelso to get into the cockpit. Sitting on Kelso's lap, he opened the throttle of "Happy Jack's Go Buggy," bumped down the rough field, and lifted off to fly back home. The November 22, 1944, incident was not publicized at the time, since it was against standing regulations![23]

Another advantage of the Mustang was its relatively low cost. Air Force data indicates an average unit cost in 1945 of $50,985, compared to $83,000 for the P-47, and $97,147 for the P-38.[24]

PRODUCTION DETAILS

Cutting down the rear fuselage for the D's canopy reduced speed only slightly, but directional stability was affected. This was corrected by adding about three square feet of area to the vertical tail fin. A small dorsal fillet was added, starting in June 1944, to the P-51D-10NA and later models, and was retrofitted to earlier aircraft. A new K-14 gun sight was used by October on the P-51D-20NA and later blocks; 4,000 had been ordered June 7, 1944, as company charge number NA-122. Metal-covered elevators were added in February 1945. A total of 7,996 D models were delivered.

Most were built in California, which had closed its B-25H production line to concentrate on Mustangs, but Dallas built 200 P-51D-5NT, followed from September 1944 to March 1945 by 1,337 P-51K-NT. These were similar to concurrent D models, with the reception of Aeroproducts electric propellers with hollow steel blades instead of the solid aluminum blades of the usual Hamilton hydromatic propellers. Starting in March, 1,264 P-51D-20/30NT with Hamilton propellers followed until the war ended in August. Photoreconnaissance versions included 163 F-6K and 136 F-6D delivered

Cutaway drawing of internal equipment on P-51D-5. *NAA*

from Dallas from November 1944 to August 1945.

These aircraft were not without troubles, as the designer tells: "After we got into the production of the P-51Ds, we ran into a new problem. While acceptance-test flying the D's, we suddenly experienced the failure of engine-mount attachment bolts. The cause was hydrogen embrittlement.

"We discovered that one of our engine-mount bolt manufacturers had a subcontractor who didn't know that chrome-plated bolts had to be reheated after plating to gas off the hydrogen that otherwise caused hydrogen embrittlement. Some of the airplanes came in with the engine hang-

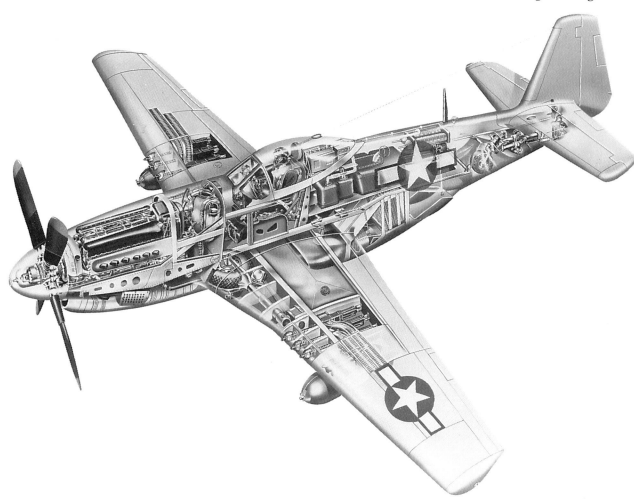

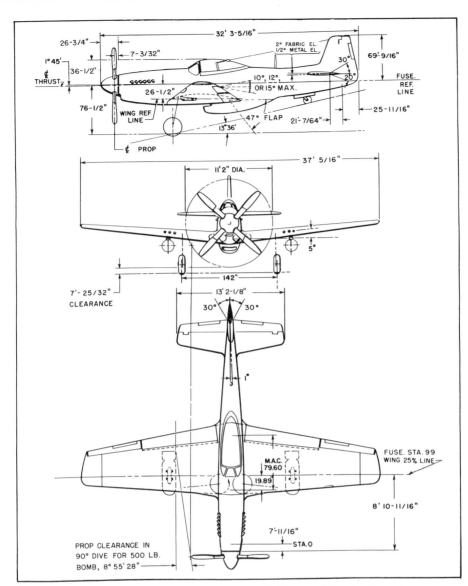

Dimensioned
manufacturer's
drawing of
the widely
used P-51D-20
Mustang. *NAA*

ing on one bolt. Within one week we had all the engine-mount bolts replaced in every P-51 around the world.

"When the P-51D came out, we had some problems with wings ripping off. One of the victims of that was our good friend Colonel Tommy Hitchcock. There were some airplanes in England [that] lost the wings for some unknown reason. He tried to find out for us what had happened, which he should not have done. It was really our business and it was dangerous. But he put the airplane in a power dive and

suddenly the wings came off. He was killed on April 18, 1944, a great loss to us and to the Air Force.

"We found out that the covers of the ammunition boxes which were located spanwise along the wing, despite the fact that they were made of eighth-inch aluminum alloy plate, buckled, and by changing curvature of the wing, increased the wing lift suddenly and off came the wings. That was a very unusual thing, because structurally they were sound. We found out that they deflected enough to change the lift on the

A P-51D-5 formation from the 352nd Fighter Group. *SDAM*

whole wing suddenly and cause failures of the wings. That was corrected and after that, we had no more problems."

WINNING THE EUROPEAN WAR

As the Mustangs increased in number, they took a steadily greater role in long-range bomber escort. For many an American airman aboard their bombers, the sight of a Mustang escort was his main hope of sur-

vival, and some would remember the Mustang as the most beautiful plane they had ever seen.

On June 21, 1944, a force raiding Berlin went on to fly a "shuttle" route in which 65 P-51 escorts flew 1,470 miles on to Russia in 7.25 hours. From there they were able to fly back, making another attack on the way. By January 1945, 14 of the 15 Eighth Air Force escort fighter groups flew P-51s, and only one had the P-47. The Fifteenth Air Force, which flew bomber missions from Italy, was escorted by four P-51 and three P-38 groups from July 1944 to VE day.

Close escort is fine, but this close?
SDAM

Four Mustangs of 361st Fighter Group illustrate the P-51D-10, P-51D-15 (rear), and P-51B-10 (below) configurations. *USAF*

Above, "Glamorous Glen III," the P-51D-15 flown by
Chuck Yeager, the first Air Force pilot to become an ace
with five victories on one mission. *SDAM; Below,* **this
F-6D-10, 44-14841, has both cameras and bombs.**
SDAM

In addition, the Ninth Air Force had P-51s with 3 of the 18 fighter groups assigned for ground support missions. The top Mustang group was the 357th, with 609 air and 106 ground kills from February 11, 1944, to April 25, 1945. Top AAF Mustang aces were George Preddy with 25 victories, John C. Meyer with 24, and Don Gentile with 23.

Besides protecting bombers, the Mustang's penetration missions forced the Luftwaffe to keep its fighters at home, reducing air cover for German forces in France and on the Eastern Front. Average bomber-loss rate dropped from 6.5 percent in the second quarter of 1943, before in-depth fighter escort, to only 1.9 percent by the second quarter of 1944, when fighter escort was usually available. As Luftwaffe opposition weakened, the Mustangs struck at enemy planes on the ground.

Postwar experts disagreed on measuring the American strategic bombing offensive's effects on the whole German war effort, but it is clear that the Mustang enabled the air battle over Germany to be won.

Examination of the P-51's combat record indicates that it accounted for almost half of the enemy aircraft destroyed in Europe by AAF fighters. Flying 213,873 sorties and losing 2,520 planes in combat, Mustangs claimed 4,950 aircraft destroyed in the air and 4,131 on the ground. Thunderbolts flew 423,435 sorties, lost 3,077 in combat, and claimed 3,082 destroyed in the air and 3,202 on the ground. Lightnings flew 129,849 sorties, lost 1,758 in combat, and claimed 1,771 destroyed in the air and 749 on the ground.

The deeds of the Mustang pilots on these missions have inspired many fine books, and they are a fascinating source of the war stories that are outside the realm of a design history such as this. Colonel James H. Howard's gallant single-handed defense of a B-17 unit on January 11, 1944, earned the Medal of Honor. This veteran of the Flying Tigers was flying his P-51B-5, 43-6315, named the "Ding Hao." Yet that was only one of many successful fights over Germany that ended only on May 8, 1945, when an F-6C downed the last Luftwaffe plane destroyed in combat.

On one mission, when Mustangs escorted B-17s to attack a factory in Stuttgart, among the nearby families taking shelter in their basements was a housewife with her two-year-old daughter. Little Christel, her mother remembered, cried at the distant booms. Neither realized that the child would grow up to marry the designer of the American fighters overhead.

At the time, of course, designer Edgar Schmued was concerned only with the success of his aircraft: "I have seen many gun camera pictures of those missions and every one I have seen denoted a victory for a Mustang. It was absolutely necessary to carry that much fuel to make the flight from London to Berlin and home again. The P-51 was the *only fighter* which had enough range for this mission. Whenever the escort mission was completed, the airplanes turned around. Then they were working on their own in destroying enemy installations on the way home. Needless to say, this trip to Berlin and back was very hard on the pilots and some of the pilots were so worn out when they came home that they had to be lifted out of the cockpit.

"A P-51D was modified as a two-seater for General Arnold because he wanted a very fast airplane to get around. We built an

A two-seat TP-51D-25-NT, 44-84662. *NAA*

airplane by taking out the back fuel tank and armor plate. We installed a second seat with no controls, since it was simply a passenger seat. That was what General Arnold wanted, and that's what he got." Ten such TP-51D two-seaters were converted at Dallas, and several others were converted in England by removing the fuselage fuel tank. After the war, many civilian Mustangs were converted in this manner.

Britain designated bubble-canopied fighter versions of the Mustang IV and IVA, receiving about 281 P-51D and 590 P-51K types from the Dallas plant. They equipped 16 RAF squadrons in Britain and six in Italy at the war's end. Australia was sent 83 P-51K, 100 P-51D-20NT, and 114 P-51D-25NT Mustangs from Dallas, along with 100 sets of NA-110 parts to build Mustangs

there, assembling 80 from these parts as the Commonwealth Aircraft CA17 with the V-1650-3, first flown April 29, 1945, and 140 as the CA18.

There was still a war with Japan to be won, and the Merlin Mustangs were to be seen on many fronts. The capture of Iwo Jima provided a base for three P-51D groups, the 15th, 21st, and 506th, to support B-29 attacks against Japan. In China, the Fourteenth Air Force had the 23rd, 51st, and 311th groups, while the Tenth Air Force in India had the First and Second Air Commando Groups. The Fifth Air Force on Okinawa had Mustangs in the Third Air Commando, 35th and 348th groups. Before long, the Mustang achieved the same air superiority in the Pacific war as it had in Europe.

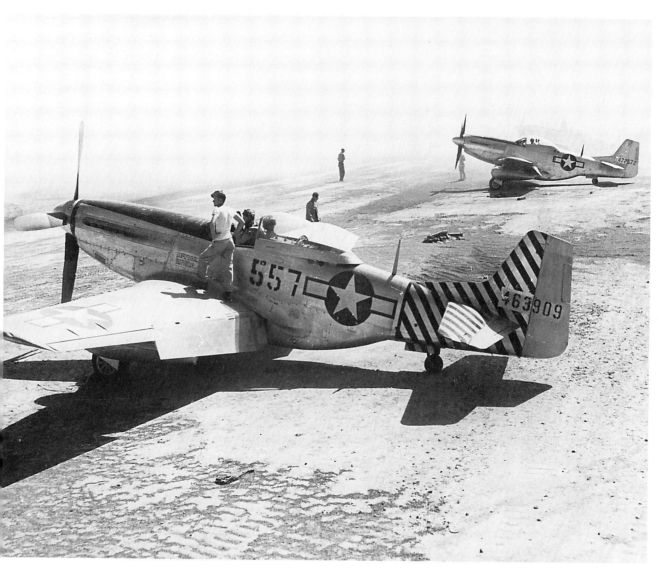

Mustangs in the Pacific; a P-51D-20 on Iwo
Jima with the 458th Fighter Squadron, 506th
Fighter Group, in July 1945. *SDAM*

CHAPTER SIX

Stripped-down and Souped-up Fighters

The XP-51F, pictured on April 10, 1944, was the first lightweight Mustang prototype. *NAA*

It was fortunate that the Mustang was proving such a success in battle, for none of the experimental single-seat fighter projects begun by the Air Force between 1940 and 1942, from XP-54 to XP-75, was able to meet AAF needs. Vultee's exotic XP-54 pusher, with which Dick Palmer had won the last of the Air Corps fighter competitions, was begun the same month as the first Mustang, but didn't fly until January 15, 1943, 31 months later. A program to build 2,500 General Motors P-75s had been approved on June 7, 1943.

Both types had big 2,300-hp engines, but proved to be inferior in performance to the P-51. Like most such wartime designs, the XP-54 was limited to the prototypes, while the P-75A program was canceled in October 1944 after a $50-million production fiasco. Air Force fighter officials were totally dissatisfied with the results of tests.[1]

All of the pusher prototypes ordered from the R40-C competition in May 1940 had been disappointing. Vultee's XP-54 had started out with an estimated top speed of 510 mph, but had in fact finally tested at 381 mph. The tailless Curtiss XP-55 was even slower, while Northrop's radical XP-56 had an unhappier fate. Test flights begun on September 6, 1943, ended with the wreck of the first prototype. Another XP-56 was built in 1944, but tests were stopped because they were "too hazardous."

Of all the single-seat designs between the XP-54 and XP-75, only the Bell XP-63 Kingcobra achieved production. Retaining the Airacobra's general layout and 37-mm cannon, the XP-63 had a larger wing with a laminar airfoil and an Allison V-1710-47 engine with a two-stage supercharger that raised critical altitude from the P-39's 12,000 feet to 22,400 feet. Although flight tests begun December 7, 1942, did show an improved high-altitude performance, the Air Force didn't deploy Kingcobras overseas, but lend-leased them to Russia and France.

Lockheed decided to concentrate on its P-80 jet fighter project as its twin-engined XP-58 heavy escort fighter had been made unnecessary. Republic did succeed in developing a good long-range version of the Thunderbolt, the P-47N, for use in the Pacific war. Their XP-72 interceptor prototype, with its big 3,450-hp R-4360-13 Wasp Major radial, was ordered on June 18, 1943, but the Air Force became too interested in jet propulsion to invest in production of a propeller-driven short-range fighter.

North American's Mustang team did not rest on its laurels, but on January 2, 1943, launched the NA-105 lightweight version. As chief design engineer, Edgar Schmued was sent to see British techniques, leaving the United States on February 9, 1943, for a two-month visit to Britain.

"The American air attaché in England was, in this case, Colonel Tommy Hitchcock, a very famous polo player and sportsman, who flew the P-51 with pleasure. He did help out on searching out problems that somebody had discovered and he verified them, if he could. He was really very instrumental in making my visit to England successful. He saw to it that I had all the papers, reservations, and the priority to go to New York to start on a flight to England on a Boeing 314 Clipper.

"It was a slow flying boat, but extremely comfortable. After waiting eight days in wintertime New York for the ice to clear, I finally got on the plane and flew to Lisbon. We were put up in a hotel overnight, and the next day we went off to Ireland.

"There was something very funny about the Irish. They really seemed to be under-the-table allies of the Germans and they did not like the idea that I, as a former German, was working to help the British in their war against Hitler. But it was always clear to me that once you change your nationality, your loyalty belongs to your new country. Their treatment was not particularly friendly. I was isolated as an individual and only at the last moment was I permitted to board the airplane that took me to London.

"I was most happy to get all the support from the British that I could have asked for. They were the most genial and nicest people I have ever met. They were building the first Vampire, a fighter airplane designed by De Havilland, and they insisted that I see this brand-new airplane with the Whittle engine, the first jet engine they had built. I told them that 'I did not come here to pry into your secrets,' but they insisted that I see it. Colonel Hitchcock and I made a trip to De Havilland and saw the Vampire in the mock-up stage. That's as far as they had gotten. In the meantime, they were testing

the Whittle engine for this particular airplane. I was very impressed by the work they had done in this very modern way of building.

"In the meanwhile, the British had developed a new version of the Merlin, numbered the RM.14.SM. It was a Merlin engine which had a manifold pressure of 120 inches and developed 2,200 hp. This was the answer to our many prayers; more power without increasing weight. Every airplane designer likes to hear that and so did we.

"I went to Derby to visit the Rolls-Royce people and get all the dope on the new 14.SM engine. When I arrived at the factory, there was a large room reserved for the meeting. I sat in the middle and in half-circle formation sat all the experts of Rolls-Royce. I was shooting questions out and somebody, without directing, picked up his slipstick [slide rule], started working, and 15 to 20 minutes later gave me the answer.

"It was a marvelous demonstration of co-operation and ability to manage. I obtained all the information I needed to use their new 14.SM engine in the P-51, including the cooling and the installation requirements. I had all the information that I could possibly have asked for." Bill Lappin, of Rolls-Royce, wrote on March 23, "It has been a most valuable thing to have Schmued visit us, and after meeting him a few times, one has no difficulty in realising why the Mustang is a good aeroplane."[2]

Schmued also investigated an Air Force concern. "Then came the idea from the field that our airplanes were too heavy. American airplanes were heavier than the British, and they wanted to know why. That was not an easy thing to answer. So I had our

Field Service Department in England check with British manufacturers, especially the Spitfire people, to get a detailed weight statement of their airplane. The British wondered what we wanted to do with it, because they didn't have any detailed weight statements; no British company had any detailed weight statements. They really didn't know how much the components of their airplanes weighed.

"Our Field Service Department, under Phil Legarra, sent his field servicemen out to the various places where Spitfires were repaired and individual pieces were available. They started weighing all the pieces they could get their hands on and provided me with the data that I requested. I finally got a weight statement of the Spitfire.

"There were a number of reasons why the British airplanes were lighter than ours. First, the high angle of attack-load factor was 12 in America, but was only 11 in England. Second, there was a side-load factor on the engine mount in America of two g's, which the British didn't have at all. You honestly cannot get side-load factors in normal flight on the engine installation. Then the landing-gear-load factors which we used were six g's, but were only four g's in England. We used all these lower factors to help whittle out a good deal of weight in a new design, which we called the P-51F & G.

"I went home, after being flown around by Colonel Hitchcock, who took care of me completely. Wherever I wanted to go, he flew me with his private plane, a reverse-staggered Beech biplane. I enjoyed him tremendously. He was very bright, a true sportsman, and I was really happy to have known him."

Sam Logan reports that when Schmued returned, "He called us to the front of the room to describe what he had seen. He had walked from his hotel in London to a meeting during a German attack, with the anti-aircraft guns firing. Someone hollered at him from a window, 'Don't you know what goes up, comes down?' When he saw all the shrapnel on the street the next day, he realized what a chance he had taken.

"He arranged shipment to us of some German aircraft parts and the powerful Rolls-Royce Griffon engine along with a five-blade Rotol propeller for installation and test on a Mustang. We were spellbound by his firsthand report." Logan was to design the carburetor air intake ducts and cowlings, as well as the engine cooling system on the new lightweight Mustang.[3]

"While this was happening," Schmued said, "I got home with the information on the new RM.14.SM engine, of 2,200 hp. What could we do with it? I had written a report in the meantime about why British airplanes like the Spitfire were so much lighter than ours, in answer to our complaints that the American airplanes were too heavy. One copy of this report got into the hands of General Hap Arnold, head of the U.S. Air Force. He called Dutch Kindelberger and said, 'Well, Dutch, if you've got such smart people, go ahead and build one.'

"That was our go-ahead to build the P-51F. It was a marvelous exercise for us because we already had an airplane that was very, very light. Now by using some of the British load factors and design requirements and our design improvements, we actually whittled 600 pounds off the empty weight of the airplane, and what an airplane we would possibly have built. We took some great pains to save weight everywhere.

"For instance, the part of the engine cowling at the engine mount was actually a structural member of the engine mount, with a substantial weight saving. It also provided a better attachment of the engine cowling. The fuselage skins, aft of the firewall, used to be .065 aluminum alloy. At that time we had heard that the Aluminum Company of America had a stronger new alloy, 75 ST, so we asked them to send us the material for our new airplane. They told us you can't get that material before next year.

"We then decided we are going to make our own 75 ST material by using 25 ST and stretch-forming and heat-treating it so we got the same values as the 75 ST material. But we bought ourselves a great deal of problems with that. When you rivet a .065-inch-thick skin, you can cut-countersink for the head of a rivet, but you can't do that with the thin .042 skins we had to replace the .065 skin. There was no way of countersinking it.

"The only thing we had left was dimpling. We took these high-quality materials, 75-ST sheets, and started dimpling. We discovered, to our dismay, that every time the punch came down, a little slug fell out. Instead of dimpling, we punched a hole in the sheet.

"Our Research Department was then asked to develop a method that we could use for punching these dimples into the sheet without cracking them or breaking them through. They came up with what they called a 'coin-dimpling' process. In this case, a punch came down against the surface and held the sheet of aluminum alloy tight against the surface underneath while the

Exploring design improvements, engineers tried a higher tail fin on the first P-51D-5. A little Disney cartoon has been added to the logo. *NAA*

punch came down and formed the dimple.

"So further improvements were made on the P-51F by having a pilot seat and a canopy operated by hydraulic pressure, which were new at that time and state-of-the-art. Furthermore, by using British load factors, we reduced the weight of the P-51F from 7,500 pounds to 6,800, a substantial weight saving over the P-51D airplane."

An Air Force contract approved on July 20, 1943, provided for five NA-105 aircraft. The first of three prototypes designated XP-51F, 43-43332, was flown by Bob Chilton on February 14, 1944. While the dimensions and V-1650-3 engine were the same as the B series, refinements included a thinner wing, smaller landing wheels, and a smooth leading edge. Weight was listed as 6,296 pounds gross on the first flight. When loaded to 7,340 pounds, performance included a top speed of 491 mph at 21,500 feet and a 42,100-foot service ceiling. Range with 180 gallons of internal fuel was 1,112 miles.[4]

Four .50-caliber guns with 1,000 rounds, 142 pounds of armor, 93 pounds of bullet-proof glass, and a three-bladed Aero-products propeller were provided. The second XP-51F was flown by Chilton on May 22, weighing only 5,492 pounds empty and 6,993 pounds with 105 gallons of fuel.[5] First flown on May 20, 1944, the third XP-51F was shipped to Britain on June 30. There, as Mustang V, FR409, it was nicknamed "Margie Hart," after a well-known London stripper who, just like the P-51F, stripped off excess weight.

According to Schmued, "Dutch Kindel-berger had asked me to obtain two new Rolls-Royce 14.SM engines in England to be used in a P-51. He told me to make any reasonable deal with the British to obtain some 14.SM engines. The British agreed to let us have these 14.SM engines if we in-stalled one with a five-blade Rotol propeller in an airplane that was to be given to the British. Designated XP-51G, this airplane was clocked at Vmax 498 mph, the fastest airplane of the P-51 series built.

"I asked Dutch how about quoting 500 mph, but he said no, it is only 498 mph. The integrity of this man would not accept a two-miles-per-hour stretch of the truth. Unfortunately, the higher rating of the 14.SM engine was not continued in the Merlin series, so there are, I believe, hardly any 14.SM engines left with the remarkable rating of 2,200 hp at 120-inch manifold pressure. Probably much to the dismay of speed pilots, who like to have as much power as they can get."

This version of the Mustang was not the world's fastest propeller-driven fighter; that honor was claimed by Republic, who re-ported that their special XP-47J did 505 mph with 2,730 hp on August 5, 1944. Many years after the war, however, the world's speed record for propeller-driven racers would be captured and held by Mus-tangs.

The first XP-51G, 43-43335, was initially flown with a standard Aeroproducts propel-ler on August 9, 1944, by Joe Barton. A wooden five-bladed Rotol propeller was in-stalled for the fifth flight; test pilot Bob Chilton described the aircraft as now direc-tionally unstable. Nevertheless, a total of 37 test flights were made with that propeller and the XP-51G was accepted by the AAF on September 26.

According to an Air Force specification, the XP-51G weighed 5,749 pounds empty and 7,858 pounds gross. The imported en-gine, called the Merlin 145, was rated at 1,675 hp for takeoff and 2,080 hp at 20,000 feet. This Mustang did 492 mph at 20,700 feet, climbed to 20,000 feet in only 3.85 minutes, and had a 44,700-foot service ceil-ing. When fueled with 105 gallons, range was 510 miles at 315 mph.[6]

Joe Barton first flew the second XP-51G on November 14, and after 54 flights, it was shipped to Britain the following February with an FR410 serial. While the RAF also put aside serial number KN987 for a P-51H, it appears that this aircraft was not actually shipped.

Deke Warner was in charge of the flight-test instrumentation for these planes. "With the rapid advances in airplane per-formance that resulted from the designs of Ed and others like him, we were constantly being challenged to come up with new and improved ways to measure and record test data. Innovation and inventiveness was the order of the day in our flight-test instrumentation section.

"On many occasions I would informally discuss some of my ideas with Ed, and he would come up with good commonsense advice. Fortunately, I used to pay a lot of attention, as I found out that when he said that one of my ideas was not as good as I thought it was, he was usually 100 percent right! He also made many practical suggestions for innovative ways of solving our instrumentation problems . . . some of them so simple that I wondered why *I* hadn't thought of them!

"Ed was a remarkable person . . . knowledgeable to the nth degree and stubborn as a mule when it came to sticking up for what he believed in and refusing to knuckle under to pressure from higher-ups who disagreed with him."[7]

Production lightweight airplanes developed from the P-51F were called the P-51H, and Arthur Patch was the project engineer. They began as the NA-126 project on April 20, 1944, and a contract for 1,000 P-51Hs to be built in Inglewood was approved on June 30. A Packard V-1650-9 with 1,380 hp for takeoff used water/alcohol injection to provide two minutes of war emergency power of 2,220 hp at 10,200 feet and 1,800 hp at 25,000 feet for the 11-foot 1-inch four-bladed Aeroproducts propeller.

Weighing 6,586 pounds empty, 9,500 pounds gross, and 11,054 pounds overload, the P-51H had a 37-inch span and was 33 feet 4 inches long. Top speed was 487 mph at 25,000 feet, 50 miles faster than the D model, but climb was little changed: 30,000

This XP-51G with five-blade propeller and imported Rolls-Royce engine was the fastest wartime Mustang. *NAA*

The fifth production P-51H-1, which did 487 mph. *NAA*

feet in 12.5 minutes with a 41,600 foot service ceiling. Fuel capacity included 210 usable gallons in the center wing tanks, plus 50 gallons behind the pilot.

Six .50-caliber guns and 1,820 rounds were provided, along with rails for six five-inch rockets and racks for two 500-pound bombs. Armor included $7/16$-inch behind the pilot's head, $5/16$-inch behind his back, and $1/4$-inch at the front firewall. Instead of bombs, two 110-gallon drop tanks could provide a maximum bomber escort radius of 945 miles with a 40-gallon reserve. Total range was 940 miles on internal fuel, or maximum ferry distance of 2,400 miles at 241 mph.[8]

The first P-51H-1, 44-64160, was flown by Bob Chilton on February 3, 1945, but was wrecked three days later when propeller failure caused a crash landing. Production went on without waiting for tests, with 221 P-51Hs delivered by July 30, and 370 by VJ day, September 2. With the war over, Mustang production drew to a close when the 555th and last P-51H rolled out of the California factory on November 9, 1945. None of these airplanes was used in the war.

Dallas had expected to build 1,700 of this version, as the P-51L with a V-1650-11, but victory ended the project. The last plane off the Texas assembly line in August 1945 was a single P-51M, 45-111743; actually a P-51D-30NT with a V-1650-9A, without water injection and with a Hamilton propeller. Sixty-three nearly completed examples on the production line were scrapped without acceptance. Total Mustang production amounted to 15,486, the largest number of any American fighter but the P-47, which reached 15,683.

One more effort to improve this fighter remains to be described. On June 30, 1944, the AAF ordered two XP-51J prototypes, 44-76027/8, to be built to test the new Allison V-1710-119, which had two-stage supercharging for high altitudes. The first XP-51J flight, by Joe Barton, was on April 23, 1945. A four-bladed Aeroproducts propeller and four .50-caliber guns were used. Design weight was 5,749 pounds empty and 7,400 pounds gross.

Inset, **a view of the P-51H-1 in flight.** *NAA*

An Air Force attempt to utilize a new version of the Allison engine resulted in this XP-51J, pictured on April 26, 1945. *SDAM*

A high-tailed P-51H-5, flying with one of the last P-51D-30 Mustangs, shows the subtle visible differences between the types. *SDAM*

This aircraft was similar to the H model, but the Allison was expected to yield 1,500 hp at takeoff and 1,720 war emergency hp at 20,700 feet, and provide 491 mph at 27,-400 feet, a climb to 20,000 feet in five minutes, and a 43,700-foot service ceiling.[9] Since that power plant had many mechanical problems, it was unpopular with Schmued and Chilton. Only seven flights were made on the first prototype, and two on the second, before they were turned over to the AAF on February 15, 1946.[10] One XP-51J was used later to test the V-1710-143 engine that was to be used in the F-82E.

At the war's end, there were 5,541 Mustangs in the Air Force inventory, but no H models had gone overseas. Fighter groups deployed against Japan used P-51Ds. Postwar fighter groups like the 56th at Selfridge AFB and the 57th in Alaska used the P-51H, and both P-51D and P-51H Mustangs were used by many National Guard squadrons.

THE DESIGNER AT HOME

Americans of German birth were often regarded with suspicion by security officers, who, on one occasion early in the war, entered Ed Schmued's home while he was at work, to look for evidence of Nazi sympathies. His fellow engineers assured them of his complete commitment to Allied victory.[11]

Dutch Kindelberger insisted that Ed and his fellow immigrants were essential to the company's war effort and that he had no doubts about their loyalty. Fortunately, German-Americans in California escaped the mass removal that befell Japanese-Americans, and were allowed to make their contribution to Axis defeat.

Ed seldom spoke of the land of his birth, but years after the war he wrote about German engineers who were working in other countries. "These men are products of a proud and cultured nation. They have trod as boys and young men the damp, brick-paved streets of German towns in winter. They have enjoyed the comradeship and songs of the beer gardens in summer. And, most important, they have known the stern discipline and exacting scholastic demands of the German academies and universities. Experience tells me how they think. . . ."[12]

With wartime working hours, Edgar had only a little time to enjoy his home at 5327 Overdale Drive, a two-story house in the Los Angeles suburb of Windsor Hills, where he lived from March 1940 to January 1956. His son, Rolf, had finished school and came to work at North American in 1940. Rolf became an enthusiastic member, along with some of Ed's coworkers like George Gehrkens, of the Flying Horsemen, a uniformed fancy riding team seen at local parades, one of many employee activities sponsored by the company.

Rolf married Carol Calvert, a teacher, in June 1943, and Edgar's house was quiet until June 1944, when Ed married 32-year-old Helen Fairfax, a vivacious blonde from San Antonio, Texas. They adopted a baby

daughter, Sandra Helen, on June 1, 1945, and Helen concentrated on making a home for the little family. Ed was usually too preoccupied with his own "romance" with airplanes to want to go out much, so social activities were confined to visits with a few friends, like dentist Dr. Graydon "Hoffie" Hofferber and his wife, Alice.

Edgar was reported to be an avid badminton player with a court in his backyard, but he had his own drawing board at home to pursue his inventive inclinations. Bill Wheeler recalls that "in all the years I knew him, there was never a time that he didn't have a drafting board in his house somewhere. In fact, there is still one down there in his last home in Oceanside."[13]

Bob Chilton still remembers Ed's car. "During World War II, Ed Schmued owned and ran his go-to-work car, which was a La Salle coupe. If you remember a La Salle, in those days it was a small Cadillac, built by the Cadillac Motor Car Company. It was really a neat-looking and good-sized machine, almost as large as the big Cadillacs of the day.

"He kept driving his La Salle coupe after the end of the war. Then the General Motors organization gets into gear and they design a hydromatic system that they put into the Oldsmobile. Automatic gearshifts. One day somebody asked, 'Ed, why don't you get one of those new Oldsmobiles? It's got automatic gearshift and the whole thing.' Ed says, 'Nah.' 'But why not?' He says, 'I don't want any General Motors engineer telling me when to shift gears!' "[14] Ed's feelings about General Motors, owners of the Allison engine plant, did not improve over the years.

CHAPTER SEVEN

Reaching for Range:
The P-82 Twin Mustang

An F-82E used in 1948–50 only by SAC's long-range 27th Fighter-Escort Group. *SDAM*

Expansion of the aircraft industry reached its peak two years after Pearl Harbor. At this point in the war, North American Aviation employed 25,068 people at the Inglewood factory, plus 59,539 at the Dallas and Kansas City plants. The company would build more aircraft, fighters, bombers, and trainers, than any other American manufacturer during the war.

While North American's Engineering Department had grown, Raymond Rice was still chief engineer, with Edgar Schmued as assistant chief engineer for design, and Carl "Red" Hansen as assistant chief engineer for administration. Edgar Schmued's preliminary design office on the new engineering building's first floor had a glass enclosure around his desk and a conference table, while three desks and about a dozen 7-by-4-foot drafting tables were lined up in two rows outside.

Julius G. Villepique, who had become assistant chief design engineer, and project engineer Howard A. Evans had their desks right outside his door, while Margaret Boles was department secretary. Specialist engineers in the department included Dick Prible for wing and empennage; Vern Tauscher, hydraulics; Fred Payne, landing gear; Charles Ulrick, armament; and several other engineers and draftsmen.[1]

"Ed was very direct in the way he took care of his people," remembers Sam Logan.

"One day he called us all up to the front of the room and said, 'I believe a happy, productive group is a well-paid group. If any of you feel you aren't making enough, please come and see me.' We all went back to our tables, and I watched to see if anyone went into his office—they didn't. I cranked up my courage and went in. I told him that I was newly married, making $170 a month, and if I deserved it, I would appreciate an increase. He just rotated his chair, picked up the phone, and said, 'Wescombe, change Logan to $190 a month.' Then, turning to me, he asked, 'Is that better?'

"An example of how he protected his people occurred in a discussion with someone from an outside group. That man made a derogatory remark about the very creative design specialist, Julius Villepique. Ed turned to the critic and very sharply said, 'I'd rather have someone who has ideas than someone who doesn't.'

"Another approach that intrigued me was the day when there was a major impasse in a design conflict in the area of the fuselage/wing intersection. After listening to all sides of the problem, Ed said, 'Give me five minutes alone.' He went into a corner of the room with a paper while we all stood for five minutes in silence. He came back with his solution sketched out, and without further discussion said, 'Here, do it this way,' and walked away."[2]

Interaction among the engineers was not

Preliminary design engineers Richard Pribil, Julius Villepique, Tim Walston, Edgar Schmued, and Merle Beaupre. *NAA*

confined to work. One New Year's Eve, Julius and Vern were celebrating at home, but were frustrated by the lack of decent liquor, wartime shortages limiting them to a cheap brand of whiskey. Vern then "rang Ed's doorbell, and he came to the door in his robe and said, 'What do you want?' I said, 'We're having a party.' Ed told me to wait there and came back with a bottle of Scotch and said, 'Enjoy yourselves. Happy New Year!' Since he didn't drink, as far as I knew, I often wondered where he got that bottle; did he save it for years?"[3]

On Thursday, October 21, 1943, Schmued called in Evans and Villepique to show them his sketch and anticipated weight breakdown for a twin-engine fighter. Villepique wrote that Schmued requested studies of two design possibilities: one a conventional twin-engine airplane with a main fuselage housing the pilot, armament and nose wheel, and nacelles on the wings for the engines and main landing gear. "The other study was to be a new type wherein two fuselage units, each housing a pilot and engine, and supporting tail surfaces, would be mounted on a 400-square-foot wing. . . . Evans lost the coin toss and had to be content with the conventional-type fighter. Although a proposal was submitted on his later design study, it could not compete with the manifold possibilities offered by the dual fuselage arrangement."[4]

Wrote Ed Schmued: "Many people think the F-82 is nothing else but two P-51 fuselages joined together by the wing. This is not the case. It was a completely new design. Nothing of the P-51, except the design principles and power-plant group, was used on this new venture. All the things that were good on the P-51 were also applied here.

"I would like to say how the F-82 started. In 1935, I with two friends—Ward Beeman, a mathematician, and Paul Balfour, a pilot—had tried to put a brochure together to form an aircraft company. In this effort, we developed designs of a low-cost trainer, low-cost fighter, and of a twin-fuselage fighter. Then we tried to get some interest, but it was not possible.

"Dutch Kindelberger eventually heard about it and told us that either you stop working on this project, or you have to quit North American. Since the prospects were very slim . . . we decided we would back off on this project. So for years I kept these drawings at home, until the day I was going to take them to North American and show them to Dutch Kindelberger and let him do with it what he wanted."

With RD-1120, a charge number issued for the twin-engine fighter design study on October 22, 1943, preliminary design began.

By November 24, weight and balance calculations were made, and Villepique had drawings of the control, fuel, coolant, lubrication, and armor systems completed by December 15, while a three-view was drawn by Tim Walston. On New Year's Day, 1944, a Saturday, the design proposal brochure was completed by Paul Anderson of the specification group, and his aide, Frank Compton, with art by Reynold Brown. Villepique rushed it to the company print shop. Engineering time charges at this point amounted to 712 hours, including 506 by Villepique and 127 by Walston.

Kindelberger had been enthusiastic about the proposal from the start, and when the design brochure was submitted to Ray Rice and Lee Atwood on Wednesday, January 5, it was approved and mailed to the Air Force the next day. General Arnold was visiting the plant on January 7, 1944, and when shown the proposal, told them to go ahead. The same day, General Order NA-120 was issued for engineering, a mock-up, and a wind-tunnel model.

Sam Logan writes that Ed personally presented the key features of the design, pointing out that "instead of pulling three fuselages through the air like the P-38, the future P-82 would only have two; having two pilots on long flights would allow one to rest; and since the two fuselages could be very close together, the airplane would be very maneuverable."

Said Ed Schmued: "Actually, we built a mock-up to find out if the off-center position of the pilot in a rapid roll would affect the two crewmen in any way. We found that there was no effect whatsoever. The pilot always had the feeling that the ship was rotating around his own fuselage. This was a big item and it was very quickly resolved by means of that mock-up."

Ed Horkey describes how that mock-up worked: "There was some concern that since one man would be the pilot, he would make rolls wherein he would cross-control subconsciously in such a way to make it most comfortable for himself. This would then mean that the man on the other side of the fuselage would go through quite a wild maneuver.

"To check out this theory, we built a machine like a Ferris wheel. There was quite a fore and aft axis, and a boom went out from the side of this and then at the end of the boom (equal in length to the distance between P-82 fuselages) we had a mock-up cockpit. We could control this either from the cockpit or by an operator on the ground. Of course this soon degenerated into a fun project in that people would take bets on who could make each other sick by controlling from the ground and subjecting the observer to some wild maneuvers.

"When we got to flying the airplane, we quickly realized that what goes on is that when one rolls an airplane, he doesn't really roll about an axis through his body. He really rolls about an axis above the airplane. In other words, the airplane goes through the air like a big corkscrew. I have had many flights in the P-82 and this factor never bothered me, or was ever mentioned by others."[5]

Air Force procurement was authorized on January 15, and on February 8 a letter-contract supplement ordered two XP-82 and two XP-82A prototypes, and one static test airframe. The purpose was to develop a "long-range fighter with dual engine reliability, with pilot and copilot, capable of escorting bombers," as well as a ground-attack suitability.[6]

A production version, the NA-123, was begun on March 8, 1944, and on March 15 Edgar Schmued applied for three design patents, including a ground-attack and a single-seat interceptor (eliminating the right-hand cockpit) configuration, which were granted after the war.[7] George Gehrkens became the P-82 project engineer when he returned from England in February 1944.

The Air Force was so eager to get the twin Mustang into production that after an XP-82 mock-up inspection was conducted from June 19 to 23, contracts were approved on June 30, 1944, for 500 P-82Bs, along with the first 1,000 P-51H models and two P-51J prototypes to try the new high-altitude version of the Allison engine.

After the first XP-82, 44-83886, completed its engineering acceptance inspection on May 25, 1945, an unexpected difficulty emerged. Bob Chilton tells the story: "The common chain of events for all our first flights was to feel out the machine with taxi tests, followed by ground runs at gradually increasing speeds. Joe Barton was scheduled for the first flight and he was the person doing these preliminary runs. Mines Field was one mile square with the main runway in roughly an east-west direction with about 4,500 feet of runway. There really was not an awful lot of room to do lift-offs, but we had done it satisfactorily with Mustangs and there was no trouble—so there should not have been any problem in getting the XP-82 airborne and back down again.

"But there was a problem. The airplane wouldn't fly! It refused to fly! Joe tried it

The second XP-82 Twin Mustang prototype. *NAA*

again and again, several days in a row. He would get up speed, pull back the stick—and the tail would come back to the runway. He would charge down the runway as far as he dared, then pull back the stick as far as he dared, then as far as he could. That airplane just would not come unglued!

"So then we sat down with the big guns, like Ray Rice, chief engineer, and Larry L. Waite, chief of engineering's Technical Section, Ed Schmued, Ed Horkey, and Ed Virgin, the chief test pilot. Then I tried to get it off the ground. I was the expert on P-51s and Merlin engines, so it was automatic that I would be able to get it out of there. I couldn't.

"Joe tried it a few more times. It still didn't work, so Ed Virgin and Joe decided to come in on Saturday when there would be more time and they had the runway all to themselves. Joe had his parachute on just to get himself up into a normal position. Ed climbed into the right fuselage and sat there in the bottom of the seat, where he could watch things happening and try to feel for himself what the problem was that prevented flight. Conditions were the same, but they had off-loaded a major part of the fuel just to get a faster acceleration and thus more runway time.

"So they charged out—this time they were going to make it fly. Joe had to do it—the boss was sitting there watching (without his parachute). Joe pulled back the stick, farther and farther, as they picked up speed, then harder on the stick. (He said later that it was almost fully back.) Suddenly, like almost instantaneously, the airplane jumped off the ground and was 50 feet in the air. Joe recovered nicely and completed a short flight without trouble.

"The engines were set up with propellers rotating toward each other. Due to the direction of travel, a stall was set up with the airplane center section. Then they swapped engines left to right and right to left. I flew it ten days later and it became like a normal P-51."[8]

As aerodynamicist Ed Horkey explains the problem: "What was happening was that we had propellers rotating in different directions on the left and right engines. For some reason, which I can't remember, we started with the blades moving upward in front of the center section. What this does, particularly at high angles of attack, is to create upward flow approaching the leading edge of the center section of the wing. You also have normal upflow ahead of the wing. The two upflows would add together and we got an early stall.

"The center section area represented a large portion of the wing area. So what was happening was that we were stalling out early and just not getting enough lift. It wasn't any mysterious vacuum holding it down or anything like that. It was just a standard stall of the wing section. I remember taking a ride during this period in one of the fuselages, and we had tufts on the wing. You could see the stalled flow. It would also happen at high-speed turns. We changed the rotations to go down in the middle and we had the problem solved."[9]

After that first hop on June 12, 1945, Chilton resumed tests on June 26, and the first flight by an AAF pilot was on July 6. The second XP-82 made its initial flight on August 30, and was also powered by Packard V-1650-23/25 Merlins with 1,380-hp takeoff and 1,500-hp military power. Allison V-1710-119 engines were planned for the XP-82A, but both A models were canceled while that power plant was tested on the P-51J.[10]

Bob Chilton reports on P-82 testing. "I was out on a routine test mission on a P-82 one day and for some reason this required getting out in the hot country and getting away from the city scene. I was up over Edwards Air Force Base and it was too noisy and too many airplanes there, so I went farther out and finally I was up working over Death Valley, pretty high. Then I decided I deserved to play a little trick. I wanted to go down and see what Death Valley was. I had never really seen it close down; we'd flown over it, of course. I started from the west and came down in a rollover dive to get the altitude out of the way. I'm smoking along, headed right at the big Death Valley hotel thing, whose name I've forgotten.

"It sat up on the rocks over the far east side of the valley floor with a massive big rock wall built all along the face of it, 100 to 200 feet long. A great big massive rock wall, it was a good 20 or 40 feet high. That's where the people sit on their stools or chairs in the morning, with their feet propped up on that big wall. I was probably up around 450, 475 mph or so steaming across the desert at about 20 feet, just about even with the altitude of that wall.

"I was just cruising along looking at the thing and then I noticed all this little row of dots along the wall and I realized that those were people. Then I saw these dots bouncing up in the air in various places along the wall, and so then I got a little cute and just held it there to see just how fast they would hop. These things were just jumping out of their chairs. Those dear, dear, people! And then I went zooming over their heads,

pulled it up to go right over the center of that great big chateau, and then I disappeared. I just never came back. It was a nasty thing to do, I thought about it later. I was deeply ashamed, really. Well, it makes a good story, but it was dumb!"[11]

Ed Horkey adds an interesting report. "Ed Virgin and Joe Barton were flying a P-82 and, somewhere during the takeoff, assumed that both were at the controls. They were not! Luckily they found it out in time.

"George Welch and I flew to San Francisco and Ames one day. We set a new speed record, but unfortunately had not mentioned our intention, so the speed could not be recorded. On the way back I asked George for the controls to go down close to Buena Vista Lake [near Bakersfield, California] to check duck populations for a potential hunting trip. I told George when I was through, assuming he would take over. It soon became apparent that he hadn't, so some radio intercom action took place!"

A description of the first Twin Mustang includes a 50 foot 11 inch wing span, a 408-square-foot wing area, 39-foot length, and 13-foot 6-inch height. The XP-82 weighed 13,402 pounds empty, and 19,100 pounds with normal 600-gallon load. Top speed with 1,810 hp from each engine with water injection was 468 mph at 22,800 feet, climb to 25,000 feet took 6.4 minutes, and service ceiling was 40,000 feet. Range was 1,390 miles in 4 hours with internal fuel, or up to 3,445 miles in 14.4 hours if drop tanks increased fuel load to 1,045 gallons.

The armament consisted of six .50-caliber M-2 guns with 400 rpg in the wing center section, and eight more guns could be added by attaching a pod under that sec-

A cutaway drawing of the XP-82's interior. *NAA*

tion. These guns were replaced on the second plane by the faster-firing M-3 model in 1946.[12]

Each cockpit had gun controls, so that this fighter not only had two-engine reliability but also had two-pilot reliability. If one pilot was hit, the other could still fight and fly to a safe landing. While one man flew the plane, the other could navigate or watch for an enemy attack. "Green" pilots could be trained in combat under the guidance of a veteran, thus reducing risk.

The war's end cut back the production contract to 20 planes, with the first P-82B, 44-65160, flown on October 31, 1945, by

Chilton. Two more were accepted in January 1946, and the rest by March. Similar to the prototype, they became famous for a nonstop flight from Honolulu to New York made by Lt. Col. Robert E. Thacker and Lieutenant John Ard in "Betty Jo," 46-5168, after it was stripped of armament and provided with extra tankage for 2,215 gallons. Taking off on February 28, 1947, the P-82B flew 4,968 miles in 14 hours 32 minutes at an average speed of 342 mph.

The 10th and 11th planes were completed as black-painted night fighters, the P-82C flown March 27, 1946, with SCR-720 intercept radar in the center pod, and the P-82D, flown two days later with an APS-4 radar.[13] Another P-82B, 46-5172, was converted by Air Force technicians at Eglin Field, who added a photographic pod with seven cameras under the center section. Called the RF-82B by its crew, it was first flown November 15, 1948, by Lin Hendrix.[14]

While the postwar Air Force was to get jet fighters, these fighters burned fuel so rapidly that piston-engined aircraft were

This P-82B, "Betty Jo," flew nonstop from Hawaii to New York. *SDAM*

still desirable for long-range and bad weather operations. North American began the NA-144 project on December 12, 1945, and got a letter contract approved on February 5, 1946, that called for 250 Twin Mustangs; 100 as escort fighters and 150 as night fighters. To get an American-designed power plant, 750 Allison V-1710-143 (left-hand rotation) and -145 (right-hand rotation) engines were ordered in March.

When the NA-144 was first flown on February 17, 1947, it was known as an P-82A, but became the F-82E with the new designation system adopted in 1948. Not until the flight test was under way did the troubles begin to appear. As the Air Force Historical Office case history explained in

great detail, "The major problem in the F-82 program was the failure of the government-furnished engine."[15]

A multitude of engine troubles so disrupted the program that total costs rose from $35 million to over $50 million, and usable aircraft were over a year late getting into service. Only one plane had been delivered by November 1947, when North American had to request an increase in partial payments, which was granted because the airframes, finished but minus engines, had to be stored at the former Vultee plant at Downey. This cost rent, maintenance of the delicate electrical systems, insurance, and plant protection.[16]

Schmued describes the central problem: "The engine we had intended for this design was a Merlin. The United States Air Force was tired of paying a $6,000 royalty to England for each Merlin engine built in this country by Packard, on a royalty basis. So they decided, then, to substitute an Allison V-1710 for the Merlin.

"Now the Merlin engine had a very high rating, 2,270 hp with 90-inch manifold pressure, and the Air Force told the Allison people they had to duplicate this performance. It was obvious that the way their engine was built was not suitable for these high manifold pressures. The British built a backfire screen into their engine, which made it run properly. But the Allison people refused to do that.

"To help the situation along, we actually modified an Allison engine with a backfire screen that worked fine. But then, the secretary of defense was powerful enough to override the Air Force and told Allison not to do anything. Which, of course, left the F-82 with a rating far below that of a good

trainer. The manifold pressure was reduced to 60 inches to keep this thing from backfiring into the blower case and damaging the engines. This was a very sad situation, because it really ruined the project. The secretary of defense [James Forresta] favored General Motors and, I think, he had a good idea of how to protect the Allison people.[17]

"The Allison people were already on the way to build jet engines and did not really like to go back and build reciprocating engines. That pretty nearly ended the project. We flew each of these airplanes with the Allison engine at high manifold pressure, and pretty nearly on every flight, we lost the engine for sure and sometimes it was dangerous enough to lose the airplane and the pilot. It was really pathetic to see a good design simply ruined by politics and the lack of cooperation by the Allison people in building a good engine.

"We had demonstrated the Allison engine with backfire screens, but it didn't make any difference, because Allison never agreed to install them. We just couldn't get the support from the Department of Defense. The secretary completely failed to support us in this particular endeavor, and therefore the airplane didn't meet expectations. It was the only airplane at that time that could fly from New York to Hawaii without refueling and then perform as a fighter, if necessary. It was a great airplane and it was ruined by personal interests. It was pathetic."

Actually, all of the airplanes were shop-completed by April 30, 1948, as per contract, but the final delivery with engines was not made until April 12, 1949. Even then a critical parts shortage grounded many aircraft, and "33 hours of mainte-

An unusual Twin Mustang configuration was this P-82B tested with a camera pod. *SDAM*

nance were required for each hour flown."[18]

When working right, which was seldom, the V-1710-143 was supposed to provide 1,600 hp for takeoff, 1,250 military power at 30,000 feet, with a war emergency rating of 1,700 hp at 21,000 feet. The F-82E's wing span was 51 feet 3 inches, wing area 418 square feet, and length 39 feet 1 inch. Empty weight was 14,914 pounds, and maximum takeoff weight was 24,864 pounds. Internal fuel was 576 gallons, with another 620 gallons possible with drop tanks.

Four 1,000-pound bombs or 25 five-inch rockets could be added under the wings to the gun arrangement, which was the same as the XP-82. Top speed was 465 mph at 21,000 feet with a 20,741 pound combat weight, and range was 2,504 miles.[19]

Only two F-82E escort fighters had been accepted by November 1947, while 96 followed through July 1948, with another in October and the last in December. Flyaway cost per aircraft was $215,154. Most served with the 27th Fighter-Escort Group as Strategic Air Command's only fighters, until they were replaced by F-84E Thunderjets in the summer of 1950.

The Air Defense Command had been somewhat anxiously awaiting the night-fighter versions to replace its wartime P-61 Black Widows. North American's contract called for 91 NA-149, or F-82F, with APG-28 search radar, 45 NA-150, or F-82G, which had the older SCR-720 radar, and 14 F-82H, which were G models winterized for Alaska.

The F-82G, 46-355, was first flown on December 8, 1947, and accepted in February 1948, followed on March 11 by the first F-82F (46-405) flight. Most had been delivered when the first F-82H was flown February 15, 1949, and the last Twin Mustangs were received in March. With their thermal anti-icing, cabin heating, automatic pilot, radar altimeter and beacon, glide path and localizer receivers, they were the first true "all-weather fighters" of the Air Force.

Armament included the six .50-caliber guns in the center section, and 20 five-inch rockets or bombs could be carried below the wings. The radar nacelle under the center section extended F-82G's length to 42 feet five inches; empty weight was 15,997

A large radar pod was fitted to black-painted F-82F and G all-weather fighter versions. *NAA*

pounds and maximum takeoff weight 25,-891 pounds, when the full 1,196-gallon fuel load, including two 310-gallon drop tanks, was carried. Top speed was 461 mph at 21,-000 feet with a 21,810-pound combat weight; combat ceiling was 37,200 feet and the F-82G climbed to 25,000 feet in 7.5 minutes. Combat range was 2,240 miles in 7.95 hours, or combat radius about 1,015 miles. Stalling speed was 127 mph and a ground run of 2,060 feet was required for takeoff.[20]

The black-painted Twin Mustangs entered service with the Air Defense Command in September 1948, and were used by the 52nd and 325th All-Weather Fighter Wings based at Mitchel Field in New York and McChord Field in Washington to protect the northeastern and northwestern

This 68th All-Weather Fighter Squadron F-82G is taking off from Japan for patrol over Korea, as Captain Johnnie Gosnell's wife and children watch. *USAF*

states. Alaska had the 449th Squadron with the P-82H until 1953, while the 68th Squadron was at Itazuke in Japan and the 4th Squadron at Kadena in Okinawa. Persistent engine problems kept over 50 percent of these planes out of commission during most of 1949. While the twin Mustang had missed World War II, it would find unexpected action in 1950.

CHAPTER EIGHT

Facing the Jet Age, 1945-1952

North American's first product for the civilian market, the NAvion, had Mustang lines. *NAA*

At the war's end, North American faced the same enormous cutbacks as the rest of the industry. Orders for almost 8,000 planes dropped to 24, and by early 1946 less than 5,000 persons remained on the payroll, of some 85,000 three years before.

Trying to carve out a postwar market share, the company went after as many airplane development programs as it could. Everything came through Ed Schmued's Design Department. As Bill Wheeler and Ed Horkey described the situation, Ed was a team member who was basically more intimately involved in the airplanes at the start of things, and then, as they got into the design phase, he was off on other plans. Ed was certainly not into as much detail as he had been on the P-51 and earlier planes. He was more generally involved with the overall design effort, and as usual supported any new ideas.

Considering the civilian market for the first time, North American began project NA-143 in 1945. Ed Schmued designed a four-place low-wing cabin monoplane whose resemblance to the Mustang was unmistakable. Powered by a 185-hp Continental E-185-3 engine, the first "NAvion" (NX18928) demonstrator was first flown January 15, 1946, by Ed Virgin and Bob Chilton.

With retractable tricycle landing gear and a roomy cabin, the NAvion (pronounced *nay-vee-on*) is described as "nigh on to indestructible, could operate from even the smallest fields . . . was very easy to fly well, was stable as a rock, had very good manners, and was comfortable enough to be enjoyed for hours at a time."[1]

These aircraft had a 33-foot 5-inch wing span with a 184.3-square-foot area, were 27 feet 8 inches long, and originally weighed 1,551 pounds empty and carried a useful load of 1,019 pounds with 40 gallons of fuel. Weighing 2,370 pounds, they cruised at 150 mph, with a 160-mph top, and landing speed with 40 degrees flap was 53 mph.

The price was set at $6,100 and orders began to come in, but North American had invested $7.5 million in the project, and sales did not meet expectations. Even after the price was raised to $6,750 in 1947, the company was still losing money and unsold NAvions were accumulating at Inglewood. The aircraft first thought of as moderately priced had become a Cadillac in cost, as well as quality. NAA suddenly announced that production would end on April 14, 1947, after 1,112 planes had been built.

Since the plane was popular with those pilots who could afford it, the Ryan Aeronautical Company of San Diego bought the design in June 1947 and built another 1,238 planes at a profit by May 1951, when Ryan became fully occupied with Korean War contracts.

After a demonstration by Bob Chilton at

Fort Bragg, North Carolina, the Air Force, on September 19, 1947, purchased 83 NAvions waiting at North American and designated them the L-17A liaison plane, serialed 47-1297/1379. "I did a big sales job by demonstrating a landing and a takeoff among a lot of trees that none of the other guys would do, so they decided that must be the airplane they wanted."[2] Another contract, approved on the following June 9, obtained another 163 L-17B (48-921/1078, 49-1961/5) from Ryan. These designations were later changed to U-18A and U-18B (the "U" is for Utility aircraft).

Forty years after the first flight, over 1,600 Navions (no longer NAvion after Ryan bought them) were still being flown by private owners, whose pride in their sleek birds united them in their own "American Navion Society," which held annual fly-in conventions.

JET FIGHTERS IN AMERICA

Aside from production of these NAvion planes and the Twin Mustangs, North American's designers worked on prototype contracts for the next generation of warplanes, using jet propulsion. American experience with these new power plants began when General "Hap" Arnold saw the first British jet, the Gloster G.40, on a visit to England. On September 4, 1941, the General Electric Company was asked to produce Whittle jet engines from British drawings.

That company's experience with turbosupercharger manufacture had made it the obvious choice to deal with the intensive temperature changes affecting the metal engine components. To design and build the first American jet aircraft, General

Arnold selected Bell Aircraft, because of its proximity to the General Electric plant and designer Bob Wood's penchant for unorthodox aircraft.

Bell replaced its pusher fighter design (XP-52/59) development with the twin-jet XP-59A. Carefully guarded with a top-secret security classification, the XP-59A was first flown October 1, 1942, at Muroc Dry Lake, which replaced Wright Field as a fighter test area and would later become Edwards Air Force Base. While the P-59 series did not have the performance needed for actual fighter operations, it played an important test and training role.[3]

The second British company in the jet-fighter business was De Havilland, who had produced their own Goblin engine for their Vampire design. This single-engine fighter had been shown to Ed Schmued during his visit in March 1943, six months before the Vampire's first flight. The De Havilland engine was also selected by the Air Force to power Lockheed's first XP-80. Flown at Muroc on January 8, 1944, "Kelly" Johnson's jet fighter became the first American plane to pass the 500-mph mark and go into mass production.

When Americans finally became aware of German progress in jet and rocket propulsion, they realized that Germany had beaten the British into getting types into actual combat. A Heinkel He 176 powered by a rocket was flown as early as June 1, 1939, and the He 178, actually the world's first turbojet-powered aircraft, was flown on August 24, 1939. Because Nazi leadership was slow to recognize their opportunity to produce superior fighters, production deliveries of the rocket-powered Messerschmitt Me 163 and twin-jet-powered Me 262 fighters were delayed until the summer of 1944.

Encountering German fighters over 100 mph faster than the Mustang was an unnerving experience for the Air Force. The German jet pilots tried to concentrate on attacking bombers and avoided the American fighters when possible. So fast were the enemy jets that bomber gun turrets could not track them. Americans countered by continuous attacks on the German airfields, and the skilled Air Force pilots utilized superior Mustang endurance and maneuverability to score some successes over the enemy jets.

An Me 262 provided on March 30, 1945, by a defecting pilot was brought to America for tests that confirmed its 540-mph top speed at 19,680 feet. But no matter how fast the German jets were, the Luftwaffe could not reverse the collapse of both the German front lines and the economy due to the advancing Allied armies and the continuous bombardment.

A ROCKET-POWERED MUSTANG

An attempt was made in the United States to improvise a rocket boost for the Mustang by installation of a rocket in the tail end of a P-51D-25NA, 44-73099. The rocket was made by Aerojet, had 1,340 pounds of thrust, and was mounted behind the radiator, back to just in front of the tail wheel. Two pressurized 75-gallon drop tanks contained the highly corrosive and inflammable fuel, aniline in one and red fumic acid in the other. On April 23, 1945, the rocket Mustang went up to 21,000 feet and was flying at 429 mph corrected air speed with the Merlin engine. Igniting the rocket by mixing the fuels suddenly increased the corrected air speed to 513 mph.

Said Bob Chilton, who made the first flight: "We gained almost 100 miles per hour in 59 seconds, with supposedly one minute's worth of fuel. It was a very successful operation that worked just exactly like it was supposed to. The problem was that Horkey couldn't design an external fuel tank that didn't add a lot of drag. And as a result, with all this extra thrust, we couldn't keep up any speed."[4] Four more flights were made by May 3, but by the time the Air Force took delivery on May 25, Germany was defeated and the rocket was unnecessary.

A more radical proposal from the confidential design office proposed a jet-powered Mustang development using both a turboprop engine in the front and a turbojet behind the pilot, with tricycle gear and swept-forward wings. This idea, as well as a projected P-51H adapted for carrier operations, was dropped in favor of straight jet projects.

THE START OF THE F-86 SABRE

North American's first jet design, the NA-130, was actually a four-engine bomber project begun on September 13, 1944, that replaced the NA-116, a propeller-driven, four-engine, twin-boom proposal started the previous April. After the war, a contract for three prototypes designated XB-45 was finally approved by the Air Force on May 2, 1946.

Another company design study, RD-1265, begun on November 22, 1944, proposed a high-performance jet fighter. This became the NA-134 on December 27, actu-

This P-51D-25 was tested with a rocket engine in April 1945. *NAA*

ally destined for the Navy, which ordered three XFJ-1 prototypes on January 1, 1945.

The navy's experience with North American fighters included testing a P-51D-5NA, 44-14017, on the aircraft carrier *Shangri-La.* This Mustang was given Navy bureau number 57987 and modified at Mustin Field, Philadelphia, with arresting hook and catapult launching gear. Beginning on November 15, 1944, Captain Robert Elder made 25 landings and takeoffs. The capture of Okinawa and Iwo Jima, however, provided Mustang groups with bases within reach of Japan and made the carrier exercise of only academic interest.[5]

On May 18, 1945, an Air Force letter contract was received authorizing three XP-86 aircraft. This design, known in company records as the NA-140, was then essentially similar to the XFJ-1. Shortly afterward, on May 28, 1945, the Navy approved a contract for 100 production FJ-1s (NA-141).

Both the XFJ-1 and XP-86 were designed around a General Electric J35 axial-flow engine. This was situated in a straight-line flow of air from a circular nose inlet to the compressor, and of exhaust gases from the combustion chamber to tailpipe outlet. This nose intake arrangement appeared to give better efficiency than the side inlets on the P-80, while maintaining full advantage of the high-speed wing. Tricycle landing gear permitted higher landing speeds.

Both North American designs used a low, thin straight wing, but the navy design's high-speed potentialities were compromised in favor of low-speed carrier operations. The XP-86, being land-based, used substantially the same airfoil section and plan form, but had a thinner wing, elliptical nose inlet, and a very slim fuselage with a high fineness ratio. A 10-percent ratio of wing thickness to chord was used to extend the critical Mach number of the XP-86 design to approximately 0.9, compared to about 0.8 on the P-80 and about 0.76 on the P-51.[6]

A mock-up of the straight-wing XP-86 was built and received Air Force approval on June 20, 1945. This configuration called for a wing span of 38.2 feet, length of 35.5 feet, and height of 13.2 feet. At a gross weight of 11,500 pounds, estimated performance included a top speed of 574 mph at sea level and 582 mph at 10,000 feet, a rate climb of 5,850 feet per minute, and a service ceiling of 46,000 feet. The combat radius of 297 miles with 410 gallons of fuel was increased to 750 miles when a 170-gallon drop tank was added to each wing tip. Four speed brakes were attached above and below the wings.[7]

The first wind-tunnel test results on the P-86 model obtained in early June confirmed that the airframe design limited the speed the plane could yield, so that the P-86 could not reach the Air Force's desired 600 mph or even surpass the rival Republic P-84's speed. It was at this point that project aerodynamicist Larry P. Greene, who reported to Harrison A. Storms and to chief aerodynamicist Edward Horkey, became interested in German wind-tunnel reports on the advantages of wing sweep-back. This material had been snapped up by an American team after German surrender in May 1945.

One such paper written in 1940 on "Swept Wings and High Speeds" indicated that a test on small models showed advantages at about 0.9 Mach number. Since no one in 1940 could build aircraft of such

speeds, that information seemed purely theoretical. In 1942, however, a German wind-tunnel test compared a swept-wing and a straight-wing configuration on the Messerschmitt Me 262 twin-jet fighter. It demonstrated that sweeping the wing, while delaying and reducing the drag rise, also introduced certain undesirable stability effects. Messerschmitt abandoned the fully swept version and continued building Me 262s with a straight-wing center section and slightly swept outer panel. Not until 1944 did German research show consistent advantages for sweep in high-speed flight.

Greene and his associates picked out and laboriously translated the more promising reports into English in order to find ways to improve the P-86. They were not entirely unacquainted with the stability problems of swept wings, for the Curtiss-Wright XP-55 pusher, a pioneer American swept-wing design, had suffered them both in the wind tunnel and in the destruction of the first prototype. If they were to utilize a swept wing successfully, they would have to improve on German experience, and the Germans had used great ingenuity with little success.

Of all the wing modifications tested by the Germans, the leading-edge slat appeared the most likely to overcome the low-speed stability problems inherent in swept wings, especially if the slats could be made to operate automatically. There was no evidence that the Germans had developed a satisfactory automatic slat—that is, independent of pilot control. Automatic-slat development for the P-86 had to be a completely American effort.

A swept-wing configuration was proposed to Raymond Rice, NAA's vice-president and chief engineer, by the aerodynamics group. After "some considerable reluctance" the advantages were recognized, and Ed Schmued received a research and development order, entitled RD-1369, on August 14, 1945, for a new design study of a swept-wing P-86.

A .23-scale model of a swept-wing version of the P-86 was built in two weeks, and on September 18, the model was installed in the tunnel. A piece of bent metal around the wing's leading edge, representing partial span slats, suggested that satisfactory stability in the low-speed area might be possible, while with the slats removed, the sweep conferred considerable benefit at high subsonic speeds, especially by raising the wing's critical Mach number.

A new plan for a swept-wing P-86 was submitted to the Air Force, which on November 1, 1945, approved the proposal to redesign the XP-86 configuration. Taking advantage of the captured data, the P-86 used the wing plan form designed by the Germans for the proposed fully swept Me 262. Although this wing shape had been discarded by the Germans, far more data on its high-speed tests was available than on any other. This bold decision to adopt the swept wing changed the P-86, soon to be called the Sabre, from a mediocre fighter into a great one.

These improvements lengthened the development time scale, but added greatly to the new fighter's value. Unhampered by these changes, the navy's straight-wing XFJ-1 first flew on September 11, 1946, piloted by Wallace Lien. Top speed with a General Electric J35-GE-2 of 3,820 pounds thrust was 542 mph at 16,000 feet, and service ceiling was 47,400 feet, quite an advance over North American's propeller-driven fighters.

Meanwhile, the XP-86 was in the hands of project engineer A. F. "Tony" Weissenberger and assistant Arthur G. Patch. While the design study from November 22, 1944, to June 3, 1945, took 15,332 man-hours to complete, the prototypes would require 619,138 engineering hours and 301,706 drafting hours from June 3 to their first flight. By January 1946 the engineer effort peaked with the equivalent of 445 full-time personnel on the project, and the basic release of manufacturing drawings was made on August 9.[8]

As on the Mustang, work on a production version began without waiting for flight tests, the NA-151 project being initiated on November 20, 1946. A letter contract for 33 P-86A airplanes was approved by the air force on December 20, and the engineering drawings were released to manufacturing on June 30, 1947.

In 1947, the company's jet program was well under way, with the first XB-45 flight on March 17, powered by four J35-A-7 engines. It had already won the first Air Force production contract for jet bombers, 96 B-45A Tornados, approved on January 20. The Navy also wanted a fast nuclear strike force, one that could operate from carriers. North American's preliminary design group had begun work on the NA-146 project on June 10, 1946, quickly resulting in an order for three XAJ-1 prototypes, joined by the first production contract on July 1, 1947, for the AJ-1 Savage bomber. Combining two R-2800-44W Wasps with a J33 jet engine in the tail to boost top speed, they became the navy's first heavy attack planes.

The first production FJ-1 Fury was flown

on July 8, 1947, although the contract had been cut back from 100 to 30 planes. These fat-bodied fighters went to VF-5A at San Diego, beginning on November 18, commanded by Evan "Pete" Aurand. This unit became the first navy jet squadron to operate from a carrier in squadron strength, and Commander Aurand made the unit's first landing at sea on the USS *Boxer* on March 10, 1948. With a 4,000-pound-thrust Allison-built J35-A-2 (which required overhaul every 10 flying hours), the FJ-1 had a top speed of 547 mph at 9,000 feet and was the last navy fighter armed with six .50-caliber guns; later types used 20-mm cannon.

Since internal fuel capacity of 435 gallons on the XFJ-1 was insufficient for a transcontinental record run planned for the Bendix race, a pair of 165-gallon drop tanks was added to the FJ-1's wing tips to increase ferry range to 1,496 miles. Field-service engineer Ray Forsnar bet Ed Schmued a dinner that these tanks wouldn't come off in flight. When they did fail to separate properly, it was "the only time Ed was ever wrong," claimed Ray.

That problem was corrected with tail fins on the tanks, but another problem arose when the FAA would not allow the tanks to be dropped over land at 30,000 feet. The

North American's first jet fighter was this barrel-shaped XFJ-1 for the navy. *NAA*

Navy pilot solved that by painting the tanks in Air Force colors and dropped them at 30,000 feet while setting a new record. "No report of dead cows or farmers was ever received," says Forsnar.[9]

The most important fighter event of 1947, however, was the first flight of the XP-86 at Muroc on October 10. George S. Welch was the test pilot, an Air Force veteran of the

The navy's first carrier-based strategic bomber, the XAJ-1, used a jet engine for added power. *NAA*

Pearl Harbor attack, who had downed 16 Japanese planes before he returned to civilian life to begin 10 years with NAA. Powered by an Allison J35-A-5 rated at 4,000 pounds static thrust, the unarmed proto-

**The FJ-1 Fury was the first jet fighter to oper-
ate from a carrier in squadron strength.** *NAA*

type weighed 9,730 pounds empty and 13,-
790 pounds for flight tests with 435 gallons
of fuel, about 45 percent heavier than the
P-51H. The wing had a 35-degree sweep-
back, a 37.12-foot span, and an area of 287.9
square feet. These dimensions, along with a
37.54-foot length, remained the same for
the F-86A and E production models. Top
speed was measured at 599 mph at sea level,
618 mph at 14,000 feet, and 575 mph at
35,000 feet.[10]

After the XP-86 was handed to Air Force
pilots for evaluation, Major Kenneth O.
Chilstrom reported that it was superior to
any jet fighter yet offered to the Air Force.
The production contract for 221 got final
approval on October 16, 1947, and the first
F-86A-1 followed the last FJ-1 down the
assembly line; by June 1948, the Air Force
had finally replaced P for Pursuit with F for
Fighter.

Similar to the prototype except for a new
5,200-pound-thrust General Electric J47-
GE-1 engine and armament of six .50-cali-
ber guns, the first production F-86A-1

Sabre, 47-605, was flown by George Welch on May 20, 1948. By September, Air Force pilots had measured top speed, at 13,960 pounds takeoff weight, as 677 mph at sea level and 595 mph at 34,500 feet, with a 49,000-foot service ceiling. A pair of 120-gallon drop tanks could be added under the wings to extend ferry range to 1,052 miles and permit a combat radius of 330 miles. On September 15, Major Robert L. Johnson set a new official world's speed record at 670.-981 mph, flying F-86A 47-611 over a measured course at Muroc.

New fighter projects continued to emerge

Swept wings were introduced to the Air Force by the XP-86 Sabre, flying here with the second XB-45 jet-propelled bomber. *NAA*

from preliminary design, including the NA-157 long-range fighter begun on December 17, 1947, and the NA-164 all-weather interceptor begun on March 28, 1949. The former project was first called the F-86C and then became the YF-93A. While the first prototype was flown by Welch on January 25, 1950, it was not selected by the Air Force for production. More successful was the NA-164, the world's first single-seat all-weather interceptor, with radar, and rockets instead of guns. It was known as the YF-86D when flown on December 22, 1949, then as the F-95A, and finally ordered into mass production as the F-86D (NA-165).

How much engineering had grown can be seen by comparing the hours necessary for the F-86D interceptor with that of the Mustang in 1940. Aerodynamicists had spent 72,520 hours before the first flight of the F-86D, 12 times more than the 6,000 hours spent on the first Mustang.

The second F-86D-1 all-weather interceptor appeared in June 1951 with rocket armament and a radar-directed fire-control system.

Wind-tunnel tests took 21 times longer than had been necessary for the Mustang up to its first flight. Stress engineering was 116,075 hours for the F-86D, but only 2,985 hours for the P-51. Flight-test engineering before the F-86D's first flight required 84,817 hours compared to just 725 hours for the Mustang. And the F-86D model was preceded by 66,512 hours of "research," an item completely missing from the Mustang's totals.

The bill for engineering hours before the first F-86D flight totaled 1,131,992 hours, more than 14 times that of the first Mustang. Electronics equipment of the interceptor alone cost more than had four P-51 airframes.

POSTWAR MUSTANG SERVICE

After World War II ended, so many Mustangs became surplus to Air Force needs that foreign air forces took advantage of the chance to add the war's best fighter to their inventory. This process began even before the end of the war in Europe.

Sweden had become interested in the Mustang after examining P-51Bs that had run out of gas and landed in that neutral nation in May 1944. After Sweden asked for some Mustangs to replace obsolete Italian-made fighters, the Air Force agreed to fly 50 P-51Ds to Sweden in March 1945. The P-51 was known as the J26 by the Swedish air force, which interned or purchased 161 Mustangs by 1948. Israel got 25 of these in 1951 and used them in the 1956 war.

China had been promised 164 Mustangs to replace the P-40s in their air force, but only 10 P-51Cs had arrived by June 30, 1945, and of 50 allocated Mustangs arriving in Asia by VJ day, 29 had been diverted to American forces and only 21 received by the Chinese. Deliveries continued after the war to equip three Nationalist Chinese fighter groups for the civil war.

Nationalist Chinese fighter strength was 200 P-51Ds (of which 65 percent were operational) and 53 P-47Ds on July 31, 1947. After the Communist victory, some served the PRCAF (People's Republic of China Air Force) until replaced by Soviet jet fighters. One P-51D-25NA, 44-73930, is still on display in a Peking museum, with a placard stating that it flew over to the celebration proclaiming the People's Republic on October 1, 1949.

Canada purchased 130 P-51Ds after the war, beginning in March 1947, and during 1948, Switzerland and Italy got 100 each. Fifty Mustangs acquired by the Netherlands East Indies, now Indonesia, in 1945 and others obtained by the Philippine air force were involved in fighting local rebels.

The Dominican Republic became the first Latin American country to get the Mustang when six were ferried from Miami from June 6 to September 29, 1948, and 42 P-51Ds were received from Sweden in 1952–53. When the Dominican air force disposed of its last 12 surviving Mustangs in 1984, they were sold to an American dealer for $300,000 each, almost six times their price brand-new 40 years earlier! Eight more Latin American countries would use small numbers of Mustangs between 1950 and 1975.[11]

MUSTANG RACERS

The Mustang began its career as a racer in the first postwar National Air Races, which began on August 30, 1946. Paul Mantz had purchased 475 surplus government aircraft after the war and had stripped and modified a P-51C-10NT, 44-10947, to get 2,270 hp from its V-1650-7 and increase internal fuel capacity to 875 gallons by filling the wing's interior with fuel, the so-called wet wings.

Flying his glossy, bright red racer, registered NX1202, in the 2,048-mile Bendix race from Van Nuys, California, to Cleveland, Ohio, Mantz came in first with a 435-mph average speed. Jacqueline Cochran came in second with a P-51C-10, NX28388, carrying drop tanks and her lucky race number, 13, while another Mantz-owned wet-winged P-51C-10, NX1204, flown by Tommy Mayson, won third prize.

Mantz used the same Mustang to win the 1947 Bendix with a 460-mph average speed and went on to take his third first-place victory in 1948 with another P-51C-10, registered N1204. Mustangs placed in the top four slots in all three races, and Paul Mantz

The first famous civilian Mustang was P-51C-10 44-10947, registered NX1202, in which Paul Mantz won the 1946 and 1947 Bendix races. In 1951, as Excalibur III, it became the first single-seat aircraft to fly over the North Pole. *SDAM*

was the only Bendix race pilot to win three consecutive times. He did not return in 1949, so the Bendix was won by Joe DeBona in an F-6C, registered N5528N, while second and third places were taken by Mantz Mustangs N1204 and N1202, flown by other pilots.

The 300-mile Thompson Trophy low-level races run at Cleveland, with their tight turns around pylons, provided tougher competition from a special Bell P-39Q and Goodyear F2G-1 "Super" Corsairs with big

Jacqueline Cochran's P-51C racer, NX28388. *SDAM*

Paul Mantz won his third transcontinental Bendix race in this P-51C-10, 42-103831, registered NX1204. *SDAM*

4,000-hp R-4360 engines. These contests ended sadly in 1949 when Bill Odom's P-51C, modified with unusual wing-tip radiators, crashed into a home, killing a mother, her baby, and the pilot. This tragedy, along with the demands of the Korean War, stopped national closed-course unlimited air racing in America. Not until unlimited racing was revived at Reno in 1964 would Mustangs show how fast they could be made to go, with imaginative modifications.

The ill-fated racer "Beguine," with unique wing-tip radiators. *SDAM*

MUSTANGS CALLED BACK TO WAR

The United States Air Force defense posture, before the Korean War, was based on long-range strategic bombing with nuclear weapons, protection by all-weather interceptors, with jet fighters for short-range air superiority. Close support for ground troops was so little considered that the "A" classification for Attack aircraft had been dropped.

As Mustangs, redesignated F-51s in June 1948, were sold abroad or salvaged for spare parts, they were replaced by jet fighters, and

the Air Force inventory dwindled. More Mustangs were assigned to the Air National Guard as mission aircraft than any other aircraft. From 1946 to 1957, 75 of the 98 ANG squadrons used F-51D, F-51H, or RF-51D aircraft.

When the Korean War began on Sunday, June 25, 1950, there still were 897 F-51 and 38 RF-51 Mustangs in the Air Force inventory and 764 Mustangs in the Air National Guard. The F-51D was chosen for war because there were not enough P-51H spare parts in the inventory to sustain long-term combat operations. Just as the Mustang had been called into Air Force service in 1942 as

When the Korean War began, the Air Force still had lots of Mustangs, like this P-51D-30 at Luke Field in September 1950. Pilot Roy Schellhous later flew jet fighters in Korea. *SDAM*

the A-36, it was again recalled to war as a close-support aircraft.

The first North American aircraft to fight, however, were the F-826 Twin Mustangs of the 68th and 339th All-Weather Fighter Squadrons, which on the war's third day, June 27, shot down the first three enemy Yak-9 fighters destroyed by Americans. Flying from Itazuke, in Japan, the long-range F-82s had been protecting the evacuation of American civilians from Seoul. They flew 1,868 sorties over Korea before being replaced by jets.

MUSTANGS IN KOREA

On Thursday, June 29, 1950, Mustangs entered the Korean War when 10 F-51Ds, painted in Republic of Korea markings, were flown in by American pilots. Led by Major Dean Hess, they were to protect Suwon airfield, where General MacArthur had just arrived to take command of the defense of South Korea. All four enemy fighters attempting to attack the airfield that day were shot down while the general watched.

The next Mustangs available for Korea were about 30 F-51Ds stored in Japan for the Air Force, so the 51st Provisional Squadron was hastily organized and flown to the airstrip at Taegu. Fortunately, most of the pilots were veterans, for they had to begin flying combat missions against ground targets on July 15 and were soon joined by the 40th Fighter Squadron at P'o-hang. An RAAF squadron with 26 Australian-built Mustangs and a South African squadron, using USAF P-51Ds, also came to Korea.[12]

On July 23, 145 more Mustangs, requisitioned from Air National Guard units, arrived in Japan aboard the carrier *Boxer* and the Air Force could build up its Mustang force in Korea. Nearly all of the 62,607 F-51 missions during the Korean War were for

These Mustangs in Korea display the markings of the South African and Republic of Korea air forces, although the latter were flown by American pilots. *USAF*

close support of the ground forces or for tactical reconnaissance. They dropped 12,-909 tons of bombs and 15,221 tons of napalm, fired 183,221 rockets, shot down 19 enemy propeller-driven planes, and destroyed 28 planes on the ground.

The last Air Force F-51D combat mission was flown on January 23, 1953, some eight years after that model was built. Total Mustang losses in Korea were 335 planes with 264 pilots killed or missing, including 172 F-51s lost to ground fire, 10 to enemy jet fighters, 44 missing or unknown, and the rest to accidents.

The reason for these losses was given by Ed Schmued: "Unfortunately the P-51 was a high-altitude fighter. It was used in ground support work, which is absolutely hopeless, because a .30-caliber bullet can rip a hole in the radiator and you fly two more minutes before your engine freezes up. Flying a P-51 in ground support was almost a suicide mission. It is unfortunate that the airplane had been used for ground support, but in the Korean conflict we were short of airplanes and anything had to do. This was the reason for using the P-51 in low-level operations."

These difficult missions, along with those of the B-26 and B-29 bombers, as well as the F-80C jet fighters, did break the back of the North Korean invasion and enabled the United Nations forces to roll back the enemy and advance into North Korea. It seemed that the war could be over in five months. But a Chinese army was gathering above the Yalu River, covered by squadrons of swept-wing MiG-15 jet fighters, and a new level of warfare was about to begin.

In November 1950, the inexhaustible resources of Chinese manpower turned the tide of ground warfare, forcing the Americans and their allies back to the narrow midpoint of the Korean peninsula. Sustained air attacks on enemy supply lines were essential to match the enemy superiority in numbers. But just as in 1943 when German fighters were on the verge of defeating American strategic bombing, enemy fighters over Korea seemed about to block American air power.

MIG ALLEY FIGHTS

The MiG-15 was so superior in performance to the straight-winged F-80 that the older Lockheeds could not be depended on to protect slower propeller-driven bombers. Fortunately, the MiG pilots lacked the experience and skill that had made German fighter pilots so deadly, and they were often outmaneuvered by the Lockheeds in the first jet-vs.-jet battles. But 14 F-80s were lost at a cost of 6 MiGs, and 10 F-51s were downed for only a couple of "probables."

Mustang fighter bombers bounced by MiGs had to evade their attackers by twisting and turning; trying to escape by speeding away was usually fatal. Unlike 1945, the jets could not be hit at their bases, since these were across the Yalu River in China.

Just as in World War II, it was a North American fighter, the F-86 Sabre, that turned the tide. The enemy had many fighters available and the MiGs had the possibility of winning air superiority, protecting Communist forces from air attack, and opening the skies to their own bombers,

Four-plane formation of the F-86A Sabres that quickly established their superiority in MiG alley. *USAF*

but this much-feared development never occurred. Had there been no Sabres, the enemy could have won control of the air over Korea. United Nations forces would then almost certainly have had to leave Korea, and the war would have been lost.

When the MiG threat first entered the picture, the 4th Fighter-Interceptor Wing was ordered to Korea on November 8, 1950. Most of their F-86A-5 Sabres left San Diego on the escort carrier *Cape Esperance* on November 29, unloaded in Japan, and flew to Kimpo airbase, near Seoul, in December. These pilots were highly experienced veterans, including some World War II aces who had been flying jet fighters before most of their Chinese adversaries had been up in any aircraft. Their 4th Wing had achieved a spectacular record of 1,000 victories fighting in Spitfires, Thunderbolts, and Mustangs against the Germans, and now their Sabres were tuned up by a year of tactical practice.

Loaded with six .50-caliber guns and two 120-gallon drop tanks, four Sabres took off for their first combat mission on December 17. They had one advantage over their propeller-driven predecessors six years before: no seven-hour escort missions. Forty minutes after takeoff, they were flying south of the Yalu at 32,000 feet when they saw four Chinese MiG-15s. They attacked, and Lt. Col. Bruce H. Hinton scored the first F-86 victory. On December 22, the enemy struck first and downed the first F-86 lost, but four hours later, six MiGs were shot down by the Sabres.

"MiG Alley," as pilots called the area near the Yalu, saw the first air battles with jets on both sides. Although the enemy had the advantage of always being able to choose the time and place of each fight,

avoiding battle whenever they wished, the North American F-86 pilots consistently outfought the MiGs. They proved that the best aircraft the enemy then had to offer was not enough to win a single significant air battle.

By the end of the war on July 27, 1953, four USAF Wings (the 4th, 8th, 18th, and 51st) with Sabres flew 87,177 sorties, destroyed 792 MiGs in the air, along with 18 enemy propeller-driven types, and lost 78 Sabres downed by MiGs, 19 to ground fire, and 26 to unknown causes or missing. Accidents brought total F-86 losses in Korea to 224.[13]

During the Korean War, Colonel William F. Barnes was the Air Force plant representative. He met each Thursday morning with contractor and Air Force staff members to discuss the most pressing problems. "Edgar Schmued was the North American engineering representative to these meetings, and it was his knowledgeable, clear explanation of the proposed solutions that was the most convincing in expediting the modification's acceptance."

Since Wright Field's contractual approval was required for each modification, "Ed and I would get on the phone to the System Program Office (SPO) chief. Ed would explain the fix, and I would verify that we had thoroughly investigated the solution and verified it by test. In most cases, Ed's straightforward, honest explanation would convince the SPO chief that approval should be granted, thus advancing the incorporation point by as many as 25 airplanes."

Fighters built by another manufacturer, Republic, also profited from Ed's ability. Early in 1951, three F-84s had crashed while making high-speed passes before crowds at air shows. The accident-investigating teams concluded that there was a stability and control problem that the manufacturer needed to correct.

While the builders accepted some responsibility, they felt that the pilots had overstressed the aircraft. The Air Force insisted that something must be done, and assembled an industry-wide meeting at the manufacturer's plant on Long Island, New York. At Air Force request, North American named Ed Schmued as their representative at the meeting, and "Bill" Barnes was also present, due to the experience he had gained with stability problems while performing acceptance tests on the F-86D. Barnes recalls that during several days' discussion, the company still seemed to decline responsibility.

Finally, the meeting's chairman, Colonel Mark Bradley, went around the room asking each industry representative to state what he felt to be the problem's cause and recommended solution. There was a wide divergence of opinion until, as Colonel Barnes wrote, "Ed Schmued stood up and, in his distinguished Germanic accent, succinctly stated that he felt the rather light longitudinal stick force resulted in overcontrol in rough air, particularly when flying in tight formation.

"This induced wing bending movements which excited the wing-tip tanks on that airplane, which then aggravated the ailerons into flutter and subsequent wing structural failures. Ed recommended that a four-pound bob weight be designed into the longitudinal flight-control system to increase the stick force and that fins be added to the tip tanks." After Ed's suggestions

were approved by Colonel Bradley and implemented, that aircraft's accident rate declined drastically.[14]

Back at North American, part of the Sabre's success came from improvements made to its flying qualities. The F-86E, introduced into Korea in June 1951, had a new horizontal tail surface whose stabilizer and elevators were operated as one unit, greatly improving control effectiveness. Fred R. Prill was the project engineer.

The next version to appear was the F-86F, powered by a 5,910-pound-thrust J47-GE-27, which reached Korea in June 1952, and steadily improved until the F-86F-30 came in January 1953 with extended leading-edge wings to improve high-altitude maneuverability. Performance of the F-86A-5 had included a top speed of 679 mph at sea level and 601 mph at 35,000 feet with a combat radius of 330 miles, but the F-86F-30 did 695 mph at sea level and 608 mph at 35,000 feet, with a combat radius of 458 miles.

While the lighter MiG-15 was a good interceptor, with a better rate of climb and ceiling, and heavy-caliber guns, it had a dangerous spin tendency that caused some to self-destruct before the eyes of American opponents. But the most important reason for Air Force success was the experience and skill of the pilots, like Captain James Jabara, the first American jet ace, and Captain Joseph McConnell, Jr., who scored 16 victories.

A "Blue F-86" for the Navy was begun as NA-181 on January 30, 1951, and three XFJ-2 prototypes were ordered on March 8. Essentially the same as an F-86E, but armed with four 20-mm guns, the first was flown on December 27 by Bob Hoover. Two more XFJ-1s followed with carrier arrester gear,

catapult points, and lengthened nose-wheel leg, but without guns.

Anxious for swept-wing fighters to match the MiGs, the Navy ordered the FJ-2 production version, to be built in Columbus, Ohio, after an order of Air Force F-86Fs were finished at the new North American facility. The first FJ-2 wasn't delivered until December 1952, and only 25 were accepted by the end of 1953. All 200 FJ-2 Fury fighters went to eight Marine squadrons, and the Columbus engineers concentrated on development of the FJ-3 series with the J65 engine.

Production of the F-86F continued at Inglewood for the Air Force until December 28, 1956. North American built 6,250 Sabres, while 1,815 were made in Canada and 112 in Australia, and 26 foreign nations used the Sabre. The Sabre's last big fight was in the September 1965 war between Pakistan and India.

A SUPERSONIC SUPER SABRE

The Korean War inspired Air Force demands for the F-100 Super Sabre, the first supersonic fighter in production anywhere. It had started in preliminary design in 1949 with research studies called the Sabre 45, for the 45-degree sweep planned for the wings. On January 19, 1951, engineering work began on the NA-180 day fighter, which had the 45-degree sweep, a Pratt & Whitney J57 two-stage turbojet rated at 14,800-pound thrust with afterburner, and

the first use of heat-resisting titanium in an airplane.

An Air Force mock-up inspection was made on November 7, 1951, and the company was encouraged to initiate a production version, the NA-192, on November 20. A letter contract for two YF-100 prototypes was issued on January 3, 1952, and the first 23 production aircraft, designated F-100A-1, were ordered on February 11, with an inspection of the revised mock-up on March 21.[15]

The design emerging from these contracts promised to be the fastest, but also the heaviest and most expensive ($1,014,910 per F-100A) single-seat fighter ever built up to that time. It would also become the last production fighter series built at North American. Weighing 18,279 pounds empty and 28,965 pounds gross when loaded with 1,307 gallons of fuel and four 20-mm guns in the long fuselage, the YF-100 would exceed the speed of sound on its first flight by George Welch on May 25, 1953.

But over 10 months earlier, Edgar Schmued had left North American Aviation to become an "independent consulting engineer." His resignation became effective on August 1, 1952.[16] The Engineering Department at North American was then far larger than that which had produced the Mustang. A new era in aircraft design had arrived, an era in which individualism was submerged in a team effort.

North American Aviation could now boast that it produced more military aircraft than any other single company in the world and had become a corporate giant of the first rank. But success of a particular design on a national scale now seemed to depend less on simple merit and more on the political situation.

These F-86F Sabres are with the 4th Fighter Wing in Korea. *SDAM*

Edgar Schmued near the end of his service at North American. *CS*

Before Ed left, faces at the top of North American's engineering hierarchy were still familiar; Raymond Rice was still chief engineer, with Carl Hansen and Ed Schmued as assistant chief engineers for administration and for design, respectively, but now the organization chart listed eight chief engineers, each with his own large staff, as well as an administrative engineer and a field service manager.

Howard A. Evans was chief designer and Julius S. Villepique was group leader, confidential design. Richard Schleicher was still chief structures engineer and Ed Horkey chief technical engineer. Dick Prible was chief components engineer, while other chiefs headed the Project, Power-plant,

and Electrical sections. Cutting across these departments were project engineers and supervisors for the AJ-1, A2J-1, B-45, XFJ-2 and FJ-2, F-86D, F-86F, F-86H, YF-100, and F-100A. Part of the engineering staff had moved to Columbus, Ohio, where deliveries had begun in May 1952 on the F-86F-20, and where production F-86H and Navy fighter developments would be built.

The problems with the F-100 seemed to suggest that corporate structure itself might become a difficulty. "By the time initial flight testing of the prototype was completed on September 25, [1953] three major deficiencies were confirmed, all of which required correction before the F-100A could be considered an acceptable combat weapon system." Although the F-100A was said to have reached "Mach 1.34 during level flight at 35,000 feet," its entrance into operational service was delayed. On November 10, 1954, all F-100A aircraft were grounded following six major accidents, one of which claimed the life of company test pilot George Welch.[17] It would take a lot of work and modifications before the F-100 became a successful fighter.

While Edgar did not say much to his colleagues about his reasons for leaving, it was apparent that his inclination toward working with individuals at their own drawing boards, as well as his concern with the increasing size and cost of fighter designs, had made him uncomfortable with the bureaucracy of a company that had become an industrial giant.

Aerodynamicist Ed Horkey offers this viewpoint: "During the war everybody pulled together, but there was some undertow of political alliances. Stan Smithson in production and Ed Schmued were very close to Kindelberger. There was another faction of Atwood, Rice, etc."[18] Not until many years later, in a letter to an official of Rockwell International, the corporation that had bought out North American in 1967, did Ed express his real feelings.

"At the time I resigned from NAA, Mr. Kindelberger's health appeared to be failing, and I faced the possibility of seeing the Atwood-Rice team taking over the management. . . . Their adverse attitude towards me made it mandatory to find employment elsewhere. At that time I had made suggestions to improve the combat capabilities of the F-100. These were turned down and it gave me the opportunity to resign from NAA with a legitimate reason. (The U.S. Air Force later demanded the changes I had proposed.)"[19]

Since Ed was 52, below the retirement age of 55, no pension was offered to him for his 22-plus years with the company. The departure party held for Schmued when he left North American is remembered as "the biggest ever held for a company executive." According to Al Kustra, then general supervisor of the chief engineer's office, "Everyone loved and respected him. He was truly a very sensitive, warm, and compassionate person. When he had to send any one of his staff on a business trip, he felt sorry for the family left behind. So he would do what no other executive had done, to my knowledge. He would send a box of candy or flowers to the wife with a note."

This supersonic YF-100 began the last successful North American fighter family. *NAA*

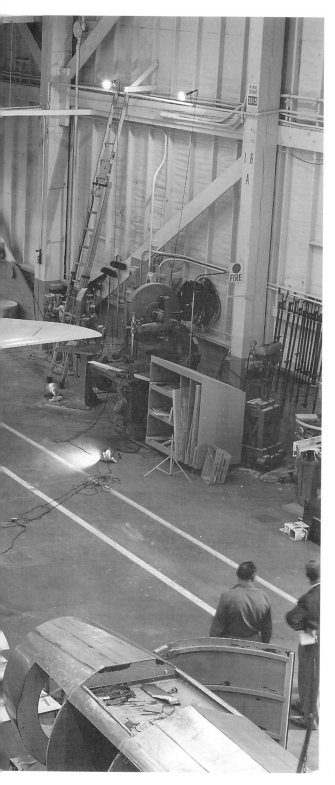

CHAPTER NINE

Northrop Launches a New Fighter

The Northrop Fang mock-up. Serial number is fictitious. *Northrop*

dgar Schmued's original intention was to work as an independent consultant, acting as vice-president of an organization called the Aircraftsmen Company, with Julius Villepique as chief engineer. Their first project was a small-caliber spin-stabilized rocket that would be more accurate than the small fin-stabilized rockets then being used by Air Force interceptors. A rocket development program was outlined in a November 14, 1952, report.

Preliminary design data was also begun on a "ramming fighter" that could intercept enemy bombers by climbing to 40,000 feet in 3.5 minutes, attack at Mach 1.53 speed (over 1,000 mph), and hit them with its steel nose, for a 100-percent kill probability, the pilot then ejecting from his armored cockpit. An alternative nose section could be installed to fire 16 of their new spin rockets.

Designed around a 6,100-pound-thrust Westinghouse XJ46-WE-2, the delta wing, 14-foot-4-inch-span fighter weighed 8,680 pounds at takeoff and 7,472 pounds when landing on its landing mat. Endurance with 400 gallons of fuel was 46 minutes, including 5 minutes at full power. Schmued and Villepique later applied for a patent on a rearward-firing rocket-launching system on April 26, 1954, that was apparently intended for a two-place aircraft.[1]

Edgar's new work was suddenly interrupted when he was recruited by Northrop Aircraft Inc., at Hawthorne, California (a few miles southeast of Inglewood), to give that ailing company a new start in fighter design. He was named vice-president in charge of engineering, and was then 52 years old.

Suddenly Ed found himself as part of top management, in the role played at North American by his old boss, Raymond Rice. Now Ed would be pointing at goals, making policy decisions, and choosing and coaching department heads, instead of doing his own drawings. He had become part of "a radical re-orientation of Northrop," according to *Interavia* magazine:

In engineering circles and amongst air industry financial underwriters, the feeling is that Schmued may prove to be "just what the doctor ordered" for Northrop's research and development ailments. Close friends feel that during his North American association his talents, to a certain degree, were submerged. At the same time, they feel that his weathering of personal disappointment with North American was maturing, and that any unusual new designs he may propose to Northrop will display a profitable tempering of enthusiasm by a strong appreciation of development and production problems gained at North American.

John K. Northrop, the company's founder, who retired November 20, 1952, was replaced as company president by Oliver P. Echols, who had been the wartime general in charge of the Air Force Material Command. Although the factory was busy with 20,000 employees working on large contracts for the F-89 two-place, all-weather jet fighter and the SM-62 Snark long-range cruise missile, both programs had serious problems. Even more worrisome was the lack of any promising designs aimed at the future military market. In his own words, Ed felt that "Jack Northrop left me an incredible mess of mismanagement and technical incompetence."[2]

Vice-president Schmued "wasted no time hiring a chief engineer. He placed a telephone call to Dr. William F. Ballhaus, chief of preliminary design at Convair, Fort Worth." A 34-year-old graduate of Stanford and Cal Tech, Ballhaus had previously been at Douglas, where he had been project engineer of the XA3D-1 carrier-based bomber. "Schmued began with such an attractive offer that Ballhaus, renowned even then as a tough bargainer, accepted almost immediately. Chided by a Convair associate as to why he would leave a much larger company to join Northrop, Ballhaus responded, 'Just think what a *chief engineer* can do!' "[3]

Ballhaus soon recruited fellow Stanford graduates Welko E. Gasich as chief of preliminary design and Thomas V. Jones as assistant to the chief engineer, while Ward Dennis was hired to head up weapons systems analysis. The hiring philosophy was to attract good talent and pay them well, getting more useful work out of a few high-priced men than out of a larger number of lower-paid inferior engineers.

While building this team to create new military programs for Northrop, Schmued also brought in so many North American veterans like Villepique that, as a joke, the Hawthorne office was dubbed "South American." A new concept in engineering organization, with a staff of about 3,000 by 1954, combined the project and group systems. Instead of separating the teams in remote offices, Schmued told a reporter, "We will put everybody into one large room. If I want to check the state of the art in general design, I walk across the rows. If I want to determine the status of a particular project, I walk up and down the rows of desks and tables." Pure research contracts belong in universities, he added. "We only want to work on projects that have a direct bearing on products."[4]

Among the nine builders of American jet fighters during the Korean War, Northrop had been noted for big, complicated, all-weather fighters like the wartime P-61 Black Widow and the F-89 Scorpion, which the Air Force had grounded on September 22, 1952. A faulty wing-structure design had forced a modification of the aircraft, and not until November 1953 was full production resumed and previous aircraft returned to service use.[5] After its redesign and modification, the F-89 had an important place in the Air Force inventory as the only plane that could handle the long-range interception problem.

The new design team determined to reverse the trend of increasing cost and size. Schmued's first project at Northrop was the lightweight N-102, with a thin delta wing. Before Ed went to Northrop, the company's heavy fighters had had names like the P-61 Black Widow and the F-89 Scorpion. Ed said "no more naming our airplanes after vermin," so the N-102 became the "Fang."

This single-seat day fighter could be powered by the latest power plants, either the Pratt & Whitney J57 used by the F-100, the Wright J65 of the Douglas A4D-1, or the General Electric J79 projected for the Lockheed F-104. Armament could consist of a single 20-mm T-171 gun with 600 rounds or eight different installations, including a choice of forty 1.5-inch rockets, two 20-mm T-160, or two 30-mm T-182 guns, according to the preliminary specification issued in July 1953.[6] As assignors to Northrop, Schmued and Gasich applied for a patent on the proprietary Fang design on December 5, 1955.[7]

Wing span of the Fang was 30 feet 6 inches, its length was 45 feet 10 inches, and its wing area 366 square feet. If a J79 giving 14,350-pound thrust with afterburner was fitted, the takeoff weight was 18,760 pounds and a Mach 2 top speed, 59,300 feet service ceiling, and 2,030-mile ferry range was expected.[8]

Other Fang design features included exceptional maintenance accessibility through the use of removable panels or doors and a hinged windshield and cockpit canopy as a means of providing easy access to instrumentation. It was estimated that the Fang could be serviced from landing to takeoff in six minutes. A full-scale wooden mock-up was assembled and painted white with a fictitious serial number.

The design was hampered by the size of the big and expensive engines then available, which left little room in the fuselage for anything else and increased the consumer price. No orders were in sight, so the design team moved to another concept, and the mock-up was presented to the Northrop Aeronautical Institute in 1956.

A PHILOSOPHY OF WEAPONS DESIGN

Thomas V. Jones, who at 36 became corporate vice-president, developmental planning, saw the problem of future design in economic terms. He originated the "life-cycle cost" philosophy of weapons design, that each weapon should be measured in terms of the cost over its entire life span. Applied to fighters, this meant small size, light weight (since cost rises per pound), and simple maintenance.

At the end of World War II, Mustang fighters cost some $50,000 each, a small portion of the national war budget. When the Korean War began, the F-86A cost $178,000 each, but only five years later the Air Force was spending over $1 million for each new fighter, and it was apparent that each future decade would bring rapid escalation. Even in 1957, Tom Jones wrote, "Today it is perfectly possible for a designer to develop a completely feasible weapon system which would absorb the entire defense budget of the United States." But, as company consultant Lt. Gen. Ennis C. Whitehead said, "Common sense tells us we must have national solvency along with national security."[9]

During the rapid expansion of World War II and the Korean War, the country "was on a technological binge," said Jones. Successful weapons systems may end a hot war within a limited time period. But during the prolonged cold war, weapons had to be built and kept up for decades. This is an appalling burden for advanced large nations and can be ruinous for smaller or less-industrialized ones.

Edgar Schmued's own thoughts on this policy were expressed in his article in the

Los Angeles Times, July 31, 1955. "What can make the best weapons platform this country can put into the air today, better than something a potential enemy might produce 10 years from now? There are many factors involved . . . but there is one of considerable importance that often is overlooked. I like to refer to this special element of aeronautical superiority as 'engineered growth potential' or 'longevity.' For short, I refer to it as the L-factor.

"To make the best use of the L-factor an engineer must put the professional standards of his job first. Like a doctor, there are times when he must prescribe something which is not palatable to the patient, or in this case, the customer.

"Military airplanes are bought through competitions, and price is important. The best airplane may cost considerably more than a skimpy design good enough for the immediate need. But the really conscientious engineer will put the long-term good of the customer and the country first.

"Think back on the military airplanes which have impressed the world as the best in their categories during the last two decades. Almost invariably you will find that these were airplanes with an extended life of aerial superiority. Airplanes that were able to hold their own for only a short period of time, in calendar terms, never seem able to acquire the reputation for greatness.

"It is not difficult for an engineering manager to direct the design of an airplane that will be the best for a year or so. But it takes considerable skill, and also the ethical qualities respected by all professional men, to design an airplane that will be superior to the enemy's best aircraft for as long as 10 years. It is the L-factor that spells the difference between one year of superiority and ten.

"The engineering manager is confronted with the need for the L-factor as soon as he relates his design proposals to the nation's economy. When we look at our financial resources in relation to defense costs, we find we are not as rich as we once thought. Our dollars do not buy as many airplanes as they once did. The reason is the increased complexity, increased weight and the requirements for new, more costly methods of manufacture and more costly materials.

"If we are to remain strong in the air, we must continue to improve our military aircraft rapidly. But if we are not to upset our economy we must keep our defense costs under control. . . .

"The armed forces—like the average housewife—have to manage their budgets with a great deal of care and caution. Most contracts for new airplanes are awarded on the basis of design competitions. Contractors are invited to enter design proposals based on requirements for a definite type of airplane to perform a specific mission. The winning contractor is picked from these proposals. The unit cost of the airplanes—usually directly related to weight—is a powerful factor in award of the contract.

"Thus an engineer is tempted to enter the competition with the very smallest airframe that can possibly do the job, because the lighter the airframe the lower will be the cost. This is why airplanes that are acquired through the normal bidding processes often suffer at the outset from being too skimpy—and thus short-lived. . . ."[10]

The Northrop organization would build its future success on this life-cost concept by designing less-expensive high-performance aircraft. They recognized that many allied countries had neither the funds nor the trained manpower to fly and maintain ever more complex aircraft. It is better to have an effective force in readiness than a smaller force of higher-performing aircraft that are mostly grounded for maintenance. But this concept was more radical than it appeared and would take more than six years to gain acceptance.

The difficulty with the concept is that wartime fighter leaders naturally think in terms of maximum performance, without regard to cost. Military engagements are seen in terms of "iron on the battlefield" at decisive moments. But modern international tensions are often beyond short-term military solutions, and military technology must fit economic realities. Weapons must provide "(1) a force effectiveness which (2) will perform a given mission at (3) a cost which does not preclude the performance of other essential missions."[11]

Northrop itself had prepared a high-cost design and was one of three companies involved in the Air Force's General Operational Requirement (GOR) 114 competition, dated October 6, 1955, for a Mach 3 two-place, long-range interceptor. Rival North American's last fighter design would win a contract to develop the XF-108, but Tom Jones was not too disappointed. He suspected that the costs involved would kill that project, especially as funds were being poured into intercontinental ballistic missiles that would leave little use for such big interceptors. He was right, for the whole program was wiped out in September 1959, before a prototype was built, after the expenditure of $141.9 million.[12]

DESIGNING THE T-38 AND F-5

Northrop instead concentrated its effort on the N-156, a lightweight fighter originally planned to fit a Navy desire for a supersonic aircraft that could operate from small carriers. Such performance might be made possible, in the first place, by General Electric's development of the J85, a small lightweight jet engine originally intended for air-breathing Quail decoy missiles. A pair of such engines, if satisfactory power was offered, could be the basis of the small, supersonic, but inexpensive fighter they wanted.

The navy changed its mind about small ships and decided to use only big supercarriers, but the original N-156 was further developed, using the area-rule concept of narrowing the fuselage at the wing roots and cambered leading edges on the wing. An extensive process of investigating the future world fighter market was begun to determine exactly what features would make potential customers interested in buying the plane.

By January 1955, Northrop could present the government with a proposal for a single-place N-156F fighter and a two-place N-156T trainer, each offering supersonic (Mach 1.3) speed with twin 3,600-pound-thrust J85-GE-5 engines. It was the trainer that interested the Air Force that year, for they wanted to replace their Lockheed T-33s with a supersonic trainer appropriate for the new generation of aircraft.

Two-place versions of the North American F-100 and Lockheed F-104 were becoming available, but were so expensive that a Northrop technical proposal in March 1956 to build the N-156T was attractive. Northrop had sent a briefing team, led by

Mock-up of Northrop N-156T helped win T-38 trainer contract. *Northrop*

**The first YT-38 is seen with N-156F mock-up
in background.** *Northrop*

John R. Alison, vice-president of Marketing (Major General USAF, retired), and including Edgar Schmued and Welko Gasich, on a tour of Air Force bases. They found the officers impressed by the trainer version, but unenthusiastic about the fighter proposal.

On June 15, 1956, the Air Force declared Northrop the winner of the supersonic trainer competition, with a letter of intent for two service-test and one static-test aircraft. After the mock-up board review in October, a contract for the first four YT-38A Talon trainers was placed in December 1956.

When General Clarence "Bill" Irvine, then head of Air Force aircraft procurement, came to Hawthorne to see the T-38 mock-up, he was escorted by Schmued and Gasich. A longtime admirer of the Mustang and Sabre, General Irvine liked the clean lines, and put his arm around Ed's shoulder, saying, "Now, that's a Schmued design if I ever saw one."[13]

Ed winked at Welko, who grinned back. The exchange reflected an early difference of opinion in the design team; Schmued had originally favored putting the engines in pods suspended below the wings so that power plants might be more easily changed in the future, but had yielded to the insistent arguments of his preliminary design chief that the engines be enclosed within the aft fuselage.

With the trainer on the way, the company turned its attention to the N-156F, concentrating on marketing a fighter whose life-cycle costs promised huge economies compared with other Century series fighters (F-100 to F-106), which used over twice the fuel and required far more maintenance. By December 14, 1956, preliminary design had completed the F-156F drawings (PD-2879D) and established the configuration that, except for the vertical tail, would become famous as the F-5. But at the moment, no customers had yet appeared.[14]

In time, the T-38 and F-156F designs would provide the company with three decades of good business, once the marketing task was accomplished. Meanwhile, Northrop completed production of its big Scorpion night fighters with the last F-89H finished in August 1956, while its Palmdale facility was busy with fitting MB-1 Genie rockets to 350 modified F-89Ds, which became the F-89J, the first nuclear-armed interceptor.

Ed Horkey also consulted for Ed and Northrop's president on the Snark missile as well as the T-38 and F-5. He remembers that as far back as 1952, "Ed was telling me about some new material . . . kind of a radar absorption crystalline or similar material you could apply, or spray, on ducts or large surfaces that would make them nonvisible to radar. He even showed me some data on it. I'll bet that Ed's inputs eventually went into the Northrop stealth bomber. This puts him about 20 to 30 years ahead of his time."[15]

With the original major design problems solved, Schmued now felt confident he had accomplished his goals for Northrop, for not only was the company on the road to success, given some patience, but air defense at a more reasonable price was now possible. Now he could return to his 1952 objective of independent design and invention. He retired from full-time management duties on October 15, 1957, continuing to serve the company as technical consultant for another year.[16]

His salary as a Northrop vice-president had been $48,500 per year, dropping to $25,000 as a part-time consultant. He and Helen had bought land in Rolling Hills Estates, at the suggestion of their friend, Dr. Hofferber. In January 1956, they moved into a new two-story house built by Cliff May at 5051 Palos Verde Drive North, so that after 20 years in California, Ed might sample a bit of the state's comfortable lifestyle. Their daughter Sandra was 12, and the experiences of parenthood could be augmented by the less-demanding role of grandparent to his own son's six-year-old boy, Laurence.

THE F-5 GOES INTO PRODUCTION

Ed's engineering consulting for Northrop gradually took up less time since the company already had the basic design done. Briefing teams tried to convince Pentagon leaders of the advantage of using larger numbers of a low-cost plane that, admittedly, was not an F-104 in speed. Overseas sales were pursued, against foreign competition from the French Mirage and the Soviet MiGs also becoming available for Third World countries.

Using company funds entirely, without government help, an F-156F prototype was begun, using many parts in common with the T-38. Then, in May 1958, a letter of intent to purchase was issued by the Air Force for three N-156F aircraft to be tested for the Mutual Assistance Program, with which the Defense Department supplied aircraft to allied nations.

Delays in engine development threatened the Northrop programs for a while, but on April 10, 1959, a day ahead of an Air Force deadline, the first YT-38, 58-1191, was flown at Edwards Air Force Base by Lewis Nelson. Tom Jones was elected the new president of Northrop on May 19, while Welko Gasich became vice-president-technical. They promptly organized a roll-out ceremony for the first N-156F, 59-4987, with "Freedom Fighter" painted on its sides, which attracted an audience of reporters and air attachés from more than 40 countries.

Lewis Nelson made the first N-156F flight at Edwards on July 30, 1959. Powered by two 3,500-pound-thrust J85-GE-1 engines, the small single-seater had a thin wing built in one piece stiffened by aluminum honeycomb, and with midwing ailerons, leading-edge and trailing-edge flaps. The horizontal tailplanes didn't have traditional elevators, but moved as a single unit.

Yet no sales were in sight, even though two prototypes flew well, and the program languished with only one engineer remaining officially assigned to the project. But allies abroad did need to schedule a supersonic replacement for their F-84 and F-86 fighters. The N-156F could make Mach 1.4, compared to .92 for the F-86F it was intended to replace, or 1.3 for the F-100, which cost much more to operate.

Another strong argument for Northrop was the growing success of the T-38, which was the first supersonic plane in American service to complete its flight tests without a major accident. A total of 1,187 T-38s

Above right, **a braking chute slows N-156F ground roll.** *Northrop*

Right, **test flying the first N-156F.** *Northrop*

The YF-5A, 94989, with first two F-5A production ships. *Northrop*

would be delivered by the time production ended in January 1972, providing advanced training for a generation of pilots. Thirty years after its first flight, the T-38 would remain the only supersonic trainer in the Air Force and have the lowest accident rate of any type in the inventory.

On April 23, 1962, the secretary of defense finally made the long-awaited decision to choose the N-156F as the new fighter for the Mutual Assistance Program. An initial letter contract was made on October 22 for 71 F-5A fighters and 14 F-5B two-place trainers, and the unfinished third N-156F, 59-4989, was reworked and flown as the YF-5A on July 31, 1963.

Deliveries to Williams Air Force Base began April 3, 1964, of production F-5A fighters using two General Electric J85-GE-13 engines giving 2,720 pounds thrust at military power and 4,080 pounds for five minutes with afterburner. Similar in appearance to the original F-156F, the F-5A had a 25.8-foot span with wing-tip tanks, 47.2-foot length, 13.2-foot height, and wing area of 170 square feet. Empty weight was 8,085 pounds, and built-in armament was two 20-mm M-39 guns in the nose with 280 rpg, firing more than twice as fast as the wartime M-2 cannon.

A pair of AIM-9B Sidewinder missiles were carried on the wing tips when armed for an interception mission filled with 583 gallons in internal fuselage tanks and weighing 17,452 pounds at takeoff. Combat radius was 270 miles and with fuel burned off to a combat weight of 11,477 pounds, top speed was 925 mph at 36,000 feet, and combat ceiling was 50,600 feet. Ferry range was 1,318 miles in 2.3 hours with 1,129 gallons and a 17,452-pound takeoff weight.

The added fuel was carried in a pair of 50-gallon nondroppable wing-tip tanks and three 150-gallon drop tanks.

For ground support missions, the five hardpoints under the fuselage and wing provided a variety of munitions, including a 2,000-pound MK-84 bomb under the fuselage, up to a maximum of 5,500 pounds. With full fuel load and two 750-pound M-117 bombs, takeoff weight was 19,726 pounds and combat radius 420 miles. After expending bombs and fuel, reducing combat weight to 14,021 pounds, top speed at sea level was 731 mph.[17]

The F-5A's most impressive numbers had to do with economy. The aircraft cost $756,000 each, about half that of its sales rival, Lockheed's F-104G. Maintenance cost was less than that of any rival jet, and, "in its first year of operation, the F-5A logged more than 1.75 million miles without any accident."[18] That safety record was unmatched! Northrop could now offer an enormous improvement in the cost of an air defense for small countries.

The rest of the F-5 story is beyond the scope of this design biography, since it happened after Edgar Schmued's departure from Northrop. Nevertheless, it must be said that the original concept was widely accepted. On February 1, 1965, the first F-5As to go abroad arrived in Iran, and on October 23 a dozen USAF pilots brought specially modified Northrops to Vietnam to try them in combat. Jerry Scutts has written a book-length study of F-5 service.[19]

So successful was the F-5 series, from the A to F models, that 30 foreign air forces purchased them, and Canada, Spain, South Korea, and Taiwan coproduced them in their own factories. Both the U.S. Navy's

Fully loaded F-5A has 2,000-pound bomb on center line, two 150-gallon drop tanks, two 750-pound bombs, and wing-tip tanks.
Northrop

"Top Gun" and the Air Force fighter training programs used these Northrops as adversary aircraft painted in "Lizard" and other color schemes intended to simulate potential opponents, believing that if their pilots learned to defeat F-5s, they could master any MiG met in combat. A total of 2,602 had been delivered when production was completed in January 1987, nearly 30 years after the first N-156F had been designed. Few fighters can claim a better longevity!

Scientific Advisory Board (SAB) of experts led by Dr. Theodore Von Karman had been established by the Air Force to advise the chief of staff on long-range scientific trends. Edgar Schmued was brought on in 1952, and the self-taught engineer was almost the only civilian member without a Ph.D. He met some of the finest scientists in America, and became friends with General J. H. "Jimmy" Doolittle, who was SAB chairman from 1955 to 1958. After Ed's commitments to Northrop tapered off, his security clearance was elevated to top secret by Air Staff Headquarters on June 20, 1957, and he became Chairman of the Guidance and Control Panel, where he remained until 1962.

As an adviser to Lt. Gen. Donald L. Putt, Deputy Chief of Staff, Development, Ed prepared secret reports on subjects like "Air Defense Systems Against Bombers and Air-Breathing Missiles." Most of what Ed worked on was very classified, but in February 1958, for example, he received reports on "Lead Collision Fire Control Systems," "Future Nuclear Weapons," "Lethality of Soviet 122-mm AA Projectiles Against B-47 Aircraft," "The Soviet Threat of Technological Superiority," and "MB-1 Warheads."

In October 1959, the B-70 bomber design's radar reflection, infrared characteristics, and infrared countermeasures were a concern, for protecting bombers from enemy missiles had become extremely difficult. Increasing SAB emphasis was put on the accuracy of intercontinental ballistic missiles, and in October 1962, with delivery of the last B-52 and B-58 bombers, quantity production of manned bombers would cease in America for two decades. An Exceptional Service Award given Edgar by the USAF cited his "exceptionally meritorious service from 1952 to 1960 in the field of guidance and control."

WORKING AT HOME

As a self-employed technical consultant, Schmued worked with corporations like Aeronutronics (who paid him $400 a day in 1959). Herb Weiss, who was working there in 1963, remembers their experiments "with a magnetic sensor, which required making a very thin slice of a fragile crystal. Our machinist had been trying without success to cut out a slice as thin as was wanted, but his tries just ended in broken pieces.

"Ed took a sample of the crystal home with him, and in the morning gave us several slices, exactly as we had wanted them; he had cut them in his home workshop. How did he do it? Something about embedding the crystal in a 'matrix' before starting to cut; in other words, skill, know-how, and craftsmanship."

Once, he reviewed the proposed design

of a gas valve. "Won't work," he said, "do it like this," and sketched out how he would have designed it. The company did try making it their proposed way, but it didn't work, so Ed's sketch was pulled from the files, and the valve was made his way.[1]

Other clients over the next eight years included the Minneapolis Honeywell, Aerospace, Conductron, and Helio Aircraft corporations. In 1960, Ed Schmued proposed formation of a private organization called "Space Science Laboratories" to bring together in California the top talent in research and development. Although USAF chief of staff General Thomas D. White wrote that such a laboratory "could be a great national asset," capital for this ambitious project did not materialize.[2]

A heart attack in January 1961 slowed down Schmued's activity for a while, but his creative fires still burned. His writings on various defense topics included an article on the importance of encouraging the younger generation to select an engineering career. But leisure time for Edgar simply meant that he could concentrate on working with projects of his own choice, for he had been careful to build his house with plenty of room for his drafting table and an adjoining workshop.

He made up a list of possible tasks in 1962 that actually numbered 39, from "Flying Belt Engine" to "Vibrating Carving Knife." Fellow engineer Vern Tauscher recalls that Ed could machine any parts he needed in his own shop, which included an engine lathe, milling and grinding machines, and a drill press. Ed "kept his shop neat and clean," and covered his tools to protect them from rust.[3]

One of his most interesting activities in-volved the film *Flight of the Phoenix.* Starring James Stewart, it is the story of a group of men who are stranded when their twin-engine C-82 crashes in the Sahara Desert. A German engineer aboard has them improvise an aircraft from one engine and a tail boom of the C-82 to escape.

Since this aircraft actually had to be flown for the film, a realistic simulation had to be made. Movie pilot Paul Mantz built the machine, but on July 8, 1965, it crashed during the film, killing Mantz. The producers approached Edgar and asked him, as an expert on mixed wood and metal construction, to rebuild the aircraft for a final film sequence. Ed did so, with the help of Dr. Graydon Hofferber and other friends.[4]

THE LOCUST

More prosaic consultations were made for KMS Industries and Lear Jet, and Ed even copyrighted a simple reaction timer in 1971 to be used in driver education classes. But the aircraft idea that intrigued him the most was what he called the Locust. A very small, light single-seat monoplane, it would be an inexpensive sport machine for amateur pilots in civilian life. The military purpose was to provide an aircraft so inexpensive that a small nation could employ it in very large numbers. An invading army could be harassed from the air, as if by a swarm of insects.[5]

He discussed his idea with General Mark Bradley, who had been associated with Air Force fighters for 35 years. General Bradley had been the junior member of the Pursuit Board in October 1941 whose views we reviewed in Chapter Four, later became chief of the wartime Fighter Production Office,

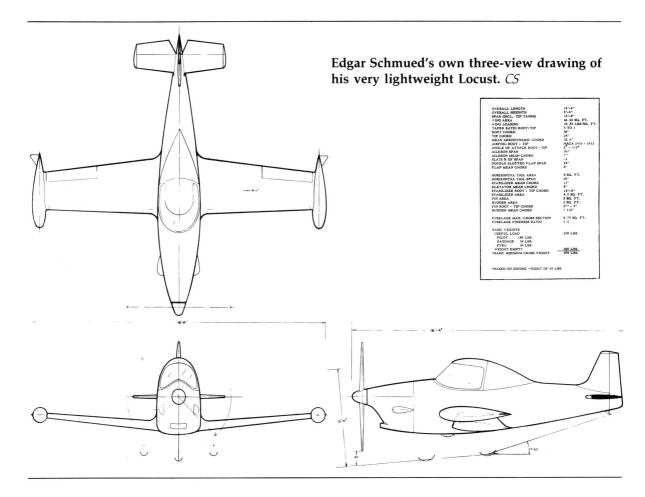

Edgar Schmued's own three-view drawing of his very lightweight Locust. *CS*

OVERALL LENGTH	15'-4"
OVERALL HEIGHT	5'-6"
SPAN (INCL. TIP TANKS)	16'-8"
WING AREA	42.66 SQ. FT.
WING LOADING	10.55 LBS/SQ. FT.
TAPER RATIO ROOT/TIP	5 TO 3
ROOT CHORD	40"
TIP CHORD	24"
MEAN AERODYNAMIC CHORD	32.6"
AIRFOIL ROOT - TIP	NACA 2416 - 2412
ANGLE OF ATTACK ROOT - TIP	2° - 1/2°
AILERON SPAN	36"
AILERON MEAN CHORD	7"
SLATS % OF SPAN	12
DOUBLE SLOTTED FLAP SPAN	54"
FLAP MEAN CHORD	8"
HORIZONTAL TAIL AREA	8 SQ. FT.
HORIZONTAL TAIL SPAN	60"
STABILIZER MEAN CHORD	11"
ELEVATOR MEAN CHORD	8"
STABILIZER ROOT - TIP CHORD	13"-9"
STABILIZER AREA	4.2 SQ. FT.
FIN AREA	2 SQ. FT.
RUDDER AREA	2 SQ. FT.
FIN ROOT - TIP CHORD	27" - 6"
RUDDER MEAN CHORD	7 1/2"
FUSELAGE MAX. CROSS SECTION	8.75 SQ. FT.
FUSELAGE FINENESS RATIO	6.2
BASIC WEIGHTS	
USEFUL LOAD	250 LBS.
PILOT 180 LBS.	
BAGGAGE 34 LBS.	
FUEL 36 LBS.	
WEIGHT EMPTY	200 LBS.
*BASIC MINIMUM GROSS WEIGHT	450 LBS.

*BASED ON ENGINE WEIGHT OF 45 LBS.

and postwar director of Air Force procurement and production. He became a close friend of Ed's after his retirement in 1965 and his move to Palos Verdes. According to Bradley, "Ed was a great guy to know. He loved to work and had an idea a minute—but the main thing on his mind was an intense desire to design another airplane . . . a small, simple, cheap, one-man aircraft."

Ed drew plans for a wing span of 16 feet 8 inches, including little five-gallon tip tanks, a 42.66-square-foot wing area, a 15-foot 4-inch length, and a 5-foot 6-inch height, an inch shorter than the designer

himself. With a 65-hp two-cylinder engine weighing 45 pounds, the Locust would weigh only 200 pounds empty and carry a 250-pound useful load. A fiberglass cockpit enclosure was provided for the pilot.

It was designed to have retractable tricycle landing gear, a stalling speed of only 40 mph with leading-edge slats and double-slotted flaps, and to be as easy to fly as a motorcycle is to ride. Top speed was estimated at 160 mph, and range at 520 miles in three hours, with only 5.5 gallons of fuel. Most important was Ed's idea that only $4 million of foreign aid could buy 1,000 such planes, as well as the simple support equipment and personnel training. Instead of a separate service organization, the pilots themselves would service and maintain their own aircraft.

All missions would be flown at very low levels to avoid radar detection and maximize chances for survival. In an attack on a missile base or gun emplacement, at least 200 airplanes would be used to saturate enemy defenses. Most of the Locusts used in such an attack would be armed with a pair of 7.62-mm NATO or .22-caliber Cadillac Gage guns slanted downward, but 30 would instead carry a pair of 3-inch armor-penetrating rockets, and 50 would have a pair of 250-pound bombs to finish off the target.

Another Locust configuration aimed to

Interior drawing of Locust. *CS*

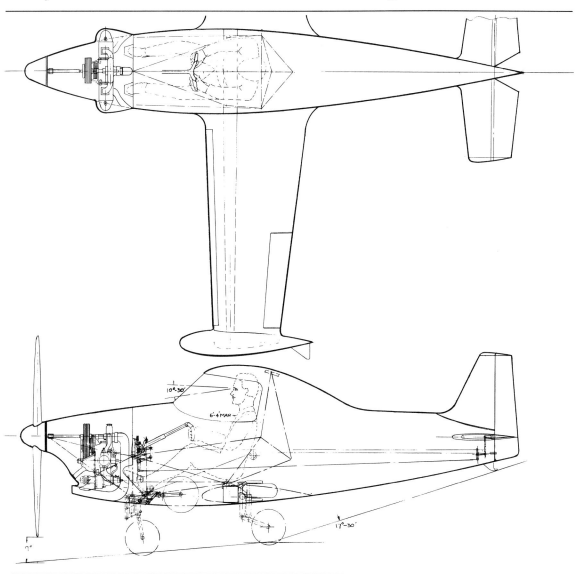

give one man an easy way of covering distance by the simplest means at a very low cost. "Like cavalry . . . the infantry has now a chance to become airborne with all the advantages of mass movements by air." Instead of risking hundreds of parachute troops on multimillion-dollar transports that could be destroyed by a single missile, a swarm of Locusts could deposit individual warriors with light automatic weapons to attack sensitive, but expensive targets. Essentially, since the Locust was built at such low cost, it could be "abandoned after it is used," a one-mission throwaway aircraft.

General Bradley wrote that "Ed presented these ideas to me and asked my opinion. . . . I had to tell him I had some pretty serious concerns about such a plan." But Ed enjoyed discussing each objection in detail. Pilot injuries in crashes would be prevented by a welded steel structure around the cockpit. The engine in the nose could be swung slightly so that the plane would turn like a motorcycle, and a simple system raised the retractable landing gear.

To produce these Locusts, Edgar Schmued produced a plan in 1970 for a company, the Schmued Aircraft and Engine Corporation, to develop a low-cost engine and airplane priced below $2,000 for both the private and military export market. This would have required an estimated $1,200,-000 in venture capital from a small group of investors.[6]

As he had done with his space-science idea, Edgar worked out his financial plan in great detail. He anticipated that countries like Israel and the Philippines would be prospective customers. They could build their own Locusts under license on a royalty basis and strengthen their own national industrial base.

The most important factor in obtaining the necessary performance was finding a lightweight power plant. His first power-plant choice was the McCulloch engine developed for snowmobiles, a 50-pound, two-cylinder unit sold for about $200. But after ownership of this company changed hands, and similar recreational-vehicle engines were considered, Ed found that the companies making them were unwilling to accept the liability risk of using their engines in manned aircraft. It became apparent that he would have to develop his own power plant, a very expensive proposition.

Schmued believed that the solution was a two-cycle, two-cylinder engine using direct fuel injection and a centrifugal blower for air scavenging, instead of the usual crank-case pump. This feature, he thought, would "cut fuel consumption in half, compared with that of the conventional two-cycle engine."[7] A rating of 55 hp could be obtained for a weight of only 45 to 50 pounds. He planned an assembly rate of 1,000 engines a year with a unit assembly time of five man-hours each. Locust airplanes, he expected, could also be assembled at a 1,000-per-year minimum rate for the same man-hours.

Once again, however, his plans were frustrated by the lack of major financial backing. Aviation progress had become more and more dependent on the corporate structures he had left behind. And now, personal tragedy again entered his life. His wife, Helen, developed malignant cancer and died on September 19, 1972. They had been a devoted couple for 28 years, and Edgar's loneliness was natural.

As he had done in 1936, Ed buried himself in his work at home, machining parts for his engine and actually beginning construction of a Locust in a rented garage.

Richard Hulse, who had been a neighbor since 1957, remembers him as a modest, quiet, smiling man, who was always a good listener. Dick was astonished by the wide range of Ed's interests, even including the measurement of the Grand Canyon and the moon by laser![8]

He continually worked on his two-cycle, two-cylinder engine and its application. An RPV (Remote-controlled Pilotless Vehicle) using two of these engines was drawn in October 1978. Weighing only 600 pounds, it could be used for reconnaissance, while a single-engine version was planned as an inexpensive decoy to create false reflections on hostile radar. Another design that year planned for a very streamlined powered sailplane with a little 20-hp engine. He worked on propeller, radiator, and landing-gear details.

Unfortunately, Ed's generosity in lending money to friends, or cosigning for their loans, blocked his own dreams. One associate's company went bankrupt, and Ed lost his own workshop and tools, which had been pledged as collateral on the friend's loan.

Considering his future retirement, he often thought of his youth in Germany and corresponded with relatives there. His niece near Stuttgart invited him to visit her family, and in 1975 Ed went to that city to try out "old-country" life. It was a far different Germany than he had left 50 years ago—prosperous, peaceful, and democratic. Ed even bought a Mercedes there, but while delighted by the food and language of his youth, he decided to return to California with his new car.

He did, however, begin corresponding with a German lady, Christel Fuchs, who worked as a confidential accountant for a large Hamburg firm. She came to California on her vacation in September 1977, but was at first a bit disappointed by America. Instead of glamorous high rises and the bright city centers, she found the rows of single-story houses of Los Angeles suburbs rather prosaic.

On the other hand, Christel immediately liked her engineer friend, although she knew nothing about airplanes or Schmued's reputation as a design genius. She had been too young to remember the raids on her hometown of Stuttgart or to have heard about the Mustang's wartime exploits, but was charmed by Ed's old-world courtesy, warmth, and attention. Christel returned for her Easter vacation in 1978 and again for Christmas, and on December 25, 1978, Edgar announced his engagement to the 36-year-old lady whose cheerful manner had quickly endeared her to him.

A SOJOURN ABROAD

The Chinese air force on Taiwan had become Northrop's biggest foreign customer when it had chosen the F-5 to replace their F-86 Sabres. The Chinese purchased 63 F-5A and F-5B models, followed by 242 F-5E single-seaters and 66 F-5F two-seaters. Wanting to create their own aircraft industry, the Chinese established an Aero Industry Development Center (AIDC) at Taichung, with a factory to assemble 120 of the Northrops, along with helicopters and training planes. When Northrop's representative in Taiwan, Maj. Gen. John R. Alison (USAF, retired), told them of Edgar's efforts to develop a low-cost and lightweight engine, they asked him to work for them.

In March 1979, Edgar Schmued went to

Ed and his bride, Christel, sign the marriage book in Taipei. *CS*

Taiwan, remaining as an adviser to the National Science Council (NSC) of the Republic of China. He married Christel Fuchs in Taipei on April 21, 1979, and they lived in a pleasant home provided by the Chinese in Hsinchu. But when Ed's chief sponsor on the NSC died, in the words of General Alison, there was conflict "between a Mandarin bureaucracy and a German doctrinaire," although General Alison felt that Ed was right from a technical point of view. Ed was "mad as hell at the Taiwanese," adds General Mark Bradley, "for having failed to keep their word and causing him to give up and go home."[9]

After leaving Taiwan and returning to California in May 1980, Ed and Christel looked for a new place to live and finally bought a home in Oceanside, California. In

spite of his retired status, Ed remained busy with consulting jobs for Aerojet and others, and planned a light, 460-pound single-seater with a 35-hp engine and a pusher propeller. When an idea came to him, even in the middle of the night, he would head for his drawing board.

Christel didn't realize how famous her husband was until she heard numerous comments about his design of the Mustang. Ed was pleased to see the stature of the P-51 continue to grow over the years, and the "Mustang Man" was sought out for a growing number of interviews. The Planes of Fame Museum at Chino, California, held a 41st-anniversary celebration of the Mustang on October 24, 1981, in which a dozen privately owned P-51s turned up to be admired by a large crowd.

Ed himself had never been up in the single-seat fighter that was his proudest achievement until that day, when he flew with Pete Regina. Pete owned a P-51B that he had rebuilt with a second seat and painted in the wartime markings of Don Gentile's "Shangri-La." Ed also participated in a panel on its development that included Steve Hinton.

Hinton had set the world's speed record for piston-engine planes at 499 mph on August 14, 1979, when he was only 27. He was flying his "Red Baron," originally a P-51D-25NT, 44-84961, finished on June 25, 1945, and rebuilt in 1975 with a 3,400-hp Rolls-Royce Griffon engine and contra-rotating propellers; very modified, but still a Mustang.[10]

The revival of unlimited air racing at Reno had inspired many private owners to modify their Mustangs for speed. Hinton brought the Red Baron to the next race at

Ed had his first Mustang ride in the rear seat of Pete Regina's P-51B at Chino, California. *Kishpaugh*

Carrying Pete and Ed, the P-51B is accompanied by a P-51A, flown by Steve Hinton, and a P-51D owned by the Planes of Fame Museum. *O'Leary*

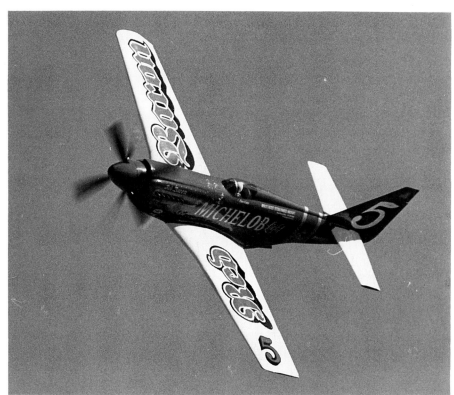

**The Red Baron
in a high-speed
turn.** *Carter*

Reno, but was nearly killed when the Griffon failed and his Mustang crashed. Other pilots persisted in the quest for speed until July 30, 1983, when Frank Taylor flew his own P-51D, "Dago Red," with a souped-up 3,000-hp Packard Merlin V-1650-9 to a new speed record for piston-engine planes of 517 mph, at Mojave, California. Ed could not help being astonished that a Mustang had set a new world's record 42 years after it was originally built.

At the 20th reunion of the Bald Eagles, the organization of retired North American Aviation employees in February 1982, Ed renewed his friendship with his former co-workers and found that the Mustang was still a favorite topic of discussion. A British writer, Paul A. Coggan, had formed Mustang International, and Ed became an honorary life member of this association of owners and enthusiasts in August 1983. Coggan assembled a complete list of all the Mustangs left in the world, which was published in 1987.[11]

Many Mustangs had begun a second life by being reprocessed as fast executive aircraft by the Cavalier Aircraft Corporation at Sarasota, originally called Trans-Florida. A dozen more had been modernized under a Defense Department contract made in February 1967 for Project Peace Condor for Bolivia and El Salvador, and similar two-place armed versions appeared elsewhere. Two Mustangs with 120-gallon wing-tip tanks, 68-15795 and 15796, were sold to the United States Army as chase planes for helicopter tests.

The Red Baron racer seen shortly after Steve Hinton set a new world's piston-engine speed record in a plane older than he was. *Bulinski*

In 1968, Cavalier had offered the Air Force a Turbo Mustang 3 ground attack type powered by the 1,740-hp Rolls-Royce Dart turboprop engine then being used on United Airlines Viscount airliners. After two more prototypes were built with 2,245-hp Lycoming T-55-T-9 engines, Piper Aircraft took over this project as the Piper PA-48 Enforcer. No production contracts were won.

As Mustangs were retired from military service, many had been sold to private owners and refurbished, often with a second seat for a lucky passenger. Some are still flown in "stock military" condition, with markings as authentic as their new owners could discover, while other owners indulged their delight in turning up at air shows and fly-ins in very bright colors. By 1975, there were 148 on the U.S. civil register, and careful rebuilding was adding more. Rockwell International, corporate owners of North American since 1967, sponsored the bright yellow P-51D that Bob Hoover flew in air shows around the country.

Some P-51s had retired to museums, like the Excalibur III in the National Air and Space Museum. This is the Bendix-winner NX1202, the P-51C-10, which Charles F. Blair, Jr., bought from Paul Mantz in 1950 for $11,000 and fitted with a new V-1650-9 and the best radio equipment available. In a remarkable display of piloting and navigation skill, Blair made the first solo flight over the North Pole, 3,450 miles from Norway to Alaska in 10 hours and 29 minutes, the longest Mustang flight ever. A total of 856 gallons of fuel was carried in the fuselage and internal wet-wing tanks. On the next day, May 30, 1951, Blair continued on to New York City for another 9 hours 31 minutes.[12]

Dago Red in flight. *Bulinski*

Dago Red became the world's fastest piston-engine racer in 1983. *Bulinski*

Some museums operated flying exhibits, like the Allison-engine P-51A in RAF colors flown by the Planes of Fame Museum at Chino, California. Most remarkable, the first XP-51, 41-038, had been restored to flying condition for the Experimental Aircraft Association Museum at Oshkosh, Wisconsin. In 1982, Ed got to see this plane again when he visited the EAA fly-in of home-built and antique aircraft. *Sport Avia-*

This two-place Mustang was rebuilt in 1967 for use by the U.S. Army as a helicopter chase plane. It was the last military Mustang to retire, in February 1978. *SDAM*

tion magazine reported that he came to "study the ultra-lights and the small aircraft engines . . . for the very efficient little airplane he perceives the current economic times to demand."[13]

When 10 aviation notables were asked to nominate the top 10 airplanes of all time, the Mustang got more votes than any other type, being listed by 6 of the 10 panelists. Said general and fighter ace Robin Olds, "P-51 was the best ever . . . and in every way was a joy to fly."[14] If any airplane can

Christel and Ed at the Bald Eagle's reunion of North American veterans. *CS*

Perhaps the ugliest conversion of the Mustang was Cavalier's turboprop ground attack model. *SDAM*

A very customized civilian Cavalier Mustang seen in June 1961 with wing-tip tanks. *SDAM*

Ed visits the first XP-51, 41-38, at Oshkosh in 1982. *CS*

remain as a monument to its builders, the Mustang will do so.

On Saturday, June 1, 1985, Edgar Schmued passed away in Oceanside. At the age of 85, his heart could no longer sustain his creative spirit. Two weeks later, a memorial service was held at the hangar of Clay Lacy Aviation in the Van Nuys airport, and 250 admirers gathered with Christel, Rolf, and Sandra to hear testimonials from aviation notables.

F. J. "Buddy" Joffrion described the event: "His wife, Christel, expressed a desire to have his ashes flown out to sea in his most beloved creation, the P-51—a fitting tribute to one who had contributed in such large measure to the science of flight and to this country's war effort. The response was immediate and overwhelming. The owners of six P-51s and one F-86 eagerly offered their services.

"As the ceremonies drew to a close with a bugler playing taps, at the appointed time the seven aircraft taxied out in single file behind Clay Lacy's purple P-51D. Shortly after becoming airborne, they fell into formation and headed for Los Angeles International Airport where a low-level fly-by was performed over the site of the old North American plant, the birthplace of the P-51. From LAX, Clay led the formation out to sea, where the ashes were released by Joffrion. The flight then returned to Van Nuys for a 'missing man' formation and, after landing, the seven aircraft taxied back to precisely the same spots they had vacated 30 minutes earlier."[15]

The pilots in the June 15 entourage were Clay Lacy, John Malone, and Elmer Ward in their P-51Ds, Pete Regina in his P-51B, Skip Holm and Bob Guilford in the P-51Ds

owned by Joe Kasperoff and Charley Knapp, while the F-86 was flown by Dave Zeuchel.

The principal eulogy by Richard Schleicher has already been quoted in this book. Buddy Joffrion also pointed out that the P-51 was Ed's greatest pride and that the fighter that contributed so much to ending

the war in Europe was designed by a man born in Germany, powered by an engine designed in Britain, and built on American soil! When the last two Mustangs arrived at the ceremony already in progress, Joffrion remarked that Ed would have loved to hear their engines' sound.

Messages of condolence also arrived from

Clay Lacy leads the memorial formation out to sea. *CS*

The Mustang Man. *CS*

Air Force leaders. General J. H. "Jimmy" Doolittle wrote: "All of us who had the good fortune to know—and to know was to admire—Edgar Schmued—miss him profoundly."

General Chuck Yeager added: "Although I didn't know Ed Schmued, I sure knew his airplane, the P-51 Mustang.

"I, like a lot of other young fighter pilots, owe our necks to the design and performance that Ed put into that airplane.

"I was in the first P-51 group in the Eighth Air Force . . . the 357th Fighter Group. It was the best airplane in the skies anywhere in the world during WW II.

"Even during these days of high-tech airplanes . . . the P-51 Mustang is still a fun airplane to fly!"

Thomas V. Jones, Chairman of the Board at Northrop, wrote Christel: "We shall always think of him dearly. Ed was a brilliant, forceful, yet very kind man, and he was loved by all who knew him at Northrop. He provided inspiration for many young engineers, myself included."

Colonel William F. "Bill" Barnes wrote: "To me, Edgar Schmued was the ideal engineer. A man with the necessary technical knowledge, but more importantly, the common sense to apply that knowledge in a practical way to solve a design problem."

We conclude this book with the parting words of the USAF chief of staff, General Charles A. Gabriel: "A generation of fighter pilots grew up flying Edgar's P-51 and F-86. I was fortunate enough to be one of those pilots and know they were great airplanes. Further, most of today's Air Force have spent time in the T-38, another airplane he played a key role in developing.

"Without a doubt, Edgar's trailblazing innovations and service on the Air Force Scientific Advisory Board were major contributors to making American airpower second to none. All of us in the Air Force family will miss him."[16]

Appendix

Serial Numbers of Air Force P-51 Aircraft:

Charge Number	Start Date	Serials	Type	Qty.	Contract Approved
NA-91	7-7-41	41-37320/37469	P-51	150	9-25-41
NA-97	4-16-42	42-83663/84162	A-36	500	8-7-42
NA-99 (to NA-104)	6-23-42	43-6003/6312	P-51A	310	8-24-42
		43-6313/7112	P-51B-5	800	
		43-7113/7202	P-51B-10	90	
NA-101	7-25-42	41-37352, 37421	XP-51B	2	
NA-102	8-26-42	43-12093/12492 (c/n102-24541/24940)	P-51B-1	400	12-28-42
NA-103	10-8-42	42-102979/103328	P-51C-1	350	12-28-42
		-103329/103778	P-51C-5	450	
		-103779/103978	P-51C-10	200	
NA-104	10-20-42	42-106429/106538	P-51B-10	110	1-5-43
		-106539/106540	P-51D-1	2	
		-106541/106738	P-51B-10	198	
		-106739/106978	P-51B-15	240	
NA-105	1-2-43	43-43332/4	XP-51F	3	7-20-43
		-43335/6	XP-51G	2	7-20-43
		44-76027/8	XP-51J	2	6-30-44
NA-109	4-13-43	44-13253/14052	P-51D-5	800	7-21-43
		-14053/14852	P-51D-10	800	
		-14853/15752	P-51D-15	900	
NA-111	5-3-43	44-10753/11152	P-51C-10	400	7-21-43
		-11153/11352	P-51D-5	200	
		-11353/12852	P-51K	1500	
		-12853/13252	P-51D-20	400	
NA-122	4-11-44	44-63160/64159	P-51D-20	1000	6-3-44
		-72027/72626	"	600	
		-72627/73626	P-51D-25	1600	
		-73627/75026	P-51D-30	800	

Charge Number	Start Date	Serials	Type	Qty.	Contract Approved
NA-124	4-14-44	44-84390/84989	P-51D-25	600	
(NT)		45-11343/11542	"	200	
		-11543/11742	P-51D-30	200	
		-11743	P-51M	1	
NA-126	4-20-44	44-64160/179	P-51H-1	20	6-30-44
		-64180/459	P-51H-5	280	
		-64460/714	P-51H-10	255	

Photo Conversions Made in Dallas and Deductable from Above Totals:

57 F-6K-5-NT	20 F-6D-20-NT
63 F-6K-10-NT	10 F-6D-20-NT
43 F-6K-15-NT	1 F-6D-20-NT
	70 F-6D-25-NT
	35 F-6D-30-NT

(163)   (136)

TOTAL 299 F-6K and F-6D

Serial Numbers of Twin Mustangs:

			First Flight
NA-123	P-82B	44-65160/179	10-31-45
NA-123	P-82C	-65169	3-27-46
NA-123	P-82D	-65170	3-29-46
NA-144	F-82E	46-255/354	2-17-47
NA-149	F-82F	-405/495	3-11-48
NA-150	F-82G	-355/404	12-8-47
NA-150	F-82H	-496/504	2-15-49

Notes

CHAPTER ONE

1. See Benjamin S. Kelsey, *The Dragon's Teeth?* (Washington, DC, 1982), pp. 110–12, and fn. 2 below for analysis of Air Corps procurement system.

2. Irving Brinton Holley, *Buying Aircraft: Matériel Procurement for the Army Air Forces* (Washington, DC, GPO, 1964) p. 139.

3. *Who's Who in World Aviation* (Washington, DC, 1955), p. 29.

4. Don R. Berlin, "Development of the Curtiss P-36A," *Aero Digest,* Dec. 1937, pp. 54–56.

5. Edward T. Maloney, *Sever the Sky* (Corona Del Mar, CA: Planes of Fame, 1979), pp. 5–7. Seversky and Kartveli both died in 1974.

6. Dewitt S. Copp, *A Few Great Captains* (New York, 1980), pp. 336–339.

7. Air Corps contract data and approval dates in this paper from *Index of AF Serial Numbers Assigned to Aircraft 1958 and Prior,* Procurement Division, AAF, April 1961. San Diego Aerospace Museum (SDAM) files.

8. Page Shamburger and Joe Christy, *The Curtiss Hawks* (Kalamazoo, MI, 1972), p. 112.

9. Arthur B. Domonske and Volney C. Finch, *Aircraft Engines* (New York, 1936), pp. 212–20, describes the supercharging state of the art in this period.

10. *Army Aircraft Characteristics,* ATSC Wright F., April 1, 1946, and charts dated August 1, 1941, and 1939: SDAM Characteristics file; AAF a/c data.

11. Kelsey, p. 65.

12. I. B. Holley, Jr., "A Detroit Dream of Mass-produced Fighter Aircraft: The XP-75 Fiasco," *Technology and Culture,* July 1987, p. 582.

13. Richard L. Foss and Roy Blay, "From Propellers to Jets in Fighter Design," *Lockheed Horizons,* 1987, pp. 3–24.

14. Birch Matthews, *Airacobra in Retrospect* (TRW, 1968).

15. George R. Reiss, "He Designed a Tiger," *Popular Aviation,* July 1939, pp. 54–55.

16. Robert J. Woods, "Why a Rear Engine Installation," *Aviation,* March 1941, pp. 36–37, 142, and April 1941, pp. 46–47, 142–44.

17. Shamburger and Christy, p. 113.

18. AFHRC 145.91-412, March 28, 1939.

19. James Hansen, *Engineer in Charge* (1987), pp. 199–201.

20. Letters in SDAM P-39 file.

21. C-616 in SDAM pursuit file.

22. L. C. Craigie, Sept. 22, 1939.

23. AFHRC 145.91-412, J. C. Shively to Vultee Aircraft, May 10, 1939.

24. CP-770 amendments and C-619 in SDAM pursuit file.

25. AFHRC 202.1-31: *ATSC Case History of XP-49 Project,* Dec. 1944.

26. Warren Bodie, *Airpower,* Sept. 1976, p. 22.

27. See fn. 24.

28. AFHRC 145.91-506: Aircraft Plans Div. Pursuit Aviation.

CHAPTER TWO

1. The information in this chapter is drawn from the tapes ES made in 1985, hereafter referred to as ES 1985, as well as personal papers including security clearance forms, passport, Luise Schmued's death certificate, patents, and other documents.

2. Edgar Schmued's Austrian citizenship is certified by his *Heimatschein* from *Stadtmagistrat Salzburg,* Nov. 13, 1923. His mother was born in 1872, sister Eugenia in 1896, and the youngest sister, Else, in 1915.

3. *Reichspatentamt* No. 364634 gives his address as Landsberg, while Nos. 367736, 378653, 384901, and 391708 locate ES in Bergedorf.

4. Documents on Fokker rules and company history are in the San Diego Aerospace Museum files.

5. See North American Aviation, *Chronology of World,* and North American Aviation, Inc. *Events Prior to World War II* (1952). In SDAM files.

6. *J. H. Kindelberger* (Columbus, OH, 1972), and *U.S. Air Services,* Aug. 1939, pp. 33–34 and 44 for personality portraits.

7. CH to CS, Dec. 17, 1986.

8. ES, 1985.

9. Wesley Price, "Merchant of Speed," *Saturday Evening Post,* Feb. 19, 1949, p. 32ff.

CHAPTER SIX

1. I. B. Holley, "A Detroit Dream of Mass-produced Fighter Aircraft: The XP-75 Fiasco," *Technology and Culture,* July 1987, p. 582. The case histories produced by the Historical Office, Air Technical Service Command, now at the AFHRC, file no. 202, were used for much of this chapter's discussion.
2. Birch, p. 87.
3. Sam Logan to CS, Sept. 14, 1986.
4. Werner R. Rankin, *Final Report on . . . XP-51F, G, & J.* SR no. 5653, December 4, 1947.
5. NA-59004, Group Weight Statement, P-51F 43-43333, May 2, 1944.
6. USAF Chart dated September 1, 1944.
7. D. K. Warner letter to CS, July 29, 1986.
8. David R. McLaren, "North American P-51H," *American Aviation Historical Society Journal,* Part I, Summer 1980, pp. 124–39; Part II, Fall 1980, pp. 203–27.
9. Rankin, op cit., and Chilton interview recorded at SDAM, April 27, 1986: "I don't know what happened to the J, we practically didn't want to fly it, especially Ed, and it wasn't flown but just a very, very few times."
10. Gene Boswell, letter on P-51H, *American Aviation Historical Society Journal,* Fall 1980, p. 238.
11. Gordon Throne letter to CS, Aug. 5, 1986.
12. Edgar Schmued, "Why U.S. Planes Are Better Than Russia's," *Los Angeles Times,* July 31, 1955.
13. Recorded at SDAM, April 27, 1986.
14. *Ibid.*

CHAPTER SEVEN

1. Vern Tauscher to CS, Sept. 1986.
2. Sam Logan to CS, Sept. 14, 1988.
3. Tauscher, Sept. 1986.
4. Julius G. Villepique, whose personal papers in SDAM were donated by his daughter, Mrs. Margaret Tyson.
5. Ed Horkey to RW, Nov. 21, 1988.
6. Werner R. Rankin, *Final Report on the Procurement, Inspection, Testing, and Acceptance of North American XP-82 and XP-82A,* TR 5673, February 19, 1948: AFHRC 216.21010-103.
7. U.S. Patents Office, Design Patents 144.936/8, June 4, 1946.
8. Chilton to RW, December 20, 1986, but George

Gehrkens feels that this description is different from his memory of the events.
9. Horkey, Nov. 21, 1988.
10. Rankin, p. 4.
11. Chilton interview at SDAM, April 27, 1986.
12. Rankin, p. 3.
13. *Air Enthusiast Six,* March–June 1978, p. 130.
14. Lin Hendrix, *Wings,* April 1977, pp. 58–63.
15. Martin J. Miller, Jr., *Case History of the F-82E, F and G,* USAF/AMC, Jan. 1951, p. 7; AFHRC 202.1-49.
16. Marcelle S. Knaack, *Encyclopedia of U.S. Air Force Aircraft,* Vol. 1 (Washington, D.C., 1978), p. 16.
17. ES 1985. George Gehrkens, the project engineer, feels this characterization of the political situation by Schmued is very overdrawn.
18. Miller, pp. 18–20.
19. *USAF Characteristics Summary,* F-82E, Sept. 22, 1950.
20. *USAF Characteristics Summary,* F-82G, Sept. 22, 1950.

CHAPTER EIGHT

1. Joseph Juptner, *U.S. Approved Type Certificated Aircraft,* Vol. VIII, pp. 283–87, and Marc C. Lacagnina, "Navions: Gentle Giant," *AOPA Pilot,* Nov. 1982, pp. 73–82.
2. Chilton, recorded at SDAM, April 27, 1986.
3. Historical Office, Air Materiel Command, *Case History of XP-59 . . . (Series) Airplanes,* AFHRC.
4. Chilton, recorded at SDAM, April 27, 1986.
5. *Hook,* Fall 1977, pp. 11–12.
6. L. P. Greene, *F-86 Preliminary Design,* Feb. 25 1959, NAA Reference No. 7.2.6.1, is the most detailed description of the subject, along with a chronology by Jack Canary, March 24, 1953. This was also a source for the book-length history of the F-86, Ray Wagner's *North American Sabre* (London, 1963).
7. NAA Report NA-8564, May 15, 1945: p. 5.
8. NA-140 Model Summary, May 28, 1952.
9. Bill Barker to CS, July 21, 1988.
10. BNA54-389, May 1, 1955, and MCRFT-2126, Jan. 15, 1948.
11. John Dienst and Dan Hagedorn, *North American F-51 Mustangs in Latin American Service* (Arlington, TX, 1985), p. 1.
12. Warren Thompson, "Mustangs in Korea," *Air Enthusiast Fifteen,* 1981, pp. 49–57.
13. Wagner, p. 78; book contains a detailed analysis of F-86 Korean War operations.

14. William F. Barnes to Christel Schmued, 1986.
15. Knaak, pp. 113–14.
16. *North American Skywriter,* Aug. 1, 1952, p. 1.
17. Knaack, pp. 114–16.
18. Edward J. Horkey to author, Nov. 21, 1988.
19. ES to M. Stanton, May 8, 1984.

CHAPTER NINE

1. U.S. Patent Office, 2,856,820, patented Oct. 21, 1958, and Aircraftsmen Reports R20-2, Nov. 14, 1952, and R21-2, Jan. 5, 1953.
2. See *Northrop News,* Dec. 3, 1952, p. 1; and *Interavia Air Letter #2611,* Dec. 12, 1952, p. 4, for company reorganization. The quotation from Schmued is from a letter written on Nov. 4, 1984.
3. Charles Barr, unpublished 1986 manuscript supplied by Dr. Ira C. Chart, who provided much of the information in this chapter.
4. David A. Anderton, *Aviation Week,* Nov. 22, 1954, pp. 39–41.
5. Knaack, pp. 89–91.
6. Northrop Model Specification NS-81, July 23, 1953.
7. U.S. Patent Office, Des. 180,297, patented May 14, 1957.
8. Fred Anderson, *Northrop: An Aeronautical History* (Los Angeles, 1976), pp. 170–72; and *Northrop News,* May 9, 1956.
9. *Northrop News,* March 13, 1957.
10. Edgar Schmued, "Why U.S. Planes Are Better Than Russia's," *Los Angeles Times,* July 31, 1955.
11. Knaack, pp. 330–31.
12. Barr, p. 15.
13. Barr, p. 22.
14. Barr, p. 25.
15. Horkey to RW, Nov. 28, 1988.
16. Charles C. Cilley, Northrop Vice-President, Finance, to ES, Oct. 2, 1957.
17. *Characteristics Summary,* F-5A, USAF Nov. 1972. Nautical miles and knots have been changed into common statute miles for this book.
18. Knaack, p. 288.

19. Jerry Scutts, *Northrop F-5/F-20* (London, 1986). See also W. E. Gasich, "Northrop F-5 Tactical Fighter in the Close Support Role" (Washington, DC: Society of Automotive Engineers, April 1965); C. M. Plattner, "F-5 Combat Trials Pinpoint Advantages, Limitations," *Aviation Week,* Jan. 17, 1966, pp. 28–32; and Lou Drendel, *F-5 in Action* (Carrollton, TX, 1980).

CHAPTER TEN

1. Herbert K. Weiss to Christel Schmued, Aug. 12, 1986.
2. General Thomas D. White to ES, March 25, 1960. This and many other personal papers, as well as conversations with Christel Schmued and Ed's friends, were the sources for this chapter.
3. Vern Tauscher, letter to CS, Sept. 1986.
4. Alice Hofferber interview, Nov. 23, 1988.
5. Edgar Schmued, "A Plan for the Formation of an Engineering and Manufacturing Organization for Aircraft and Engines," 48-page typescript, Sept. 1, 1970.
6. Ibid., pp. 47–48; and Mark Bradley memo., April 27, 1986.
7. "Description of the Schmued Aircraft Engine Design," ES ms., no date.
8. Richard Hulse interviews, 1988.
9. John R. Alison, interview by author, Nov. 12, 1988, and Bradley memo cited above.
10. Paul A. Coggan, *Mustang Survivors* (Bourne End, 1987), pp. 136–48.
11. Ibid.
12. Robert C. Mikesh, *Excalibur III* (Washington, DC, 1978).
13. *Sport Aviation,* Oct. 1982, p. 29.
14. Jeffrey P. Rhodes, "The Top Ten," *Air Force Magazine,* April 1987, pp. 84–91.
15. F. J. "Buddy" Joffrion, "A Farewell to Ed Schmued," *Warbirds,* Nov. 1985, pp. 12–13.
16. Copies of all the letters cited here are in the Schmued papers at SDAM.

Glossary

The following definitions are offered to explain common aircraft technical terms used in this book. These definitions have been adapted from the USAF Dictionary.

Airfoil A wing section designed to obtain lift in its motion through the air. Its efficiency depends on the amount of lift generated without excessive drag.

Angle of attack The angle between the chord of an airfoil and a horizontal reference line of the aircraft.

Critical altitude The maximum altitude at which the maximum continuous power can be maintained, in the cases of engines for which this power is the same at sea level and at the rated altitude.

Dimpling Putting small circular depressions in the metal surface to accommodate flush rivets.

Drag coefficient A coefficient representing the drag on a given airfoil, or other body.

G The gravitational force, or pull, of the earth. To pull five G's is to subject the aircraft and pilot to a G-force of five G's during a change of acceleration or direction.

In-line engine An internal combustion, reciprocating engine in which the cylinders are arranged in one or more straight rows, either upright or inverted. In World War II engines, 12 cylinders set in two rows shaped as a *V* were the most common arrangement.

Laminar-flow airfoil A wing surface specially designed to maintain laminar, or nonturbulent, airflow about itself.

Load factor A factor representing the ratio of weight or pressure of a specified load or force to a standard weight or pressure. Used to measure or express the stress to which an aircraft is subjected under certain conditions.

Mach number A number expressing the ratio of the speed of an aircraft moving through the air, to the speed of sound in the air.

Power loading The gross weight of an airplane divided by the military rated power, or other specified horsepower, of its engine or engines.

Ram air delivery Air gathered by the forward motion of an air scoop or inlet through the air, and delivered to the engine with increased pressure.

Self-sealing fuel tanks Tanks lined with a rubberized substance that closes immediately over a small rupture in the tank, like a bullet hole.

Slats Movable auxiliary airfoils running along the leading edge of each wing, usually remaining against the leading edge in normal conditions, but lifting away from the wing to form a slot at certain angles of attack.

Supercharger A compressor for forcing more air or fuel-air mixture into an internal-combustion, reciprocating engine than it would normally induct at the prevailing atmospheric pressure. A gear-driven supercharger built as an integral part of the engine is called an internal supercharger, and may be either single or double stage. If the engine exhaust is used to drive a turbine to operate the impeller, it is a *turbosupercharger.*

Wing loading The gross weight of an airplane divided by the wing area.

Selected Bibliography

PRIMARY DOCUMENTS

Unless otherwise cited, first-person quotations in this book are from the biographical tapes and manuscript Edgar Schmued made in 1985, hereafter referred to as ES 1985, and personal information is from official documents held by his widow, Christel Schmued. Copies are in the San Diego Aerospace Museum (SDAM) archives.

Many of Schmued's coworkers provided interviews, letters, and documents, beginning with a meeting chaired by Bill Wheeler at the SDAM, April 27, 1986. They are listed in the Acknowledgments, with specific citations in footnotes.

DOCUMENTS IN SAN DIEGO AEROSPACE MUSEUM (SDAM) ARCHIVES

I. North American Aviation, Inc. Internal documents in SDAM Files:

Airplane Flight Report, NAA 73-92-1/2

Airframe Contract Record (Report "O"), as of July 27, 1956.

Chronology of World, U.S. Aircraft Industry and North American Aviation, Inc., Events Prior to World War II. 1959. Gives company dates for events and projects.

J. H. Kindelberger. Columbus, OH: NAA, 1972. Biography.

NAA Skyline/Skywriter. Company magazines, issues from 1940 to 1952.

P-51 Mustang Fighter Combat Record, NA-68-967, Nov. 19, 1968. Company organization charts, various dates.

II. Government Documents:

Army Aircraft Characteristics, ATSC Wright F., April 1, 1946, and charts dated August 1, 1941, and 1939: SDAM; AAF a/c data from this source, unless otherwise cited.

Index of AF Serial Numbers Assigned to Aircraft 1958 and Prior. Procurement Division, AAF, April 1961. Has Air Force contract data and approval dates.

Model Designations of Army Aircraft Engines, ATSC Wright F., 1945.

U.S. Military Aircraft Acceptances, 1940–1945. Washington, DC: GPO, 1946.

III. Others

Clark B. Millikan. *Comparative Wind Tunnel Tests on Two Alternative Wings for the North America NA-X73.* Guggenheim Aeronautical Laboratories, California Institute of Technology (GALCIT), Pasadena, GALCIT Report #284, Sept. 20, 1940.

Clark B. Millikan, *Wind Tunnel Tests on a 1/4 Scale Model of the NA–73 . . .* Guggenheim Aeronautical Laboratories, California Institute of Technology (GALCIT), Pasadena, GALCIT Report #286, Jan. 16, 1941.

Richard L. Schleicher. *The Low Carbon Steel Airplane.* Unpublished report, Oct. 6, 1986. Copy provided by author.

Colonel H. G. Bunker. *Air Fighting Development Unit.* RAF Station Wittering, Report No. 107, Mustang III.

III. Documents in the Air Force Historical Research Center (AFHRC) at Air University, Maxwell AFB. All Notes with AFHRC File Numbers, Including:

Report of the Army Air Forces Board, AAFSAT, Orlando, FL. "Report on North American P-51A-10," June 8, 1943: AFHRC 245.64.

Army Air Forces PGC, Eglin Field, "Tactical Employment Trials on North American P-51B-1," January 27, 1944: AFHRC 240.04-15.

Numerous case histories of USAF fighter planes produced by the Historical Office, Air Technical Service Command, are now at the AFHRC, file number 202, along with final reports of prototype development by the Air Material Command, file number 216.2101. These essential documents were used extensively as background for this report.

BOOKS

I. Development of P-51:

The most extensive P-51 story is Robert Gruenhagen. *Mustang: The Story of the P-51.* New York: Arco. Revised 1976. See also:

Birch, David. *Rolls-Royce and the Mustang.* Derby, England: Rolls-Royce Heritage Trust, 1987. A very complete study of British documents.

Coggan, Paul. *Mustang Survivors.* Aston: Bourne House, 1987.

Dienst, John, and Hagedorn, Dan. *North American F-51 Mustangs in Latin American Air Force Service.* Arlington, TX: Aerofax, 1985.

Ethell, Jeffrey. *Mustang: A Documentary History.* London: Jane's, 1981.

Grinsell, Robert. *P-51 Mustang.* New York: Crown Publishers, 1980.

Halley, James A. *Royal Air Force Aircraft, AA100 to AZ999.* Air Britain, 1985.

II. Operational Histories:

Carson, Leonard. *Pursue and Destroy.* Granada Hills, CA: Sentry, 1978.

Davis, Larry. *Mustang In Action.* Carrollton, TX: Squadron/Signal, 1981. Especially good detail drawings.

Davis, Larry. *MiG Alley.* Carrollton, TX: Squadron/Signal, 1978.

Ethell, J., and Fry, G. L. *Escort to Berlin, the 4th Fighter Group.* New York: Arco, 1978.

Farnol, Lynn. *To the Limit of Their Endurance: A Family Story of the VIII Fighter Command.* Manhattan, KS: Sunflower Univ. Press, 1986.

Freeman, Roger A. *Mighty Eighth War Diary.* London: Jane's, 1981.

Freeman, Roger A. *Mighty Eighth War Manual.* London: Jane's, 1984.

Freeman, Roger A. *Mustang at War.* Garden City, NY: Doubleday, 1974.

Mikesh, Robert C. *Excalibur III.* Washington, DC: Smithsonian Press, 1978.

Olmstead, Merle C. *The Yoxford Boys: The 357th Fighter Group.* Fallbrook, CA: Aero Publishers, 1971.

Rawlings, John D. *Fighter Squadrons of the R.A.F.* London: Macdonald, 1969.

Rust, Kenn C., and Hess, William N. *The Slybird Group: The 353rd Fighter Group on Escort and Ground Attack Operations.* Fallbrook, CA: Aero Publishers, 1968.

Spagnuolo, Mark D. *Don S. Gentile.* East Lansing, MI: College Press, 1986.

Turner, Richard E. *Mustang Pilot.* London: New English Library, 1969.

III. The Following Were Useful on Air Force and Aircraft Industry History:

Arnold, H. H. *Global Mission,* New York: Harper and Brothers, 1949.

Boylan, Bernard. *Development of the Longrange Escort Fighter.* USAF Historical Study No. 136. Air University, 1955.

Carter, Kit C., and Mueller, Robert. *The Army Air Forces in World War II: Combat Chronology, 1941–1945.* Washington, DC: U.S. Government Printing Office, 1974.

Copp, Dewitt S. *A Few Great Captains.* New York: Doubleday, 1980.

Copp, Dewitt S. *Forged in Fire: Strategy and Decisions in the Air War over Europe, 1940–45.* Garden City, NY: Doubleday, 1982.

Craven, Wesley Frank, and Cate, James Lea. *The Army Air Forces in World War II.* Chicago: Univ. of Chicago Press, 1949–55:

——Vol. II, *Europe: Torch to Pointblank, August 1942 to December 1943.*

——Vol. IV, *The Pacific: Guadalcanal to Saipan, August 1942 to July 1944.*

——Vol. VI, *Men and Planes.*

Domonske, Arthur B., and Finch, Volney C. *Aircraft Engines.* New York, 1936.

Haight, John M. *American Aid to France.* New York: Atheneum, 1970.

Hallion, Richard P. *Test Pilots: The Frontiersmen of Flight.* Washington, DC: Smithsonian, 1988.

Hansen, James. *Engineer in Charge.* Washington, DC: NASA, 1987.

Holley, Irving Brinton. *Buying Aircraft: Matériel Procurement for the Army Air Forces.* Washington, DC: GPO, 1964.

Knaack, Marcelle S. *Encyclopedia of U.S. Air Force Aircraft,* Vol. I. Washington, DC: Office of Air Force History, 1978.

Kelsey, Benjamin S. *The Dragon's Teeth.* Washington, DC: Smithsonian Press, 1982.

Maloney, Edward T. *Sever the Sky.* Planes of Fame, 1979.

Morrow, Howard B. *An American Adventure—How Good It Is!* La Verne, CA: 1982.

Norton, Donald J. *Larry: A Biography of Lawrence D. Bell.* Chicago: Nelson-Hall, 1981.

Rust, Kenn C. *Twentieth Air Force Story.* Temple City, CA: Historical Aviation Album, 1979.

Rust, Kenn C., and Hess, William N. *The Slybird*

Group: The 353rd Fighter Group on Escort and Ground Attack Operations. Fallbrook, CA: Aero Publishers, 1968.

Schlaifer, Robert. *Development of Aircraft Engines.* Boston: Harvard, 1950.

Webster, Sir Charles, and Frankland, Noble. *The Strategic Air Offensive Against Germany, 1939–1945.* London: Her Majesty's Stationery Office, 1961: Vol. I, *Preparation;* Vol. II, *Endeavour;* Vol. III, *Victory.*

Who's Who in World Aviation. Washington, American Aviation Publications, 1955.

PERIODICALS

I. Early Accounts of Mustang Development in Periodical Literature Began with the Designer's Own Article:

Edgar Schmued, "Evolution of the Mustang." *Skyways,* Jan. 1944: 23ff. The writing style, however, seems to reflect NAA's advertising department.

Other useful sources are:

Churchill, Edward. "The Mustang." *Flying,* Sept. 1944: 32ff. A contemporary survey.

Cox, Jack. "Restoration of XP-51." *Sport Aviation,* Dec. 1976: 58–64.

Lawson, Robert. *Hook,* Fall 1977: 11–12. P-51D tests on the USS Shangri-La.

McLaren, David R. "North American P-51H." *American Aviation Historical Society Journal.* Part I, Summer 1980: 124–39; Part II, Fall 1980: 203–27.

McLaren, David R. "Air Support in Korea: Mustang Style." *Aerospace Historian,* June 1986: 74–86.

Meyers, Robert B., Jr. "The Packard Merlin Story." *Rolls-Royce Magazine,* Sept. 1980: 21–25.

Reeder, John P. "The Mustang Story." *Sport Aviation,* Sept. 1983: 40–44.

Shores, Christopher. "The Allison Mustangs." *Air Classics.* Part 1, Sept. 1980: 25–36; Part 2, Oct. 1980: 58–73; Part 3, Nov. 1980: 16–72.

Thompson, Warren. "Mustangs in Korea." *Air Enthusiast* 15:49–57.

II. Periodical References to NAA Company History Include:

Cunningham, Frank. "Airplanes by the Dozen." *Popular Aviation,* Jan. 1939: 42–45.

Price, Wesley. "Merchant of Speed." *Saturday Evening Post,* Feb. 19, 1949: 32ff.

Wilson, Gill Robb. "North American Aviation." *Flying,* Sept. 1961: 28ff.

III. General Background

Hazen, R. M., Chief Engineer, Allison Division, General Motors. *The Allison Aircraft Engine. SAE Journal,* 49:5:498–500.

Holley, I. B., Jr. "A Detroit Dream of Mass-produced Fighter Aircraft: The XP-75 Fiasco." *Technology and Culture,* July 1987: 582.

McFarland, Stephen L. "Evolution of the American Strategic Fighter in Europe, 1942–44." *Journal of Strategic Studies,* London, June 1987.

Schmued, Edgar. "Why U.S. Planes Are Better Than Russia's." *Los Angeles Times,* July 31, 1955.

Index